FAITH ENACTED AS HISTORY

WILL HERBERG

Faith
Enacted as History

ESSAYS IN BIBLICAL THEOLOGY

By
WILL HERBERG

Edited with an Introduction
by
BERNHARD W. ANDERSON

THE WESTMINSTER PRESS
Philadelphia

Book Design by Dorothy Alden Smith

Published by The Westminster Press ®
Philadelphia, Pennsylvania

PRINTED IN THE UNITED STATES OF AMERICA

Library of Congress Cataloging in Publication Data

Herberg, Will.
    Faith enacted as history.

    Includes bibliographical references.
    CONTENTS: Introduction: Will Herberg as Biblical theologian.—The posture of faith: Biblical faith as "Heilsgeschichte"; the meaning of redemptive history in human existence. Judaism and Christianity; their unity and difference. [etc.]
    1. Bible—Theology—Addresses, essays, lectures. I. Title.
BS543.H45   230   76–26899
ISBN 0–664–21335–9

77-5198

CONTENTS

PREFACE

For a number of years it has been my plan to gather together some of the essays of my esteemed colleague and close friend, Will Herberg, and to publish them as a tribute at the climax of his teaching career. Of late I have hoped that the published essays could be presented to him on the occasion of his retirement from his teaching position at Drew University in the 1975/76 academic year, a position that he held with distinction for two decades. Owing to incalculable elements in the human situation, however, it has been impossible to time the event of publication with the consummation of his career as teacher, writer, and lecturer. While the tribute comes belatedly, it nevertheless expresses the deep appreciation felt by many people for the profound influence of Herberg's theological and philosophical thought.

This volume of essays represents only a small portion of the literary harvest of Will Herberg's career, and it includes only those writings in the field of biblical theology which have influenced me most. Even these gleanings, however, could not have been gathered and bound without the help of others. I want to express thanks to Professor Donald G. Jones of Drew University—who, by the way, later intends to issue Herberg's complete works in all fields—for his advice at various points; to my editorial assistant, Carol Hanawalt, and to my graduate assistant, James Butler, for their careful work on the manuscript as a whole; to Ruth A. Anderson, whose philosophical understanding of Hegel enabled her to undertake the difficult task of transcribing and editing Herberg's taped lecture "Hegel and His Influence on Biblical Theology"; and finally to the staff of The Westminster Press, who sensed the potential significance of these essays for future readers and who offered the cooperation of a publisher.

It is my hope that these essays, which appeared here and there during the past generation, will have a new impact when published in the present format. Since the time of publication coincides with the year of the American bicentennial, I hope this volume will contribute to a rediscovery of the biblical heritage which belongs essentially to the American tradition.

BERNHARD W. ANDERSON

Princeton Theological Seminary
Passover-Easter, 1976

INTRODUCTION

Will Herberg as Biblical Theologian

by Bernhard W. Anderson

"I am no heretic," said Will Herberg to a Christian audience on the occasion of his inauguration as Professor of Judaic Studies and Social Philosophy at Drew University; "at least the only heresy I am aware of in myself is the incurable heresy of being a Jew."[1] Those words were spoken in a context of wry humor, but they have deep meaning. For the influence of Will Herberg as a teacher, writer, and lecturer stems from his theological affirmation of his Jewish identity (he is a Conservative Jew), an affirmation that is made from a firm position in the biblical tradition. He is a man of biblical faith, and his profound understanding of that faith enables him both to relate to the Christian community and to explore the depth and breadth of human culture. It was appropriate, then, that later the name of his professorial chair was changed to "Professor of Philosophy and Culture." Those who have encountered him through his teaching, writing, and lecturing have been impressed with the penetration of his mind, the ecumenicity of his interests, and his comprehensive grasp of the history of human thought. He is an able interpreter of Plato and Aristotle, Augustine and Aquinas, Hegel and Marx, Kierkegaard and the existentialists, Buber and Maritain, Barth and Tillich —to take just a few examples. His essays, which run into the thousands, deal with a wide span of contemporary issues: labor relations, academic freedom, urban problems, the Great Society, desegregation, Roman Catholicism after Vatican II, the "Jesus Freaks," civil religion—and much, much more. Nothing human is alien to him.

Though having a wide-ranging mind, Will Herberg is no intellectual wanderer, driven only by curiosity like that of the ancient Athenians who "spent their time in nothing except telling or hearing something new" (Acts 17:21). While he has an amazing capacity to enter sympathetically into another perspective and expound it with clarity and power, he also displays discriminating judgment. He never drifts away from the fundamental basis of his thought: a faith which, in the spirit of Augustine and Anselm, seeks for explication, understanding, and manifestation in the world. And that faith is rooted in and nourished by the scriptural tradition in which he stands.

Will Herberg, then, is a biblical theologian—a role which has priority over his being a sociologist, philosopher of culture, apologist to the secular world, or analyst of current affairs. Hence, I have selected from his many essays a few that display his creative thinking in the field of biblical theology. Needless to say, the selection is arbitrary in the sense that the essays chosen are those which have influenced me most; other persons would have made a different selection from the treasury of his writings. The selection in this case is based on my close relationship with Will Herberg which began in 1955, when I was dean of the Theological School of Drew University and he was invited to join the faculty, and which, after my moving to Princeton Theological Seminary in 1968, continued unbroken in luncheon discussions held on a regular basis. Most of these essays have actually entered into our conversations in one way or another. Recently at one of these luncheon dates I presented him with an outline of the volume of essays, the publication of which he had already approved. On that occasion he was pleased with the selection and the tripartite arrangement that I proposed: the posture of faith, the understanding of faith, and the witness of faith in the world. Indeed, he expressed amazement that the selection and arrangement coincided with his own understanding of his work. He agreed that, while the essays were written at different times and for different occasions, without any conscious attention to an overall scheme, the proposed volume authentically represents the interrelated phases of his thinking. The reader should consider, then, that each essay in this volume stands on its own and may be read separately; but it is necessary to read the essays in all three categories if one is to appreciate the thrust and sweep of Herberg's work as a biblical theologian.

FAITH AND HISTORY

One fundamental tone resonates, like an organ diapason, through all of Will Herberg's essays on biblical theology: Man is essentially a historical being, and therefore all human thought and achievement can be understood authentically only when man's historicity is taken with radical seriousness. On one occasion, when he was expressing appreciation for Reinhold Niebuhr's work, Herberg quoted with approval the words of the Spanish philosopher José Ortega y Gasset that "to comprehend anything human, be it personal or collective, one must understand its history."[2] It is this historical sense which Herberg discovered in his own biblical tradition, for according to Jewish scriptures (or, in Christian terms, the Old Testament), "history is what is real," and Divine Reality is mediated and known historically. The theological significance of man's historicity was already evident in Herberg's *Judaism and Modern Man* (1951), which he regarded as a kind of "confession of faith." By the end of the decade, however, when he wrote "How My Mind Has Changed" for *The Christian Century* (Essay 15 in this volume), he was able to say with greater clarity and force that "historicism" is the touchstone of his thinking in all areas: philosophy, sociology, theology, and human affairs.

Herberg's thinking about history is not abstract and general.

All human thought is essentially related to the concrete realities of time, place, and circumstance; and, by the same token, the thought of a particular human being is inseparable from his own history, his life story. It is appropriate, then, to say a few things about Will Herberg's career, which has spanned about three quarters of the twentieth century. In personal conversations he has shared some of his life story with me. He was born into an atheistic Jewish home, the son of Hyman Louis and Sarah (Wolkov) Herberg. His parents, whose ancestral roots were in Russia, had migrated from Europe shortly after the turn of the century and settled in New York City. There he grew up in a trilingual immigrant home (his mother spoke Russian, German, and French) and there he gained his education. In his youth, like many sensitive young intellectuals of the time, he embraced "the Marxist faith" and became a member of the Communist Party. His rational idealism, however, was shaken by events that transpired in the early '30s, the period of economic crisis and of the gathering storm of world war. He came to realize that Stalinist Communism was a monolithic structure, indeed a political orthodoxy, which suppressed shades of interpretation. As a member of a Jewish family, he was even more alarmed when the word went out through the Party that Communists should support Hitler, on the assumption that his imminent defeat would provide the opportunity for Communism to rise. Disillusioned with Communism, owing to its cynical use of political power and its pursuit of an illusion, Herberg broke with the Party and became a fierce critic of totalitarianism in any form, as can be seen from the essays in the third part of this volume.

Concomitant with Herberg's disillusionment over the Communist faith was his discovery of the biblical tradition. At Columbia University, so he has told me, he took a course, "The Bible as Literature," which provided him with the opportunity to read the Bible all the way through—including the New Testament. Also, he became acquainted with the thought of the Jewish philosopher Franz Rosenzweig (1886–1929), and arose

every day at 5 A.M. to study his writings. But it was Reinhold
Niebuhr who, more than anyone else, helped to crystallize his
thinking. Those who lived through the '30s and '40s will remember that Niebuhr, speaking from a prophetic biblical perspective, appealed to many young secular figures in history and
political science, such as Arthur M. Schlesinger, Jr.—not because they shared his theology but because his realistic analysis
of the human situation seemed inescapably relevant in a time of
the breakdown of "liberal" faith in progress and human enlightenment. In an autobiographical passage in one of his essays,
Herberg described Niebuhr's profound influence on his thinking:

> My first encounter with the thought of Reinhold Niebuhr
> came in the later 1930's. I was then at a most crucial mo-
> ment in my life. My Marxist faith had collapsed under the
> shattering blows of contemporary history. . . . I was left lit-
> erally without any ground to stand on, deprived of the com-
> mitment and understanding that alone made life livable. At
> this point, in a way I cannot now remember, I came upon
> Niebuhr's *Moral Man and Immoral Society*. . . . It came
> with the revelation of a new understanding of human exis-
> tence in terms of which I might reconstruct my life and
> thought. What impressed me most profoundly was the para-
> doxical combination of realism and radicalism that Niebuhr's
> "prophetic" faith made possible. Here was a faith that trans-
> ferred the center of its absolute commitment to what is re-
> ally absolute—the transcendent God—and was therefore
> able to face the real facts of life unafraid, with open eyes.
> Here was a faith that called into question all human institu-
> tions and institutional vested interests, that permitted noth-
> ing of this world to parade as final or ultimate, and yet pro-
> vided an intelligent ground for discriminate judgment. Here
> was a faith that warned against all premature securities, yet
> called to responsible action. Here, in short, was a "social ide-
> alism" without illusions, in comparison with which even the
> most "advanced" Marxism appeared confused, inconsistent,
> and hopelessly illusion-ridden.[3]

In this same autobiographical account Herberg went on to say that his encounter with Niebuhr's thought was a turning point, even before he met Niebuhr personally. Promptly he read all of Niebuhr's writings that he could get hold of. This intellectual encounter "quite literally changed my mind and my life," he wrote. "Humanly speaking, it 'converted' me, for in some manner I cannot describe, I felt my whole being, and not merely my thinking, shifted to a new center. I could now speak about God and religion without embarrassment, though as yet without very much understanding of what was involved."[4] It was in this period that he wrote "The Christian Mythology of Socialism" (1943), in which he argued that Socialism (Communism) is essentially a secularization of the biblical perspective on history. Like any heresy, this one is seductive because it contains an element of biblical truth within a deceptive myth.

Like Franz Rosenzweig before him, Herberg went through a struggle over whether to become a Christian. It was at this time that he became personally acquainted with Reinhold Niebuhr, who was teaching at Union Theological Seminary in New York City. Herberg has related to me that he used to discuss with Niebuhr the possibility of his moving into the Christian community; but Niebuhr counseled against it on the ground that he should not become a Christian until first he was a good Jew. And Herberg, on his part, perceived the wisdom of this advice for, under the influence of Rosenzweig, he was beginning to see more clearly that Christianity and Judaism belong together and complement each other in "the larger plan" of God. His understanding of the complementary relationship of the two communities is set forth in his important essay "Judaism and Christianity: Their Unity and Difference."

The invitation to join the faculty of Drew University in 1955 came at the climax of Herberg's early career. After spending twelve years (1935–1948) as research analyst and educational director of a large AFL labor union, The International Ladies'

Garment Workers Association, he became a free-lance writer
and lecturer (1948–1955). Two of his major books were written
in this general period: first, *Judaism and Modern Man: An
Interpretation of Jewish Religion* (1951), a book which he described as "avowedly Niebuhrian in temper and thought";[5]
and *Protestant—Catholic—Jew* (1955), a sociological analysis
of American society. In much demand as a speaker, especially
on college campuses, he traveled widely and gained the reputa-
tion of being "the Reinhold Niebuhr of Judaism." In view of
his distinction as a theologian and his ability to open up creative conversation about, and exploration into, the meaning of
biblical faith, it was altogether fitting and proper that he was
asked to join the faculty of Drew University. Although techni-
cally he was not a member of the faculty of the Theological
School but of the Graduate School, his dynamic teaching and
penetrating thought were felt by generations of theological
students who were privileged to study under him. With in-
creasing theological and philosophical vitality, interrupted only
by the sad period occasioned by the death of his wife and close
companion, Anna, in 1959, he probed ever more deeply into
the historicity of man and what this means, theologically and
philosophically. He continued to take a lively interest in political and social affairs, as essays in the third part of this volume
will show, but he maintained increasingly that, as in the case
of Reinhold Niebuhr, a sober estimate of human nature and
the limitations of human achievement demanded a "new conservatism."[6] It is significant that his last graduate seminars at
Drew University before his retirement were on Marx and
Nietzsche. It is his conviction that biblical faith provides a
"depth understanding" of human nature and human history
which enables human beings to assume social responsibility in
the world without despair and without illusion. The alternatives, as he has remarked to me on more than one occasion, are
the nihilism of Nietzsche and the secularism of Marx.

JUDAISM AND CHRISTIANITY

Readers of these essays will be struck especially by Will Herberg's sympathetic understanding of Christianity. Christian students who have studied under him will testify that Herberg, without surrendering his stance within the Jewish community, not only gave a profound and orthodox exposition of Christian theology but, with relentless intellectual force, pressed them to take their Christian faith seriously. His ability to project himself into the Christian faith is evidenced especially in his sermon "The Incarnate Word," which was given during a Communion service. This extraordinary event deserves an autobiographical recollection, which goes back to the time when I was dean of the Theological School of Drew University. Theological students were so responsive to Herberg's teaching that the spokesman for the graduating class of 1961, Donald G. Jones, asked that Herberg give the Communion homily to the graduating seniors. The request raised difficult questions. Would Will Herberg respond kindly to an invitation to take part in a Christian service? Was it "kosher," in Christian terms, for a Jewish theologian to take part in the celebration of the Christian sacrament? After we had done much searching of heart and consultation with Herberg, it was decided to allow this unprecedented event to occur, though under a special arrangement. Herberg was not to be an officiant in the service. He was to sit in the front pew as an observer, come to the pulpit at the appropriate time for the homily, and return to his seat when he was finished. Undoubtedly the arrangement was somewhat irregular; but those who read the sermon will probably admit that the "word" which was proclaimed on that occasion was more "Christian," even more orthodoxly Christian, than many Communion sermons given by properly ordained Christian ministers. After all, God is free to speak outside of "properly ordained" channels.

This incident, however, raises the larger question of the relationship between Jewish and Christian communities. Later on I want to consider this question as a Christian biblical theologian. But for the moment I am concerned about Herberg's challenge to both communities. Exponents of each have insisted that a sharp line must be drawn between Christian and Jew. On the one hand, some exponents of the Jewish faith have maintained a strict separation, to the point of saying that "Christianity is irrelevant to being a Jew." It is difficult to rebut this thesis in view of the long history in which Christians have perpetrated terrible crimes against the Jews. On the other side, some exponents of the Christian faith have also argued for a strict separation, to the point of saying that the scriptures of Israel (the Old Testament) are essentially irrelevant theologically for Christian faith. These scriptures, so it is argued, may provide a historical background for the emergence of Christianity or they may serve as a foil to the Christian gospel, but they do not really belong to "the story of our life." And it must be admitted that there are major difficulties in understanding the relationship between the Old and the New Testament, even though both are embraced within the Christian canon. Thus we find ourselves in a dilemma, precisely at the time when the Jewish faith and the Christian faith, which have much in common, are opposed by other religions and political ideologies. In this situation, Will Herberg's witness presents a major theological challenge, not only to those who came under the immediate impact of his written and spoken words, but to future generations to whom he may speak through the publication of these essays.

Previously I referred to the influence of Franz Rosenzweig's writings on Herberg at a time when he was struggling to find a meaningful faith. Consideration of the full range of Rosenzweig's thought, as set forth preeminently in his *Der Stern der Erlösung* (The Star of Redemption),[7] is beyond our immediate concern. It is sufficient to notice that there are striking parallels, both in experience and in thought, between the two men. The young Rosenzweig, who had been brought up in the world view of progress and faith in reason, came to sense the emptiness of liberal rationalism. Existential philosophy, which started from the concrete situation of the existing person, began to have an appeal to him; but then, especially in conversations with a Christian of Jewish descent, Eugen Rosenstock, he became convinced that the Christian faith gave the only adequate answer to the question of reason and faith. He decided to become a Christian, but as a good Jew. So before accepting baptism and in preparation for entering the church, he attended the synagogue service of the Day of Atonement (Yom Kippur) in 1913. However, he emerged from this service as a changed person—one who was able to affirm his Jewish identity theologically and philosophically.[8] Out of his life and thought he then proposed a new understanding of the relationship between Jew and Christian.

Rosenzweig used the image of fire to express the complementary relationship between the two communities. In the heart of Judaism burns the eternal flame of the Torah; the flame, however, sends out rays of light (the Christian mission) which requires the source of the fire. Thus the Jew, according to Rosenzweig, belongs by birth to an eternal people who are called out of the stream of history into eternal life, a life of immediate relationship to God. The Christian, on the other hand, is by birth a pagan who must give up his natural (pagan) self in order to become a member of a special community, a people who are sent into the stream of history with a God-given mission. The Jew, he said, is called to live in the present under the Torah and to take part in the Eternal Now, the End which has already arrived. The Christian, on the other hand, is called to follow the "eternal way," to strive toward a redemption that is not complete, and thus to be ever on the way toward the divine goal. From these statements it can be seen that Rosenzweig believes that Jew and Christian hold different attitudes toward history. As he said in one of his writings, Jewish faith is free from "the curse of historicity,"[9] for in faith the Jew is placed in the dimension of eternity, where the movement of history does not impinge upon the inner life. The Christian, however, is plunged into historicity, that is, he is called "to go out and conquer the unredeemed world of the heathens" and thereby to become involved in "the fate of the nations and the unfolding of the world-historic drama."[10]

Herberg, who went through a similar intellectual and spiritual struggle, holds a view that is both similar and different. In his essay "Judaism and Christianity," he too speaks of the complementary relationship between the two communities. With the people Israel, he says, God has entered into a covenant which requires fidelity to the Torah, that is, a witness to God's transcendent sovereignty in their life. With the church, on the other hand, God has established a covenant through Jesus Christ which entails a mission into the world to proclaim the gospel. Within the economy of God's redemptive purpose, both covenantal vocations are necessary, and each complements the other. There is one major difference between Herberg and Rosenzweig, however. The expression "the curse of historicity" would never fall from Herberg's lips! On the contrary, historicism, in his own words, is the "touchstone" of his thinking. In his understanding, neither Judaism nor Christianity is metahistorical; in neither case does faith place the believer "outside history." On the contrary, both Jew and Christian agree on "faith enacted as history," to use the phrase of Herberg that has been chosen as the title for this volume.

To be sure, this enactment has the dimension of contemporaneity, as Herberg explains in "Beyond Time and Eternity," for when the Jew celebrates Passover or the Christian celebrates Easter, time and eternity are fused. This fusion, however, does not permit either to live in an Eternal Now which transcends history or in a realized eschatology in which the goal has already been attained. The "double covenant," according to his view, must be seen in the historical and es-chatological perspective which the two communities hold in common. Both Jew and Christian live in the historical interim between the Already and the Not-Yet. The Jew who celebrates the redemption that came with Exodus-Sinai looks forward to the redemption that is yet to come with the Messiah; and the Christian who celebrates God's redemptive act in Jesus Christ looks forward to the time when Christ will return in power and glory. In his inaugural address, "Theological Presuppositions of Social Philosophy," Herberg recalls that Rosenzweig also once spoke of the Jew as standing in the same position as the Christian: " 'staring ahead,' glancing neither to the right nor to the left, his eyes fixed on the 'end.' "

Herberg does not minimize the differences between Judaism and Christianity, especially on the subject of Christology. In "A Jew Looks at Jesus," he observes that the confession "Jesus is the Christ" will mean much more for the Christian than it can possibly mean to the Jew. "For," he says, "the Jew sees Jesus as emerging from Israel and going forth; he sees him from the rear, as it were," and looking ahead to the final goal of God's redemptive purpose. "The Christian, on the other hand, precisely because he is a Christian, will see Christ coming toward him, in the fullness of divine grace, to claim, to judge, and to save; he meets him as Paul met him on the road to Damascus or as Peter outside Rome, face to face, in confronta-tion." Yet this "difference in perspective," significant as it is, should not obscure the truth that in the elective purpose of God both communities belong to the one people of God and, in a profound sense, share one faith over against the religions and philosophies of the world. Each community, he says, is placed on "different sectors of the fighting front of the King-dom," but they are united not only to bear a "common witness to God" but to witness against "the perils, inadequacies, and temptations of the other." In short, the two communities are twins that are inseparably related, like Esau and Jacob who came from the same womb, one grasping the heel of the other.

THE BIBLICAL STORY

Will Herberg maintains that the fundamental historical movement of the Bible is that of *Heilsgeschichte*—the history or story of God's activity to accomplish his saving purpose. This thesis is set forth in his important essay on the meaning of redemptive history in' human existence, with which this volume begins. Since the term *Heilsgeschichte* has become controversial in theological discussions, where it is used in various ways, it is appropriate to comment on Herberg's understanding of it.

First of all, he does not understand *Heilsgeschichte* to be a strictly chronological, objective progression of events that may be periodized into dispensations or schematized in historical patterns. This view does not do justice to Herberg's existential understanding of man as a historical being who is called to take part in God's story as it moves in an eschatological sweep: creation, fall (loss of original rightness), and restoration. While he is concerned with the "pastness" and the "facticity" of the biblical history, especially as it is anchored to the crucial events of Exodus-Sinai or the crucifixion-resurrection, he maintains that this is a history which calls for participation, not for objective detachment. He does not want history to be reduced to mere pastness (chronology), on the one hand, or to mere contemporaneity (self-understanding), on the other. The biblical history is our real past; but within the believing and worshiping community that past impinges upon the present, giving the believer identity and vocation, and calling him to take part in a history which moves toward its divine consummation.

Secondly, Herberg does not share completely the view of the Old Testament theologian Gerhard von Rad, who understands *Heilsgeschichte* as a history of traditions, that is, a historical process in which the Israelite community constantly retold the received tradition in the light of the ever-new situations in which it found itself in its ongoing history with Yahweh. Von

Rad's stress on "re-telling" *(Nacherzählen)*—upon event rather than *logos*—accords with Herberg's existentialist view of dramatic participation in redemptive history; but the German theologian's view, in Herberg's judgment, does not do full justice to the biblical view of history. For one thing, the emphasis upon *process* of reinterpretation seems to be a legacy from the philosopher Hegel, as Herberg points out in "Hegel and His Influence on Biblical Theology." Further, Herberg is dissatisfied with Von Rad's sharp distinction between *Historie* (ordinary history that is open to historical study) and *Geschichte* (history as experienced and interpreted by Israel). This dichotomy could lead to the conclusion that the biblical history is *only* story, with no firm anchorage in concrete historical reality. Are the crucial events of the exodus and the resurrection only story? Or are they rooted in actual, factual history?

If there are tensions in Herberg's thinking about the historical character of scripture, other biblical theologians who struggle with the question are in no better position to resolve the problem. Undoubtedly he would agree with the late Jewish philosopher Abraham J. Heschel that "the Bible is not a book to be read but a drama in which to participate."[11] But Herberg insists on saying more. He wants to do justice both to the dramatic power of scripture and to its historical realism. The Bible is not pure story; it is also history, even though its historicity cannot be comprehended completely within the canons of scientific study.

One of Will Herberg's greatest contributions to theological discussion has been his clarification of the terms of the theological debate. First, what do we mean by the word "history"? The term is used by theologians as far apart as G. Ernest Wright, who emphasized God's revelation in history, and Rudolf Bultmann, who reduced historicity to existential self-understanding. Herberg's "Five Meanings of the Word 'Historical'" is a great contribution toward theological clarification. Second, what do we mean by the word "myth"? Here again there is such confusion that some theologians are disposed to speak of biblical history as "myth." To this semantic problem Herberg also addressed his attention.[12] He never completed his essay "Some Variant Meanings of the Word 'Myth,'" but the sketch of his definitions, supplemented with notes based on personal conversations about the proposed essay, is included in this volume as a companion piece to his study of the uses of the word "history."

In one of our recent conversations when we were discussing his definitions of "myth," Herberg remarked that the phenomenological analysis of myth should not be disparaged, for the human mind is so multileveled that it cannot be exhausted. He admitted that some of the biblical materials (e.g., the poem about the victory at the sea in Ex., ch. 15) may have the form of myth. Nevertheless, he insisted that the biblical story has a unique basis in historical experience; and that it is important, therefore, for the theologian to be concerned about what happened, even though the question cannot be answered satisfactorily, if at all, by the critical historian. These remarks indicate that for him the word "myth" in any of its senses does not do justice to the biblical *Heilsgeschichte*. The Bible tells and retells a story about God's involvement in the life of a people and their response to his presence; but it is more than a story: it is a history which at crucial points reflects concrete experiences and therefore, unlike myth, has a fundamental facticity with which the theologian must reckon. Herberg has reminded Christian students of this in forceful terms, as evidenced in "Objective Facticity and the Historicity of Faith."

DIALOGUE BETWEEN JEW AND CHRISTIAN

It is not my intention to assess the impact of Herberg's thought upon the Jewish community; I can speak only as a Christian, and as a close friend. Will Herberg is a rare person who, as a Jew, has taken part fully in the life of a university that stands in the Christian tradition, and he has had a profound influence upon his colleagues and upon generations of students, many of whom were training for the Christian ministry.

In my judgment, there are two reasons for Herberg's ability to enter into conversations that move back and forth between the perspectives of Judaism and Christianity. These reasons I shall state in the reverse order of their priority. First, he sees himself as an *American* Jew who belongs to a pluralistic society. In his book *Protestant—Catholic—Jew* he argues that in a democratic society such as ours religious membership functions to give one identity and a sense of belonging—not in the first instance to create theological division. All of us, regardless of how we denominate ourselves religiously, are Americans who share a common history (even though our parents or our grandparents may have been immigrants) and a common devotion to the American way of life. This sociological analysis creates the possibility of interrelationship and conversation that could be mutually enriching to Protestant, Catholic, and Jew. On the other hand, Herberg also sees that American civil religion, the cohesive bond in a pluralistic society, may dominate and overcome the biblical tradition which is an essential part of the American heritage. Hence, as an American he speaks to Protestants, Catholics, Jews, and others about the theological presuppositions of constitutional democracy and calls for "a biblical-realist view" in his essay "Society, Democracy, and the State."

This brings me to the second, and even more important, reason for Will Herberg's influence on the Christian community. As a philosopher and theologian, he has helped Christians to reach a deeper understanding of their own faith. He has done this, in part, by insisting that Christians take the Old Testament more seriously. In Israel's scriptures he finds the basic witness that man's existence is historical and that Divine Reality is manifest historically. Man does not experience "salvation" or "wholeness" by taking flight from history into the changeless, timeless realm of myth. Rather, the meaning of his existence is given to him in a history, a *Heilsgeschichte*, where God meets him in the concrete situations of life, calls him to decision and responsibility, judges him for his idolatries, and leads him into the future. The rediscovery of the Old Testament is a theological necessity, lest the Christian faith lapse into some form of paganism or into otherworldly piety. But more than this: Herberg has also insisted that Christians take the *New* Testament more seriously. In contrast to some theologians who interpret away the essential content of the New Testament by reducing it to lofty ideas about God and man or to a dimension of human existence (self-understanding), Herberg has rigorously pressed Christians toward what he believes is an apostolic, orthodox understanding of Christian faith which centers in the crucial event of the crucifixion-resurrection. This sympathetic understanding of Christian faith, which is strikingly evident in his Communion service homily "The Incarnate Word," is the fruit of his own religious struggle and of his Rosenzweig-like view of the complementary vocations of the Jewish and Christian communities.

In view of Herberg's forceful impact upon the Christian community, it is appropriate for Christians to take a new look at some passages in the New Testament—especially Rom., chs. 9 to 11, a passage that Herberg profoundly appreciates. In this passage the apostle Paul, the great New Testament theologian, wrestles in "sorrow" and "anguish" (Rom. 9:2) with the divine mystery of Israel as the elect people of God. In the past the epistle to the Romans has been read too much from the standpoint of Protestant concern about "justification by faith," construed to mean the salvation of the individual and his new life in relation to the God who loves him and accepts him. But the central question to which Paul addresses himself is, as phrased in an introduction to the New Testament: "How in the midst of disobedient humanity is God calling into being a New People?"[13] From the outset Paul wrestles with this question, beginning with his initial testimony, "I am not ashamed of the gospel: it is the power of God for salvation to every one who has faith, *to the Jew first* and also to the Greek" (Rom. 1:16; emphasis added). In the ensuing discussion, Paul insists on the freedom of God to justify the ungodly (4:5), to call into existence things that do not exist (4:17), and to give new life to the dead (4:17). Yet Paul is equally emphatic in saying that God does not exercise his freedom capriciously; he is the faithful God who remains true to his promises made to Israel.

Paul's discussion of the existence of the Jewish community vis-à-vis the Christian community in Rom., chs. 9 to 11, is, as New Testament scholars have pointed out, the continuation and climax of his discussion of God's freedom and faithfulness —only in this case God's freedom to "make the rules" is expounded historically. For God called his people Israel into existence with sovereign freedom, ignoring the human law of the firstborn and choosing Jacob instead of Esau. Paul argues that in the present, when the covenant is opened to the Gentiles, God retains his freedom to determine who belongs to his people. God keeps the circle open, so to speak, for the Gentile can be cut off, and the Jew can be grafted back in (11:22–23). It is striking that in this context, where Paul's exposition of divine grace reaches a climax, faith is understood as a relationship to God, not to Jesus. Apparently Paul does not suggest that the grace of God for the Jew is conditional upon his leaving the Jewish community and becoming a Christian. The decisive issue, for both Jew and Christian, is recognition of the sovereignty of God who is faithful, the God who is both the God of Abraham and the Father of Jesus Christ; for "since God is one" (see Rom. 3:29–30), both Jew and Gentile belong to the *one* people of God. Viewed from the standpoint of God's electing purpose, "there is no distinction between Jew and Greek; the same Lord is Lord of all and bestows his riches upon all who call upon him" (10:12). The final doxology, with which Paul's discussion concludes (11:33–36), appropriately lifts the discussion to the theological level of the calling (election) of God which includes both Jew and Christian.

Whether Herberg's view of the "double covenant" may be supported by the epistle to the Romans is a matter for theological exegesis of the passage itself. At least it is a fair inference from Paul's discussion, however, that in the sovereignty of God's grace Jew and Christian belong together inseparably. And if his elective purpose includes both, each may make a witness to the other and a common witness to the world.

Christians may well ponder one passage especially in Paul's epistle: "As regards the gospel they [the Jews] are enemies, *for your sake;* but as regards election they are beloved for the sake of their forefathers. For the gifts and the call of God are irrevocable" (Rom. 11:28–29; emphasis added). The phrase "for your sake" has taken on new meaning in the twentieth century, for in many ways the Christian has been a debtor to the Jew. Who can deny that Martin Buber's philosophical exploration of the "I and Thou" dimension of human existence has profoundly enriched the Christian understanding of faith?[14] Who would want to ignore Abraham Heschel's profound study of Israel's prophets, which lifts up the theme of the divine pathos?[15] And who would ignore Emil Fackenheim's philosophical probing into the biblical witness to God's presence in history, even in the face of the monstrous evil of our time evidenced in the Jewish holocaust?[16] In addition to these and other philosophical contributions, Christian faith has been influenced by Jewish artists, poets, and novelists (e.g., Elie Wiesel). All of this has been "for our sake."

It is especially impressive that in the twentieth century there has arisen a remarkable succession of Jewish thinkers who, whatever their contribution to Judaism, have had a profound impact upon Christian theology. In that splendid succession, which runs especially from Rosenzweig and Buber to the present, Will Herberg has made a distinctive and memorable contribution to which, it is hoped, this volume will bear some small witness.

NOTES

1. Herberg's inaugural address, "Theological Presuppositions of Social Philosophy," is included in this volume.

2. Will Herberg's essay "Christian Apologist to the Secular World," *Union Seminary Quarterly Review*, Vol. XI, No. 4 (1956), pp. 11–16, was part of a symposium occasioned by the publication of Vol. II of the Library of Living Theology, *Reinhold Niebuhr: His Religious, Social, and Political Thought*, ed. by C. W. Kegley and R. W. Bretall (The Macmillan Company, 1956).

3. Herberg, "Christian Apologist," p. 14.

4. *Ibid.*, p. 12.

5. *Ibid.*, p. 13.

6. *Ibid.*, p. 15. See Herberg's essay "The Great Society and the American Constitutional Tradition," included in this volume.

7. English translation by William H. Hallo, *The Star of Redemption* (Holt, Rinehart & Winston, 1971). See also Nahum N. Glatzer, *Franz Rosenzweig: His Life and Thought*, 2d ed. (Schocken Books, 1961), and the summary and criticism by Eliezer Berkovits, *Major Themes in Modern Philosophies of Judaism* (Ktav Publishing House, Inc., 1974), pp. 37–67.

8. See the introductory essay by Glatzer, *op. cit.*, pp. ix–xxxviii.

9. *Ibid.*, p. xxi.

10. *Ibid.*

11. Abraham J. Heschel, *God in Search of Man* (Farrar, Straus & Cudahy, Inc., 1955), p. 24.

12. See Herberg's review of W. Taylor Stevenson's *History as Myth: The Import for Contemporary Theology*, in *Interpretation*, Vol. XXIII (1969), pp. 497–499.

13. Howard Clark Kee, Franklin Young, and Karlfried Froehlich, *Understanding the New Testament*, 3d ed. (Prentice-Hall, Inc., 1973), p. 208.

14. See Will Herberg, ed., *The Writings of Martin Buber* (Meridian Books, 1956), and *Four Existentialist Theologians* (Doubleday & Company, Inc., 1958), pp. 155–229.

15. Abraham J. Heschel, *The Prophets* (Harper & Row, Publishers, Inc., 1962). See the tribute to Heschel, "Confrontation with the Bible," by Bernhard W. Anderson, *Theology Today*, Vol. XXX (1973), pp. 267–271.

16. See Emil L. Fackenheim, *God's Presence in History: Jewish Affirmations and Philosophical Reflections* (Harper & Row, Publishers, Inc., Harper Torchbooks, 1972).

Part One

THE POSTURE OF FAITH

The German word *Heilsgeschichte,* often used in theological discussion, is composed of two elements: *Heil,* which means "health," "wholeness," "salvation," and *Geschichte,* which means "history," "story"—thus, the movement of God's redemptive purpose in history between the horizons of Creation and Consummation, beginning and end. The term is used in presentations of biblical theology as widely different as those of the nineteenth-century scholar J. C. K. von Hofmann and of the late Old Testament theologian Gerhard von Rad. The discerning reader will observe that Will Herberg uses *Heilsgeschichte* in a distinctive way to refer to "faith enacted as history," and thus to a dramatic view of history which avoids, on the one hand, mere temporal progression and, on the other, an existentialist interpretation detached from past happenings.

The following essay was published in *The Christian Scholar,* Vol. XXIX (1956).

1

BIBLICAL FAITH
AS "HEILSGESCHICHTE"

The Meaning of Redemptive History
in Human Existence

The uniqueness—the "scandal"—of biblical faith is revealed in its radically historical character. Biblical faith is historical not merely because it has a history, or deals with historical events; there is nothing particularly novel in that. Biblical faith is historical in the much more profound sense that it is itself essentially a history. The message biblical faith proclaims, the judgments it pronounces, the salvation it promises, the teachings it communicates, are all defined historically and understood as historical realities rather than as timeless structures of ideas or values. The historicity of biblical faith has long been a source of embarrassment to philosopher and mystic, yet it cannot be eliminated without virtually eliminating the faith itself. Dehistoricizing biblical faith is like paraphrasing poetry; something called an "idea content" remains, but everything that gave power and significance to the original is gone. Biblical faith is *faith enacted as history,* or it is nothing at all.

I

How shall we understand this radically historical character of biblical faith? Is it merely a cultural trait of the "Hebraic mind," or does it reflect something deeper, something in the very grain of reality, particularly human reality?

There are, fundamentally, three ways in which man has

attempted to understand himself, to establish his being, and to relate himself to what is ultimate. One of these, culturally perhaps the oldest, is the way of heathenism. Heathen man sees reality as *nature*. Nature—divine since it is the locus of all ultimate sanctities, that beyond which there is nothing—is the context in which heathen man strives to understand himself and establish the meaning of his existence. The reality of his being is the "nature" in him, and rightness is to be achieved by engulfing himself in nature and its cyclical rhythms as an organic part of it. This is heathen man's way of realizing his humanness; heathen man feels wrong, and (if I may so put it) not truly himself, to the degree that he stands out of nature as an incommensurable element. Heathenism is thus at bottom total immanence, a primal unity of the divine, nature, and man.

Heathenism in this sense is obviously not something confined to primitive peoples remote in time and place. On the contrary, the heathen way of understanding man in his relation to ultimate reality seems to enter into the spirituality of men at all times and places, including our own. It emerges in the nature pantheism of so many spiritually-minded people of our time, as well as in the "hard-boiled" scientistic naturalism that holds nature to be ultimate and sees man as nothing more than a biological organism adjusting to its environment.

Standing in a kind of polar opposition to the heathen outlook is the outlook characteristic of the tradition of Greek philosophy and Oriental mysticism. Here it is not nature which is held to be ultimate and really real—though it is often spoken of as in some sense divine—but the *timelessly eternal* behind nature. A sharp dualism of appearance and reality is basic to this view: appearance is material and empirical, multiple, mutable, temporal, engrossed in flux; reality is one, immutable, timeless, eternal, spiritual. This ontological dualism of appearance and reality, the temporal and the eternal, is mirrored in a body-soul dualism in terms of which human being is analyzed.

The real self is the soul, and human self-realization becomes essentially the extrication of the self from nature and time (the body) and its elevation to the timeless realm of spirit. It is surely unnecessary to document the pervasiveness of this type of outlook, with its spiritualistic emphasis and its disparagement of time and history, among the religious people of our time. It is perhaps necessary to remind ourselves that, however high-minded and spiritual it may appear, this outlook, like the heathenism it replaces, is utterly alien to biblical faith, which understands human existence and ultimate reality in very different categories.

II

Biblical faith defines a view of reality and human existence that marks a sharp break with the presuppositions of both heathenism and Greek-Oriental spirituality. In biblical faith, nature is real and time no illusion, since they are the creation of God: this is the biblical witness against the spiritualistic devaluation of the natural and the temporal. Yet though real, they are not self-subsistent or ultimate, since they look to God as their creator: here biblical faith takes its stand against heathen immanentism. In exactly the same way, biblical faith refuses to dissolve man into nature, as does heathenism, or into timeless spirit, as is the effort of so much of philosophy and mysticism. In biblical faith, man is understood as (to use a modern and perhaps inexact term) a psychophysical unity, really and truly part of nature, yet transcending it by virtue of his "spirit," his freedom, his self-awareness, his capacity to get beyond and outside of himself, by virtue of the "image of God" in which he is made.

This complex, multidimensional conception makes it possible, for the first time, to understand man as a genuinely personal and historical being. Heathen naturalism assimilates man's time (history) to nature's time, and feels the uniqueness of the self—insofar as that emerges—as a threat to the oneness with nature which is blessedness. Greek-Oriental eternalism necessarily devaluates history as pure temporality and finds no place for the self, with its uniqueness and multiplicity, in the realm of the really real. It is in biblical faith that the self and history come into their own, for in biblical faith it is man's "essential dignity" that he is a self and "can have a history."[1] Indeed, the two are really one: in biblical faith, human history is intrinsically personal, and the self is a historical structure.

Here we come close to the heart of the matter. Biblical faith understands human existence and human destiny in irreducibly historical terms. If the question is asked, what is the real reality of man?—what is it the actualization of which constitutes the fullness of his being?—the heathen (turned philosopher) would say nature; the Greek metaphysician and the Oriental mystic would say that which is timeless and eternal in him; but the biblical thinker would say his *history*. History is the very stuff out of which human being is made: human existence is potential or implicit history; history is explicit or actualized existence. And it is not very different on the corporate level. In attempting to explain to someone who really does not know what it means to be an American, it would be futile to try to contrive some conceptual definition of "Americanness." Would it not prove more appropriate to tell the story of America and rely upon that story to communicate the fullness of what it means to be an American? "The human person and man's society," Reinhold Niebuhr has profoundly observed, "are *by nature historical* . . . [and] the ultimate truth about life must be mediated historically" (emphasis added).[2]

This is the biblical understanding of man as a historical being. On the basis of this understanding, biblical faith insists that man can realize himself only in and through his life in history. It is in and through history that God calls to man; it is in and through history, human action in history, that man responds; and it is in and through history that God judges.

Heathen man pursues his life in nature below the level of history; Greek-Oriental man aspires to escape from history into the realm of timeless eternity. On the contrary, biblical man, seeing human existence as essentially historical, strives to redeem history, though realizing that it is not in his time or by his hand that the work can be completed.

It is in this context that the biblical notion of *Heilsgeschichte* (redemptive history, "sacred history") emerges and becomes intelligible. Lessing, in his famous address "On the Proof of the Spirit and of Power" (1777),[3] protested that "particular facts of history cannot establish eternal truths," least of all the truths of religion; and Fichte reiterated that "the metaphysical only and not the historical can give blessedness." They were both repeating Celsus' outraged remonstrance against the "scandal of particularity," which is the "scandal" of history.[4] But he who understands the reality of human being in biblical terms will find no difficulty in understanding that the ultimate truth about human life and destiny, about man's plight and man's hope alike, is truly and inexpugnably historical, and can be expressed in no other way. (Hence the Bible is composed so largely of stories, recitals, histories.) The structure of faith is a historical structure, because being, living, and acting are, in the biblical conviction, radically historical in character.

III

Once we come to understand our existence in terms of history, and to analyze the human situation in historical terms, we begin to grasp what it means to think of faith as *Heilsgeschichte.* Examining the structure of our existence, we see that each of us has—or rather *is*—many partial histories, reflecting the many concerns and interests of life. We are Americans, members of a particular family and ethnic group, intimately associated with particular social institutions and movements.

Each of these concerns, allegiances, and associations has its own special history through which it is expressed and made explicit. But most of these histories, we ourselves realize, are merely partial histories; they define only fragments of our being and do not tell us who we "really" are. Underlying and including the partial histories of life, there must be some "total" history, in some way fundamental and comprehensive, some really ultimate history. Such a history, the history which one affirms in a total and ultimate manner, is one's *redemptive history (Heilsgeschichte)*, for it is the history in terms of which the final meaning of life is established and the self redeemed from the powers of meaninglessness and nonbeing. This is the history that defines, and is defined by, one's faith; it is, indeed, the history that *is* one's faith. "To be a self," H. Richard Niebuhr has said, "is to have a god; to have a god is to have a history."[5] If we reverse this—"To have a history is to have a god; to have a god is to be a self"—we get a glimpse of the full significance of the relation of faith and history.

Whatever history I take to tell me who I "really" am may thus be taken to define my actual faith. If I take my American history to define not merely the American aspect of my life, but also the fullness and ultimacy of my being as a person, I make "Americanism" (the American way of life) my faith and the nation my god. A moment's thought will show us how real this faith is in the lives of most of us today, and how clearly it is expressed as *Heilsgeschichte*. It has its symbols, liturgy, and ceremony, its holy days and cultic observances; it has its "sacred history" and its sense of messianic vocation. In this country, more than anywhere else in the world perhaps, the old Christian church year has been all but replaced in law and in fact by a round of holidays (Columbus Day, Washington's Birthday, Independence Day, Memorial Day, Armistice [or Veterans] Day, etc.) that mark the great events in our national history. These are the days that Americans, insofar as they celebrate anything, celebrate as the "holy days" that really count. (Christmas and Easter are virtually all that remain of the old church calendar for the mass of Americans, and even these holidays have been largely voided of their religious content.) Perhaps even more revealing is the response of a group of outstanding Americans to the request that they rate the one hundred most significant events in universal history. As reported in *Time* (May 24, 1954), first place was given to Columbus' discovery of America, while Christ, either his birth or crucifixion, came fourteenth, tied with the Wright brothers' first plane flight. This order of priority, so shocking in terms of Christian faith, becomes quite intelligible, even inevitable, once it is realized that the framework of faith in which it is made is the faith of "Americanism." This faith is defined by American history taken as ultimate and redemptive; it is only natural that those who hold this faith and this redemptive history should see Columbus' discovery of America (or alternatively, the American War of Independence) as the most important event in the annals of mankind.[6]

Marxism, the great rival of Americanism in the conflict of secular religions, is as thoroughly historical in structure, and even more obviously the reflection of the absolutization of a partial history. Marxism takes the partial history defined by the proletarian status of the modern worker as the ultimate and "total" history, and this history it proclaims as redemptive. From this standpoint, Marxism is, fundamentally, a secularized version—and therefore perversion—of biblical "sacred history," in which God is replaced by the Dialectic, the "chosen people" by the proletariat, the "faithful remnant" and even the Messiah by the Party, while the "beginning" and "end" of history, the "original rightness" lost and the "restored rightness" to come, are robbed of their transcendence and made points *within* the historical process. That Marxism is essentially a faith—an idolatrous faith—enacted as history, and therefore a *Heilsgeschichte,* is now almost a commonplace.

And so generally. Idolatrous faiths (particularly those emerging in the history-conscious West) are faiths defined by, and defining, partial histories made ultimate. They bear witness to gods that are idolatrous, in the sense that they are gods who are something of this world—some idea, institution, movement, power, or community—divinized and turned into absolutes. The idolatrous god thus has his idolatrous "sacred history"; very frequently, it is the idolatrous "sacred history" that is more vivid in men's minds than the god to whom it points.

Biblical faith, because it is faith in the living God, the God who is "beyond the gods" of the world, expresses itself in a redemptive history in which this God is central and the "holy people of God" the crucial historical community. And just as faith in the living God is the only alternative to idolatrous faiths, so, in the last analysis, the definition of life in terms of the "sacred history" of God's dealings with men given in biblical tradition is the only alternative to the idolatrous "totalization" of one or another of the partial histories which make up our lives. The ultimate existential decision is a choice between "sacred histories" as it is a choice between gods.

IV

Biblical faith, understood as history, presents us with a grand and stirring drama of human existence and destiny. It is not my purpose to describe this cosmic drama, since that has been done and magnificently done in a number of recent works on biblical religion. In its essentials, it defines a three-phase pattern in which the present "wrong" and contradictory existence of man and society is seen as a falling away from the original "rightness" of God's creation, and as destined for restoration and rectification in the final fulfillment of the kingdom of God. Within this vast orbit, it traces the history of the "people of God"—God's instrument for the redemption of mankind. All human history falls under its range and sweep, since its purpose is universal, though its center—the crucial revelatory, community-creating event (Exodus-Sinai in Judaism, Calvary-Easter in Christianity)—is particular. But no attempt is made to impose a final "philosophy of history" upon the historical material, which is drawn from legend, saga, oral tradition, and written documents. Every understanding of history is felt to be partial and fragmentary; in the end, everything is swallowed up in the mystery of divine providence. Yet, however limited and uncertain our grasp of it may be, it is the "sacred history" that tells us who we are, where we stand, and what we hope for— that, in short, gives meaning to existence.

It has been repeatedly pointed out in recent years, and not by theologians alone, that this understanding of history tends to make for a creative realism that escapes utopianism on the one side and despair on the other. It is, in fact, the only real alternative to the many historical idolatries of our time, which are now seen to be distortions, often demonic distortions, of the historical faith and hope of the Bible.

Yet even with this understanding we have not penetrated to the heart of biblical faith as *Heilsgeschichte*. For we are still, as it were, on the outside looking in. Biblical "sacred history" possesses a double inwardness. It is, first of all, an interpretation through the eyes of faith of acts and events that, from another standpoint, might well be interpreted in an altogether different way: to Thucydides, the victorious Assyrian would hardly have appeared as the rod of God's anger against a wayward Israel. But it is inward also in another and perhaps deeper sense, in the sense that, as the history of God's redemptive work, it can become actually redemptive *for me*, redemptive existentially, only if I appropriate it in faith as *my personal history*, the history of my own life. "Faith in the New Testament sense," writes Oscar Cullmann, "is the way by which the past phase of redemptive history becomes effectual for me. . . . Faith in the New Testament sense means to be convinced of the fact that this entire happening takes place *for me*." [7] Remembrance and expectation are the two foci of existence in faith.

"He who does not himself remember that God led him out of Egypt, he who does not himself await the Messiah," says Martin Buber, "is no longer a true Jew."[8] Religion is thus not the apprehension of eternal truths or loyalty to eternal values; it is rather the personal acceptance, through commitment and action, of what God has done, is doing, and will do for the redemption of mankind, and in the first place of oneself.[9] From this angle, the act of faith is double: the existential affirmation of a history as one's redemptive history and the existential appropriation of this redemptive history as one's personal background history, and therefore in a real sense the foundation of one's personal existence. "In the history of Israel," to quote Buber once more, "we see the prehistory of our own life, each of us the prehistory of his own life."[10]

But this means that redemptive history is not merely a recital that we hear and understand. It is also a demand upon us, for out of it comes the voice of God. Faith is responding to the call of God that comes to us from out of the midst of redemptive history. It is (to borrow from Kierkegaard) as though we sat witnessing some tremendous epic drama being performed on a vast stage, when suddenly the chief character of the drama, who is also its director, steps forward to the front of the stage, fixes his eye upon us, points his finger at us, and calls out: "You, you're wanted. Come up here. Take your part!" This is the call of faith coming from out of "sacred history," the call to cease to be a spectator and come forward to be an actor in the great drama of redemption. We are none of us comfortable with this call; we much prefer the anonymity and irresponsibility of being spectators, and we resent the demand that we come forward, assume responsibility, and become actors. But precisely this is the demand of biblical faith as redemptive history. Unless we receive this call and respond to it, the redemptive history that we apprehend is not redemptive. It does not really tell us who we are, where we stand, and what we may hope for; it does not really give meaning to existence. The history which redeems is a history in which one is both object and subject, both spectator and actor; but paradoxically, it is a history in which one is not object unless he is subject, one is not spectator unless he is actor, for unless one is really actor and subject, the "sacred history" ceases to be personal history and loses all religious significance. Redemptive history, to be truly redemptive, must be existential, appropriated in inwardness in personal existence as a demand and a responsibility. This is the meaning of biblical faith as *Heilsgeschichte*.

NOTES

1. Søren Kierkegaard, *Either/Or*, tr. by Walter Lowrie (Princeton University Press, 1948), Vol. II, p. 209.

2. Reinhold Niebuhr, "Religion and Education," *Religious Education*, Vol. XLVIII (Nov.–Dec., 1953), p. 373.

3. *Lessing's Theological Writings*, ed. by Henry Chadwick (Stanford University Press, 1957), pp. 51–56.

4. [Celsus was a learned pagan philosopher of the second century A.D., whose "True Discourse" may be the oldest extant literary attack on Christianity. The major part of his literary work is available to us indirectly through the eight-volume reply of Origen, *Contra Celsum*, which dates from the third century.—EDITOR]

5. H. Richard Niebuhr, *The Meaning of Revelation* (The Macmillan Company, 1941), p. 80.

6. See Will Herberg, *Protestant—Catholic—Jew: An Essay in American Religious Sociology* (Doubleday & Company, Inc., 1955), Ch. V.

7. Oscar Cullmann, *Christ and Time*, tr. by Floyd V. Filson, rev. ed. (The Westminster Press, 1964), p. 219.

8. Martin Buber, "Der Preis," *Der Jude*, Oct., 1917.

9. In other words, redemption in the biblical sense is history, though history is not, as the Marxists or liberal utopians think, redemptive.

10. Martin Buber, "The Place of Hasidism in the History of Religion," in *Hasidism*, tr. by Greta Hort *et al.* (Philosophical Library, Inc., 1948), p. 199. This is true for both Jew and Christian, though the Christian, of course, extends the "old Israel" into the "new Israel" of the church.

Basic to Will Herberg's understanding of himself as a biblical theologian is his perception of the interrelation between the Jewish and Christian communities. As Herberg himself admits, he was profoundly influenced in this respect by the thought of the Jewish philosopher Franz Rosenzweig (1886–1929), who also believed that Jew and Christian have a complementary relationship to each other in the purpose of God (see the Introduction). But Herberg brings to the discussion a positive view of historicism and an eschatological perspective which leads beyond, and at points even challenges, Rosenzweig's thought.

The following essay was originally delivered as an address before the National Association of Biblical Instructors (later to become the American Academy of Religion) at a meeting held at Union Theological Seminary in New York City, December 28, 1952, and was published in *The Journal of Bible and Religion,* Vol. XXI (1953). It is reprinted by permission of the *Journal of the American Academy of Religion.*

2

JUDAISM AND CHRISTIANITY

Their Unity and Difference

The Double Covenant in the Divine Economy of Salvation

I

No one who examines Judaism and Christianity in a broad religiohistorical perspective can fail to be impressed by the profound likeness of the two religions. However significant the differences between them may be when seen at close range, the essential similarity they exhibit becomes very striking when the two, taken together, are contrasted with the nonbiblical "religions of the world." In such a perspective, they strike one as being virtually identical in their structure of faith. Let me briefly formulate this common structure as it is exhibited in both Judaism and Christianity in their authentic forms:

1. They both affirm the living God, the God of Abraham, Isaac, and Jacob, the God of Israel, as Creator, King, Judge, and Redeemer.

2. They both see in Abraham's coming out of the pagan world in response to the divine call the crucial break with the religions and philosophies of the world and the establishment of the covenant that defines man's authentic relation to God.

3. They both assert that true knowledge of God is accessible only through his self-revelation in encounter with man and that scripture is in some sense both vehicle and record of such revelation.

4. They both see man as a unitary, self-transcending, dy-

namic, responsive, and responsible creature, in contrast to both the mystical-idealist and the naturalist views of man.

5. They both see man as originally (in the order of creation) ordained to God and therefore at one with the world and himself. They both see this primal harmony upset and all creation "spoiled" by man's sin, which is essentially self-will in rebellion against God, the idolatrous diversion of ultimate allegiance from God to something that is not God. They therefore see no way out for man from the misery of sinful existence except through repentance and a restoration of the proper relation to God in total love and obedience. And, for both, such restoration is possible only through the grace of a loving and merciful God.

6. They both share a realistic and actualistic emphasis: they both see the world, and human action within it, as real and important, though of course they hold the world to be the creation of God and therefore without any claims to ultimacy or self-subsistence in its own right.

7. For both, an ethic of obedience is central in the requirement of faith, and the demand of God is a moral demand for righteousness and love in action. In this they differ from the nature religions, which do not rise to ethics but seek a unity with the divine through harmony with the rhythms of nature, as well as from the mystical religions, which pretend to transcend ethics in a self-dissolving union with the divine.

8. Both are eschatological: they look forward to a transhistorical "end" of history, which is both judgment and fulfillment, and in which the full meaning of life and history is revealed.

9. In both, faith is defined by and expressed through a saved and saving community, which is understood as an instrument of God with a divine vocation in history. And both see Israel as such an elect community of God.

10. Both are historical religions in the profound sense that for both religion is *faith enacted as history,* incapable of being

expressed, understood, or communicated apart from the history in and through which it is enacted. For both, the context of sacred history is basically the same, the history of the People Israel. And both see the entire human enterprise as part of a great three-phase process of *Heilsgeschichte* [salvation history] —of creation, fall, and redemption. Both look back to a crucial redemptive and revelatory act in the past, which was also the community-creating event, an event that came as prefigurement and instrument of the fulfillment of God's purpose. In both, therefore, the very quintessence of faith is (to use Buber's phrase) the attitude of remembrance and expectation—remembrance of God's gracious act of redemption in the past and expectation of the full and final redemption to come.

In all of these respects, and they are surely basic, Judaism and Christianity are at one with each other and poles apart from the nonbiblical "religions of the world." Is it any wonder that Christian theologians speak of Judaism and Christianity as "not, fundamentally, two different religions but one" (Frederick C. Grant)[1] and note with emphasis "the identity of structure at all points and the identity of content in most" of the two faiths (Tillich),[2] or that a Jewish theologian (Finkelstein) refers to Judaism and Christianity as "twin religions" and indeed speaks of them as constituting "one system"?[3] There can be little doubt that the two religions belong together in a most intimate way. Yet in their very likeness they are different, and to define this difference within the framework of their unity now becomes our task.

II

It is necessary, in the first place, to note and to evaluate some of the attempts that have been made to establish criteria by which Judaism and Christianity may be validly distinguished. Martin Buber's recent and Hermann Cohen's earlier attempts[4] to make this distinction in terms of a basic difference between Jewish *'emunah* and Christian *pistis* seem to me to fail because of the discrepancy in terms of comparison; they take *'emunah* in its authentic Hebraic meaning of utter trust and self-commitment, but *pistis* they take not in its true biblical sense but as overlaid with Greek intellectualism. Nor is the distinction, made by Parkes and others,[5] that Judaism is corporate while Christianity is individual valid in any but a very relative sense; in both, the tension between the corporate and the personal is to be found, though naturally expressed in somewhat different ways. Most fallacious, it seems to me, is the attempt, familiar through the centuries, to distinguish the two religions by making Judaism, especially the Judaism of New Testament times, into a religion of dead legalism and justification through works, in contrast to Christianity as a religion of grace and faith. "It was quite generally held," Hans-Werner Bartsch comments in his summary of recent Protestant theological thinking, "that the religion of later Judaism [he means the Judaism of New Testament times] was dominated entirely by thoughts of righteousness for reward, and so provided the dark background for Jesus' proclamation of forgiveness. But now Erik Sjöberg has shown *(Gott und Sünder in palästinischen Judentum nach dem Zeugnis der Tannaiten)* that the idea of repentance and forgiveness was present in late Judaism as well. This confronts New Testament scholarship with the task of presenting the significance of the proclamation of Jesus Christ."[6] It was hardly necessary to wait for Sjöberg's researches, valuable as they are, to reach this conclusion; the same lesson might have been learned from the writings of such well-known scholars as George Foot Moore, Claude Montefiore, and Travers Herford.[7] The fact of the matter is that the demand of the law and the gospel of grace are to be found in both religions; indeed, as Luther once exclaimed, where is the man who can properly distinguish between law and gospel?

The real distinction between Judaism and Christianity

seems to me to lie elsewhere. To see the two in their proper
relation, it is necessary to relate each and both to the divine
economy of salvation as that is biblically understood.

The central category of biblical thinking is covenant. "Never
imagine that you have rightly grasped a biblical idea," Paul
Ramsey has said, "until you have reduced it to a corollary of
the idea of 'covenant.' "8 And this is supremely true of biblical
thinking about salvation. In the biblical view, man has, so to
speak, standing with God, and a direct personal relation to
him, only by virtue of his membership in the people of God,
the redeemed and redeeming community. "The individual Israelite," Alan Richardson points out quite emphatically, "approached God in virtue of his membership in the holy people.
. . . In the whole of the Bible, in the Old Testament as well
as the New, there is no such thing as a private personal relation
between an individual and God apart from his membership in
the covenant-folk."9 Man's relation to God is essentially responsive; it is God's call expressed in the grace of election that
gives man the possibility of, from his side, entering into personal relationship with God. Modern religious existentialism,
in its very welcome emphasis on personal confrontation, tends
to forget that such confrontation is, humanly speaking—there
can be no question of limiting God's grace—possible only
within, and on the basis of, the covenant. In the biblical view,
people outside the covenant, properly called gentiles, cannot—
apart from the uncovenanted grace of God, which is virtually
covenant-creating—of themselves find their way to God or
meet him in personal confrontation. In our modern intellectualistic and therefore inadequate terminology, this is equivalent
to saying that only the religion of Israel brings men to God;
other, pagan, religions, the "religions of the world," lead them
away from God.

The covenant of Israel is understood by the prophets, and
perhaps much earlier, as the covenant of a redeemed and
redeeming community; the purpose it defines is a universal

purpose and the people it brings into being is an instrument of God for the redemption of mankind. All of mankind is to be brought into the covenant and, within the covenant, restored to a right relation to God.

The paradox of Israelite religion was that a covenant of such universal scope and purpose was actualized in a particular folk or ethnic community. To affirm the God of Israel involved coming under the covenant and that meant becoming part of the Israelitish, or Jewish, people in the folk sense of the term. Despite all rabbinic efforts to establish halfway covenants and categories in order to facilitate proselytizing and thus help realize the universal vocation of Israel, this fact remained a fact and could not basically be altered. In this situation, Christianity emerged to break through the paradox and bring the "nations of the world" to the God of Israel by bringing them under the covenant of Israel in a new form. Through Christianity, God's covenant with Israel was opened to all mankind—without requiring a change of ethnic or "national" status. This is simply a historical fact, and has been noted as such by quite unbelieving historians; but it is also the conclusion of Paul, who in true Hebraic spirit attempts to discern the purposes of God in the course of historic events.

God's covenant with Israel is opened to all mankind through Christ. I hesitate to touch upon this tremendous question; I will say in advance that my comments relate to only one aspect of Christ's vocation, but that aspect is, I think, very relevant to the purposes of the present discussion.

As the one by whom and through whom the covenant of Israel is opened to mankind, Christ appears in early Christian thinking as, quite literally, an incarnate or one-man Israel, the Remnant-Man. Through union in faith with him, the gentile believer becomes part of Israel; he therefore comes under the covenant and thereby becomes heir to the promises of God to Israel. "So remember," Paul tells recent gentile converts, "that at that time when you were without Christ, you were aliens to the commonwealth of Israel and strangers to the covenants of promise. . . . But now through your union with Christ Jesus, you, who were once far away, have . . . been brought near . . . so that you are no longer strangers and foreigners but fellow citizens of God's people and of the family of God" (Eph. 2:12-19). "And if you are Christ's," he says elsewhere, "then you are Abraham's seed, heirs according to the promise" (Gal. 3:29). A modern Jewish scholar has put what he takes to be Paul's meaning in these words: "He so broadened the term 'Jew' as to include in it, as an honorable fellowship, all those who transformed their lives by being faithful Christians."[10]

Through Christ, a new covenant-community is created—the Church, the "Body of Christ." Through Christ, Israel's *Heilsgeschichte* becomes the redemptive history of the pagan-turned-Christian, who thus becomes in effect an Israelite. "Through Jesus Christ," writes H. Richard Niebuhr, "Christians of all races recognize the Hebrews as their fathers; they build into their lives as Englishmen or as Americans, as Italians or Germans, the memories of Abraham's loyalty, of Moses' heroic leadership, of prophetic denunciations and comfortings. All that has happened to the strange and wandering people of God becomes a part of their own past."[11]

Christian faith thus brings into being and defines a new covenant, which is new not in the sense of supplanting the old but in the sense of extending and enlarging it, very much as we speak of the New World side by side with the Old World. For with the emergence of Christianity, the election and vocation of Israel are not annulled. On this, Jews of course insist, and on this Christian theologians as far apart as H. Wheeler Robinson and Karl Barth agree. "Israel," says the former, "remains an elect nation by virtue of the divine choice and that choice is sufficiently vindicated by that which Israel's history has produced."[12] "Is Israel's mission thereby suspended?" asks the latter. "No; on the contrary, through everything . . . God's election holds and will hold to all eternity. . . . God keeps faith [with Israel] right through all stages of its wanderings. . . . [So] God's faithfulness in the reality of Israel is in fact the guarantee of his faithfulness to us and to all men."[13] The election of Israel remains, and its vocation remains, though it assumes a form in the Christian world different from that which it possessed in the pre-Christian world.

It is not without significance that the bringing of the gospel to the world and the opening of the covenant of Israel to all mankind came only after a vigorous conflict within the early Christian community; the restrictive conceptions which dominated this community were such that, had they triumphed, Christianity would have been doomed to remain just another Jewish sect. It was Paul preeminently who saw the purpose of God and strove to bring Christ, and therefore the covenant and the God of Israel, to the non-Jewish world. Yet it was not until the fall of Jerusalem, and the virtual elimination of the earlier Jewish-Christian "Mother-Church" of that city, that Paul's victory was assured. With the church of Jerusalem, though at the other pole, were eliminated also the Sadducees, whose existence was tied to the Temple. We may pause a moment to marvel how the very same catastrophic event—the fall of Jerusalem and the destruction of the Temple—served as the historical instrument for assuring the victory, each in its own community, of the "twin religions," rabbinic Judaism and Pauline Christianity. How unsearchable indeed are God's judgments and his ways past finding out! [See Rom. 11:33.]

III

We may now resume the original line of argument. What I have been trying to say can be summarized as follows: Judaism and Christianity represent one religious reality, Judaism facing inward to the Jews and Christianity facing outward to the gentiles, who, through it, are brought to the God and under the covenant of Israel, and therefore cease to be gentiles. This is the unity of Judaism and Christianity.

What, then, are the differences? They are differences of mediation, of vocation, and of orientation. And these differences, though they emerge within the framework of the unity of the two faiths, are of crucial importance.

In both Judaism and Christianity, as I have pointed out, there is no such thing as a direct and unmediated relation to God; this relation must in some way be mediated through one's covenant status. In Judaism, however, it is by virtue of his being a member of the People Israel that the believer approaches God and has standing before him; in Christianity, it is by virtue of his being a member of Christ. This is clearly brought out in the structure of prayer of the two faiths. Both Christian and Jew open their prayers with an invocation to God, go on to their petitions, and conclude with a kind of commendatory plea. But the Christian says "through" or "for the sake of Christ our Lord," whereas the Jew concludes with "for the sake of Israel thy people"; the one recalls the "merits of Christ," the other the "merits of the fathers" (Abraham, Isaac, and Jacob; i.e., Israel). To be a Jew means to meet God and receive his grace in and through Israel; to be a Christian means to meet God and receive his grace in and through Christ.

In the matter of orientation, authentic Judaism is therefore Israel-centered (I mean, of course, the covenant-people Israel, not the State of Israel), while authentic Christianity is Christ-centered. In neither need this centrality lead to a diversion from God, because in both it is through mediation that God is approached.

There is also a corresponding difference in their *Heilsgeschichten*, which structurally are so alike. Both Judaism and Christianity anchor their faith in a redemptive, revelatory, and community-creating event, which becomes the center of history: in Judaism, it is the Sinai-event; in Christianity, the Christ-event.[14] Both have an eschatology that is "realized" and futuristic at the same time, though the "realized" aspect is obviously stronger in Christianity and the futuristic in Judaism.

Everything converges on the problem of vocation. The vocation of both Judaism and Christianity can be defined in common terms: to stand witness to God amidst the idolatries of the world, or in the familiar rabbinic formula, *kiddush ha-Shem*— the sanctification of the Name. But the Jew fulfills his vocation by "staying with God," while the Christian can fulfill his only by "going out" to conquer the world for God. (I use the concepts and terminology of Franz Rosenzweig, the great German-Jewish philosopher and theologian whose profound insights on the relationship of Judaism and Christianity I am trying to present.) What does this distinction basically mean? I think I can best indicate my meaning by quoting from a recent essay by Roger Shinn: "Inevitably [says Roger Shinn] Hitler found in the Jews *(by their very existence)* and in *faithful* Christians *(by their religious protests)* a reminder of the universalism . . . he could not tolerate" (emphasis added).[15]

I call your attention to the words I have emphasized. What do they imply? They imply that whereas to fulfill his witness the Christian must be "faithful" and must make a "religious protest," the Jew stands witness by his very being, simply by being. Because of his anomalous status in the non-Jewish world —and this, too, cannot be understood as historical accident, but must be seen, through the eyes of faith, as reflecting the purposes of God—the Jew is forced to live the "semi-detached" existence—in the world, but never quite of it—to which the Christian aspires. Recall the picture of Christian life given in the Epistle to Diognetus: "The Christians dwell in all countries, but only as sojourners. As citizens, they share in all things with others and yet endure all things as if they were strangers. Every foreign land is to them as a native country, and every land of their birth is as a land of strangers." This is the Christian life as it should be, but it is the Jewish actuality. The Christian may very easily make his peace with the world at the expense of his faith; he then lapses into idolatry and worships the "gods of space," as Tillich puts it. The Jew, so long as he remains and is known as a Jew, cannot do that, however much he may desire to. The Jew is, whether he will or not, a standing reproach to the pagan in man and society, an unassimilable element in any culture engaged in deifying itself—and he is that simply by being a Jew and quite apart from his personal faith or desire, "by [his] very existence," as Roger Shinn puts it. The choice for him is authentic or unauthentic Jewish existence, God's witness in self-affirmation or in self-repudiation—but God's witness he remains nevertheless. Such is the "mystery of Israel."

The Jew's vocation is to "stand," the Christian's to "go out" —both in the same cause, the cause of the Kingdom. This difference of vocation, combined with the parallel differences in mediation and orientation, make for a series of other differences which are also equivalences. The liturgical pattern reflects in a particularly faithful manner the identity of structure yet difference of content to which Tillich refers. In both Judaism and Christianity, the central liturgical pattern is the reenactment of the crucial revelatory, redemptive, and community-creating event—the Exodus-Sinai-event in Judaism, the Christ-event in Christianity. Pesach, Sukkot, and Shabuot [Passover, Tabernacles, Weeks], the three great pilgrim festivals, reenact phases of the Sinai-event that brought Israel into being; Good Friday, Easter, and Pentecost, with perhaps Christmas prefixed, reenact phases of the Christ-event that brought the Church into being. In both cases, the believer reenacts these events liturgically in order to appropriate them existentially as part of his own being and history. "All this I do," says the Jew reciting the Passover Haggadah, "because of what God did for *me* in bringing me out of Egypt." And the Mishnah comments: "In every generation, a man must so regard himself as if he himself came forth from Egypt."[16] This is, of course, equivalent to the familiar Christian concept which Pascal formulates in these words: "Everything that happened to Jesus Christ must take place in the soul and in the body of every Christian. . . . Everything that happens to the Church happens also to every Christian as an individual."[17] Existential appropriation of *Heilsgeschichte* in contemporaneity is the basic principle of Jewish and Christian liturgy alike, the difference arising from the difference in the *heilsgeschichtliche* event that forms the core of each faith.

The alleged distinction between Judaism as corporate and Christianity as individual finds its relative validation but also its limitation in this context. In both Judaism and Christianity, normative religious existence is corporate; no one—not even the hermit in the desert—can be a Christian all by himself apart from the Church, any more than the Jew can be a Jew all by himself apart from Israel. In both, the personal confrontation with God, which is at the heart of faith, occurs normatively only within the context of the corporate covenant group. Yet there is this difference: the Jew is born a Jew, the Christian is born a pagan and becomes a Christian through accepting Christ. The Christian's religious experience, therefore, normatively begins with a personal confrontation and a personal act of faith, even if (as in infant baptism) that act is vicariously performed by a sponsor. For the Jew, however, religious existence is normatively corporate from the beginning, since the Jew is born into the covenant. (The pagan convert to Judaism constitutes the exception that, so to speak, proves the rule, since the pagan who becomes a Jew, like the pagan who becomes a Christian, but in contrast to the Jew born a Jew, begins with a personal act of faith and its appropriate ritual expression.) This difference is not without its effect on the *ethos* of the two faiths.

But, of course, the most familiar difference between Judaism and Christianity is a difference that is felt to be somehow related to the difference between law and grace, between *halakah* and *agape*. It is easy to misunderstand and misrepresent this difference. It is not as if law can be assigned to Judaism and grace to Christianity: both affirm law in some sense and both see law transcended and fulfilled in grace and love. Judaism is not salvation by works—the rabbis tell us that "our father Abraham inherited this world and the world-to-come solely by virtue of his faith";[18] and the observant Jew prays every morning, "Our Father, our King, be gracious unto us, for we have no works. Save us according to thy grace." On the other hand, Christianity does not disregard works—does not Paul himself tell us that everyone will be judged according to "the things done in his body, according to what he has done, whether it be good or bad" (II Cor. 5:10)? The difference goes much deeper than such superficial distinctions: it is a difference directly related to the basic difference in covenant character and vocation.

The Jew's relatively "static" vocation—he "stays with" God —is reflected in the regulative principle of *halakah*, which is central to normative Jewish faith. It is *halakah* as a holy discipline of life that maintains Israel's existence as covenant-people and therefore enables it to fulfill its vocation. But the Church's vocation is essentially to "go out"; its function is to shatter the pagan patterns of life and re-create everything in and under Christ; for that it needs the unbound weapon of the free *charisma* of grace. Yet there remains in both an inescapable polarity: Judaism has its *charisma* of grace, which was particularly evident in its periods of proselytizing activity; and Christianity has its *halakah* and law, which come to the fore when the Christian community, as in Calvinist Geneva, settles down to a relatively static existence. But the weights assigned to the two poles are very different, and that is everything.[19]

It is in terms of this difference that the ritual acting out of personal incorporation into the covenant community is defined. The Jew born a Jew is circumcised as a mark of the covenant; he, so to speak, appropriates his covenant existence through the ongoing pattern of halakic observance—that is how he affirms, maintains, and ever renews his belonging to Israel, the People of God. The Christian, on his part, becomes a Christian through baptism (or its equivalent); he appropriates his covenant existence through the one observance that, in Christian faith, replaces the entire *halakah*—the Lord's Supper. Precisely because, in Christian faith, Christ "fulfills the law," *all* ritual observances, for the Christian, are performed in the one sacrament of Christ, by which the believer renews his union with Christ and his belonging to the Church, the new people of God. Halakic observance and the Lord's Supper are thus essentially equivalents.

Within the same framework, we may understand something of the characteristic perils and corruptions of the two covenant communities. In respect to the covenant, the Jew's characteristic peril is the pride of exclusive possession—God's election was his from the beginning and his to keep for himself; the Christian's is the pride of supersession—the election is now his alone, the Jew having been disinherited. Again in respect to the covenant, but now negatively: the Jew who revolts against the "yoke of the Kingdom" expresses it in the so-called self-hatred that reflects both rejection of his vocation and bitter resentment at having been "separated" by God and forced to be "different"; the Christian, on the other hand, expresses his resentment against the claim of God through anti-Semitism. "Whenever the pagan within the Christian soul rises in revolt against the yoke of the Cross," Rosenzweig points out, "he vents his fury on the Jew"[20] as Christ-bringer. This is virtually identical with the view expounded by a number of recent Christian theologians, particularly A. Roy Eckardt, in his important work *Christianity and the Children of Israel* [1948], to which I am so much indebted.

In respect to the distinction between law and grace, the characteristic peril of the Jew is legalism, the notion that one can rely upon the meticulous performance of his obligations under the law to put him in a right relation with God; for the

Christian, the analogous peril is antinomianism, the belief that grace absolves the believer from all obligations under the law.

I will not attempt to continue the list of similarities, differences, and equivalences. My purpose is not to present an exhaustive account, but simply to stress that these similarities, differences, and equivalences are not really intelligible except in terms of the fundamental unity of Judaism and Christianity, which yet involves an essential distinction in vocation, mediation, and orientation.

IV

Let me now try to bring all the threads together by reformulating the relationship of Judaism and Christianity in their unity and difference, in their interdependence of function and witness.

"Israel," says Franz Rosenzweig, "can bring the world to God only through Christianity." [21] Despite all hostility through the ages, Jewish tradition has always "freely acknowledged the divine mission of Christianity" as "Israel's apostle" to the nations.[22] This, if one may venture to put it that way, is Christianity's service for Judaism.

But there is also Judaism's service for Christianity. "Christianity," Franz Rosenzweig continues, "could not long remain a force for redemption without Israel in its midst." [23]

It is important [Paul Tillich asserts] that there always be Judaism. It is the corrective against the paganism that goes along with Christianity. . . . The Church is always in danger of adoring the gods of space in which she is ruling. . . . The Church is always in danger of losing her prophetic spirit. . . . Therefore, the prophetic spirit included in the tradition of the Synagogue is needed so long as the gods of space are in power, and that means to the end of history. . . . Synagogue and Church should be united in our period in the struggle for the Lord of time.[24]

That the witness of the Jew through his very being a Jew is also a witness, and a very necessary witness, against the ever-present temptation of the Church to make its peace with the "gods of space," all recent history goes to show; and one must be grateful for the insight and integrity that have led so many Christian writers—Barth, Berdyaev, Tillich, Maritain, Eckardt—to draw this lesson of history and proclaim it to the Church and the world. "If, as Christians, we thought that Church and Synagogue no longer affect one another," says Barth, "everything would be lost. And where the separation . . . has been made complete, it is the Christian community which has suffered. The whole reality of the revelation of God is then secretly denied and as a result philosophy and ideology take the upper hand and Christianity of a Greek or German or some other kind is invented." [25] "Whenever the Church is in danger of drawing away from its source and forgetting its origins," the French Jesuit L. Richard asserts, "Israel is there to recall it thereto." [26] This is Judaism's service for Christianity.

Yet this interdependence is, after all, secondary. Primarily, each faith is the authentic form of religious existence for those who belong to the covenant community which it defines. "Granted that Judaism and Christianity are dialectically related, and hence that it is wrong to say that Christianity has taken the place of Judaism, a particular individual will nevertheless affirm confessionally why he must subscribe to Christianity rather than to Judaism or to Judaism rather than to Christianity. Were this not the case, the tension between the two faiths would not be real or meaningful." [27] These words of A. Roy Eckardt seem to me thoroughly valid and never to be forgotten as we stress the inescapable interdependence of the two faiths.

The last word, therefore, is difference in unity and unity in difference. "The two religions," says Franz Rosenzweig, "are equal representations of the truth—equal before God." [28] With God, truth is one, but for men it is irreducibly split *(entzweit)*, since the truth as men see it is confessional and conditioned by one's covenantal position. This is not a vicious relativism, nor does it assert for one moment that all religions are equally true or equally valid. On the contrary, as Rosenzweig puts it, man is either a pagan or a Jew or Christian. (Islam presents a problem; Rosenzweig does not regard it as a distinct way, nor do I; I think rather it is a kind of Jewish-Christian heresy.) The pagan, as pagan, does not rise to the level of the *Überwelt* [transcendent] (Franz Rosenzweig's term), where the Jew and Christian find themselves—although, of course, God in his grace may reach out to him. On this level of the *Überwelt,* Jew and Christian has each his assigned position, defined in the covenant that relates him to God. Their positions, their "standpoints," being different, their views of the one truth will be different—although they will be views of the same truth, just as two people standing in the same room but in different corners will see the room in different perspectives and therefore somewhat differently. Each will be loyal to the truth if he speaks out about the truth as he sees it, though recognizing that his truth is never quite identical with the full truth of God. "Truth is a noun only to God," says Franz Rosenzweig; "to men it is really best known as an adverb, 'truly' *(wahrlich),* as the measure of inner faithfulness." [29] "Granted that Judaism and Christianity are dialectically related," I repeat the words of A. Roy Eckardt quoted above, "a particular individual will nevertheless affirm confessionally why he must subscribe to Christianity rather than to Judaism or to Judaism rather than to Christianity." This does not derogate from the "finality" of either Judaism or Christianity, if that is properly understood; it merely prevents the idolization of either. For, strictly speaking, God alone is absolute, and our knowledge of the Absolute need not itself be absolute knowledge.

In short, each of us—the Jew on his part and the Christian on his—sees that aspect of the truth which is to be apprehended from his perspective, as that is defined by his covenantal position and vocation. Each of us must stand by his truth and confess it, recognizing that insofar as we do so in integrity and wholeness of heart, we remain faithful to the God whose truth it is. Naturally, we will see the same reality in somewhat different ways; naturally, too, each may see an aspect of reality hidden to the other, and even interpret the same things differently. But perhaps this is part of the purpose of God in placing Jew and Christian on different sectors of the fighting front of the Kingdom.

If what I have said makes any sense at all, it must follow that the authentic differences between Judaism and Christianity are not the result of ignorance or blindness, but are irreducible differences which must persist until the final clarification. Judaism and Christianity, as a young Jewish theologian has put it, are parallel lines meeting only at infinity. In the final clarification, we both believe, the two will be one—and then perhaps (let us be humble enough to admit it) neither "our" truth nor "their" error will prove to be quite as we see it today.

Again, if all this is at all valid, there can be no proselytizing between the Jewish and Christian communities. Finkelstein has connected the cessation of Jewish proselytism with the emergence of the "monotheistic faiths" of Christianity and Islam.[30] Eckardt has presented the Christian argument against the "mission to the Jews" in the book I have mentioned and in other writings. "The missionary view," he says, "is . . . challenged [not alone by "liberalism," but also] by some who accept Christian faith as in a certain sense final. . . . What is usually involved here is the contention that the Jews have a unique function in the divine economy. . . . The claim [that if the "mission to the Jews" is abandoned] it logically follows that missionary endeavor has to cease for all people, is seen as failing to realize that Judaism and other religions are not on the same plane. Christianity and Judaism have a relationship lacking between Christianity and other religions."[31] Not "mission to the Jews" or "mission to the Christians," but "Jewish-Christian conversation." [32] Each—the Jew on his part and the Christian on his—is obliged to make a confessional statement of his faith and to make it in "conversation," so to speak, with the other. Neither Judaism nor Christianity is "higher" or "more perfect" than the other—such criteria make no sense in biblical thinking; but from the standpoint of each, it is always possible to see the specific shortcomings and perils of the other, and, in all charity, to bear witness against them. "From a human point of view"—I quote Eckardt again—"certain shortcomings will be discerned in the alternate view. . . . I have no interest in trying to convert the Jews to Christianity. The intention here is to show why some of us must be Christians rather than Jews. Frank confession may help to further understanding." [33] The heart of each may ache, perhaps, that the other is not in his camp, fighting side by side with him on his sector of the front, but he must also recognize that though the other fights on another sector, he is also fighting for the living God and that it is perhaps by the providence of God that they are thus separated.

And so Jew and Christian stand separated yet united. The unity far transcends the separation, for we are united in our common allegiance to the living God and in our common expectation of, and longing for, the One who is to come. Jew and Christian—to recall Tillich's words—stand united until the end of history in the struggle for the Lord of time against the "gods of space."

NOTES

1. Frederick C. Grant, "The Teaching of Jesus and First-Century Jewish Ethics," in *The Study of the Bible Today and Tomorrow*, ed. by H. R. Willoughby (The University of Chicago Press, 1947), p. 312.

2. Paul Tillich, "Is There a Judaeo-Christian Tradition?" *Judaism*, Vol. I, No. 2 (1952), p. 109.

3. Louis Finkelstein, *Akiba: Scholar, Saint, and Martyr* (Covici & Friede, Inc., 1936), p. 6; *Tradition in the Making* (Jewish Theological Seminary of America, 1937), p. 12.

4. Martin Buber, *Two Types of Faith* (London: Routledge & Kegan Paul, Ltd., 1951); Simon Kaplan, "Hermann Cohen's Philosophy of Judaism," *Judaism*, Vol. I, No. 2 (1952), esp. pp. 145–146.

5. James Parkes, *Judaism and Christianity* (The University of Chicago Press, 1948).

6. Hans-Werner Bartsch, *Handbuch der evangelisch-theologischen Arbeit, 1938 bis 1948* (Stuttgart: Evangelisches Verlagswerk, 1949).

7. See, e.g., George Foot Moore, *Judaism in the First Centuries of the Christian Era*, 3 vols. (Harvard University Press, 1927–1930); and R. Travers Herford, *Pharisaism: Its Aim and Its Method* (G. P. Putnam's Sons, Inc., 1912), *Talmud and Apocrypha* (London: Soncino Press, Ltd., 1933), *The Pharisees* (The Macmillan Company, 1924), *Judaism in the New Testament Period* (London: Lindsey Press, 1928).

8. Paul Ramsey, "Elements of a Biblical Political Theory," *The Journal of Religion*, Vol. XXIX, No. 4 (1949), p. 258.

9. Alan Richardson, "Instrument of God," *Interpretation*, Vol. III, No. 3 (1949), p. 278.

10. Solomon Grayzel, "Christian-Jewish Relations in the First Millennium," in *Essays on Antisemitism*, ed. by K. S. Pinson (Conference on Jewish Relations, 1942), p. 27.

11. H. Richard Niebuhr, *The Meaning of Revelation* (The Macmillan Company, 1946), pp. 115–116.

12. H. Wheeler Robinson, *Inspiration and Revelation in the Old Testament* (Oxford: Clarendon Press, 1946), p. 159.

13. Karl Barth, *Dogmatics in Outline*, tr. by G. T. Thomson (Philosophical Library, Inc., 1949), p. 79; see also Maria F. Sulzbach, "Karl Barth and the Jews," *Religion in Life*, Vol. XXI, No. 4 (1952), pp. 585–593.

14. Both Martin Buber, *Israel and the World* (Schocken Books, 1948), p. 94, and Oscar Cullmann, *Christ and Time*, rev. ed. (The Westminster Press, 1964), *passim*, deny that there is any real "midpoint" or "center" in Israel's *Heilsgeschichte*, and indeed make this absence a point of difference between Judaism and Christianity. I do not see how the structure of Jewish faith permits any such interpretation.

15. Roger Shinn, "Religious Faith and the Task of the Historian," in *Liberal Learning and Religion*, ed. by Amos N. Wilder (Harper & Brothers, 1951), p. 70.

16. M. Pesahim 10.5.

17. Blaise Pascal, "Letter to M. and Mme. Perier" (Oct. 17, 1651), in *The Great Shorter Works of Pascal*, tr. by Emile Cailliet and John C. Blankenagel (The Westminster Press, 1948), p. 89; "Letter to M. and Mme. de Rouannez" (Sept., 1656), *ibid.*, p. 143.

18. Mekilta to Ex. 14:31, Jacob Z. Lauterbach, *Mekilta de-Rabbi Ishmael* (London: Routledge & Kegan Paul, Ltd., 1933), Vol. I, p. 253.

19. See the very significant article by Monford Harris, "Two Ways: *Halakah* and *Charisma,*" *Judaism*, Vol. I, No. 1 (1952), pp. 80–84.

20. Jacob B. Agus, "Franz Rosenzweig," in *Modern Philosophies of Judaism* (New York: Behrman's Jewish Book House, 1941), p. 194.

21. *Ibid.*, p. 193; Nahum N. Glatzer, *Franz Rosenzweig: His Life and Thought* (Schocken Books, 1953), p. 341.

22. A. A. Neuman, "Judaism," in *The Great Religions of the Modern World*, ed. by Edward J. Jurji (Princeton University Press, 1946), pp. 228–229.

23. Agus, *op. cit.*, p. 193; Glatzer, *op. cit.*, pp. 343–344.

24. Quoted in A. Roy Eckardt, *Christianity and the Children of Israel* (King's Crown Press, 1948), pp. 146–147.

25. Barth, *op. cit.*, p. 75.

26. L. Richard, "Israël et le Christ," in H. deLubac *et al.*, *Israël et la foi chrétienne* (Fribourg: Librairie de l'Université, 1942), p. 118.

27. A. Roy Eckardt, "Christian Faith and the Jews," *The Journal of Religion*, Vol. XXX, No. 4 (1950), p. 245.

28. Glatzer, *op. cit.*, pp. xxv–xxvi.

29. Agus, *op. cit.*, p. 191.

30. Louis Finkelstein, "The Beliefs and Practices of Judaism," in Louis Finkelstein *et al.*, *The Religions of Democracy* (Devin-Adair Company, 1941), p. 6.

31. Eckardt, "Christian Faith and the Jews," p. 236, and *Christianity and the Children of Israel*, p. 158.

32. It is gratifying to note that this conception is beginning to make itself felt among Continental Protestants; see J. H. Grolle, *Het Gesprek met Israël* (The Hague: 's-Gravenhage, Boekencentrum, 1949).

33. Eckardt, "Christian Faith and the Jews," p. 245.

Will Herberg's understanding of "faith enacted as history" calls for personal appropriation of the biblical story *(Heilsgeschichte)*. This appropriation requires not only that one become an actor in the historical arena where God is at work but that he reenact within the worshiping community the crucial, redemptive event of the story so that the past is contemporized or "made present." In the following essay, Herberg maintains that the Jewish and Christian communities, when celebrating, respectively, Passover and Easter, differ on the crucial event that is contemporized but hold analogous views on the meaning of worship.

This essay is reprinted by permission from the April 18, 1949, issue of *Christianity and Crisis*.

ETERNITY

Overwhelmed with a crushing sense of the utter meaninglessness of mere time and change, the reflective mind strives to escape into the realm of eternity. "Both in thought and in feeling to realize the unimportance of time," Bertrand Russell tells us, "is the gate of wisdom." Not the senseless flux of events but the eternal principles discovered in them constitute reality. Not the confusing succession of social customs but the eternal values hidden within them give significance to human life. History is an endless, meaningless chaos; only what is eternal, what is timeless, can have sense or value. This is the burden of the great classic tradition in philosophy, from Plato to Russell, and it is a view that has always appealed to sensitive and reflective minds.

But it is a view that we, who look to scripture for the fundamental insights of our religion, cannot share. Hebraic religion—and by this term I mean both Judaism and Christianity—Hebraic religion too searches for ultimate meaning. But unlike classic philosophy, it cannot brush aside the empirical world of time and history as meaningless, for does not scripture teach us in the plainest terms that this empirical world is the creation and the field of operation of the Living God, the sphere in which man is called to live and work? In devaluating time, philosophy devaluates life and cuts the nerve of action.

CONTEMPORANEITY

And so we turn back to time, but no longer in the simple and naive fashion in which we first accepted it. For now we must somehow effect a fusion between time and eternity, a dialectic fusion into one dynamic whole.

This dynamic whole—this dialectic fusion of time and eternity—is *contemporaneity*. Contemporaneity is at the heart of our Hebraic religion. We are accustomed to speak of Judaism and Christianity as historical religions in contrast to the non-historical religions and philosophies of Greece and the Far East. That means that Hebraic religion is not a system of abstract propositions but, in the most literal sense, a *faith enacted as history* and entirely unintelligible and incommunicable apart from that history. There is no Judaism without Abraham and Moses, without Egypt and Sinai; there is no Christianity without these and, in addition, without Jesus and Calvary. Hebraic religion abstracted from time and history is unthinkable. The devaluation of time may, as Russell suggests, be the gate to philosophic wisdom, but it is a wisdom that neither prophet nor apostle would have understood or accepted.

Yet this is not all that is meant by saying that Judaism and Christianity are historical faiths. They are not merely faiths enacted as history; they are historical faiths that every believer must reenact in his own life. That is what existential appropriation means. Every believing Jew *in his own life* stands in the place of Abraham our Father and *in his own life* reenacts the historical encounter between Israel and God. Every believing Christian reenacts *in his own life* the suffering, crucifixion, and resurrection of the Christ. In this existential reenactment by each of us of our "faith enacted as history"—in this existential identification of the believing Jew with Israel and the believing Christian with Christ—we have the organic fusion of time and eternity in contemporaneity. Is not Christ the eternal contemporary of every Christian, just as Abraham and Moses are the eternal contemporaries of every Jew?

How, then, shall we interpret the holy days that are at hand? For the believing Jew or Christian, true to his tradition, these holy days are not mere memorials, like Washington's Birthday or the Fourth of July. They are crucial moments in which eternity enters time, in which the temporal takes on the dimensions of the eternal. They are moments when history is reenacted in our own lives. In the Passover ritual, every Jew becomes an Israelite contemporary with Moses whom God is drawing out of Egypt, out of the house of bondage, to bring to the foot of Sinai to receive the Torah. "All this I do," the Passover Haggadah represents the Jew as saying in explanation of the order of service, "all this I do because of what God did for *me* in bringing me forth from Egypt." For *me*—not for my ancestors or for someone else—but for me in exactly the same way as he did for Moses and the Israelite slaves of the time. "He who does not himself remember that God led him out of Egypt," says Martin Buber, "he who does not himself await the Messiah, is no longer a true Jew." And is not the true Christian he who goes up to Calvary with Jesus to be crucified on Good Friday so as to rise again with him at Easter? Is he not the contemporary of the apostles, of Christ himself, as Kierkegaard never tired of insisting? "We are buried with Jesus Christ unto death," the apostle Paul writes in his letter to the Romans, "so that just as he was raised from the dead, we too may have a new life. . . . If we have died with Christ, we believe that we shall also live with him" [see Rom. 6:4–5]. This is the meaning of Passover to the Jew, this is the meaning of Easter to the Christian—provided Jew and Christian are not merely commemorating events long past and gone but are appropriating for themselves the divine work for the sake of which their religions exist. History and eternity are fused in the living contemporaneous moment.

Under the aspect of time, the exodus from Egypt and the reception of the Torah are at best merely historical events. Under the aspect of time, the life and death of Jesus represent the brief career of a young religious enthusiast in an obscure, far-off corner of the Roman Empire long ago. Dissatisfied with the superficialities of such an interpretation, we seek refuge in the realm of eternal verities. In the Exodus and Sinai, we find the eternal values of freedom and moral duty; in the life and death of Jesus, we find an ennobling example of single-minded devotion to, and martyrdom for, the truth. But is not this idealistic eternalization just as superficial, just as inadequate, as the temporalization of the mere historian? Could we not have taken the American Revolution and the death of Socrates as well? Whatever we may have gained, one thing is certain: we have lost our *religion*—and in losing our religion we have lost all.

No; neither the temporal alone nor the eternal alone, but the temporal and the eternal united in the contemporaneous is what we need. Standing in the place of Abraham, the Jew hears the divine call and answers, "Here I am"; standing at the foot of Sinai, he receives the Torah and exclaims, "I will do and hear." Standing at the foot of Calvary, the Christian goes up to be crucified with Christ to rise again from the death of sin on the third day. Our faith does not free us from time—that would be to free us from life. It does something much more wonderful: it enables us to appropriate and live out in contemporaneity the saving work of God in history.

In the following essay, originally delivered as a sermon in various chapel services on university campuses, Will Herberg gives a hard-hitting attack on the kind of religion that is—to use a Marxist cliché—"the opiate of the people."

4

THE STRANGENESS
OF FAITH

I know your works; you are neither cold nor hot.
Would that you were cold or hot! So, because you
are lukewarm, and neither cold nor hot, I will
spew you out of my mouth. (Rev. 3:15-16)

I preach today on a text from Martin Luther, who so well
understood the strangeness of faith. "I will say one thing boldly
and freely," Luther once declared. "Nobody in this life is
nearer to God than those who hate and deny him, and he has
no more pleasing, no more dear children than these." What
shall we make of this astounding statement? What could Luther conceivably have meant by such an incredible assertion:
no one in this life nearer to God, no one dearer to him, than
those who hate and deny him? Shall we charge it to Luther's
notorious fondness for utterances violent and extreme, or does
this paradox reveal something profound about the meaning of
faith that we in our conventional piety tend to overlook?

I think that perhaps the latter is the case. Luther's statement, however shocking and extreme it may sound, seems to
me to point to a profound truth that lies at the very heart of
authentic faith: that unless God matters infinitely, he does not
matter at all. There is something absolute about faith which
demands everything or nothing. Faith is not just one more
interest or attachment in life, side by side with other interests

and attachments; if it were merely that, it would indeed be nothing at all. "Faith," the great Jewish philosopher Martin Buber has said, "is not a feeling in the soul, but an entrance into reality, an entrance into the whole reality without reduction or curtailment." If it is genuine, it is everything; it touches everything and transforms everything, and when it is thrown into question, everything is thrown into question: all life is at stake.

That is what Luther is saying. The passionate unbeliever who "hates" and "denies" God may be all wrong in his ideas, but at least he takes God seriously. This kind of unbeliever is no mere unbeliever; he is, rather, an antibeliever whose whole life is a wrestling with God, whose whole mind is preoccupied with the problem of faith. Whatever else he may do, he does not take God for granted; he does not commit the ultimate sin of indifference. For that reason, Luther insists, he is near to God and dear to him.

THE ULTIMATE SIN

Not unbelief but indifference, not atheism but taking God for granted, is the ultimate sin. Let me put it another way: not skeptical questioning, not even passionate denial of God, is so displeasing to him as the lukewarmness of conventional piety. This is what Luther is saying; and in saying this he is merely echoing the searing words with which the Bible denounces the lukewarm in faith. Very few people nowadays read that strange book which comes at the end of the New Testament, the book of Revelation; but we miss a great deal in overlooking it. For it is filled with the burning passion of faith which kindles the imagination, despite the grotesque and often weird imagery in which it is expressed. There are those unforgettable chapters in which the seven churches in Asia are described by means of "letters" addressed to their "angels" or spiritual leaders. To the church in Laodicea the Almighty dictates the following message: "I know your works; you are neither cold nor hot. Would that you were cold or hot! So, because you are lukewarm, and neither cold nor hot, I will spew you out of my mouth." We all belong to this church of Laodicea, the church of the lukewarm; so let us take these words to heart. God can forgive anything but he cannot forgive mediocrity. Those who are mediocre in faith—neither hot nor cold but lukewarm—he spews forth.

Friedrich Nietzsche, the German philosopher, had his mixed feelings about the New Testament, but this passage at least he must have understood and approved. For Nietzsche the atheist was infuriated at the utter insipidity of so much of the Christianity of his time. Mockingly, passionately, he denounced its stodginess, its superficiality, its sentimentalism; with blinding anger he exposed the degradation of the faith into a conventional sanctification of conventional mediocrity. Who today takes God seriously? he demanded; and because he looked and looked and could find no one in whatever direction he turned, he proclaimed defiantly that God was "dead." He was wrong; God was not "dead"; what was dead was the faith of the conventional piety that had so degraded God. Yet, in his error Nietzsche was surely less distant from God's truth than were the conventional believers who so self-righteously denounced him: he took God seriously; they took him for granted.

ATHEISM: FAITH INVERTED

Where do we find our Nietzsches today? We have none and we are much the poorer for their absence. On one campus where I have spent a good deal of time there was an old professor now retired, a man of great eminence in his field. Whenever anyone spoke to me about him, it was always with an indulgent smile. "He's our campus atheist," they would say; "don't take him too seriously." Yet I learned to take him seriously enough, for he took with the utmost seriousness the questions I was there to discuss. He attended all the lectures and meetings, even the chapel service, raised every conceivable objection, and threw himself heart and soul into the controversy. The topics we discussed meant much to him, as one could readily see from his eagerness and excitement. Yes, he was an "atheist"; but he was obsessed, literally obsessed, with the things of God. His more religious colleagues dismissed him, together with his atheism, as a leftover from an age past and gone, as indeed he was. But I am afraid that some of them were as much perplexed by the passion of his concern as by his atheistic opinions. They could not see that his passion was the passion of faith curiously inverted; his very denial of God was, strangely enough, a testimony to God's reality and power. They, the more conventionally pious, had in their very piety lost the almost feverish sense of excitement at things divine which the old man, for all his atheism—perhaps even because of his atheism—still retained.

Luther would have known what to make of this man, as he would have known what to make of Friedrich Nietzsche, the man who scandalized the world of his time by proclaiming that God was dead. Luther understood men like these; he opposed them but he understood them. What infuriated Luther was not passionate doubt or denial but conventional piety. In uttering his paradoxical words about the God denier who is near to God, Luther was denouncing the conventional piety of the good, self-satisfied Christians in the pews, and attempting to shock them into a sense of their condition. For the condition of the good, self-satisfied Christian, of the religious man of conventional piety, is a perilous one indeed. He has put God in his place, somewhere on the margin of life, where he permits him to occupy a very honorable position but also a very innocuous one. Conventional piety issues no challenge and makes no demand; it merely reassures the church member that all is well with him because he, after all, is on the inside of the church, engaged in pious works and exercises, while the unbeliever is on the outside in outer darkness. In this way conventional piety tends to confirm man in his self-righteousness and good opinion of himself; indeed, it often actually supplies him with another device by which these may be sanctioned in the name of religion. For there is something strangely ambiguous about religion. It is, on the one side, man's openness to the divine, but on the other side, it is always being converted into a means of spiritual self-sufficiency, which shuts one off from God. Religion and church membership may thus well become a kind of defense that the conventionally religious man throws up to protect himself against the absolute demand of faith. That is why the great Christian theologian Karl Barth is always warning us that "the church is not only the place where man meets God; it is often also the place where man makes his last stand against God." How? By using religion and church membership to bolster his self-complacency. When that happens, the witness of the passionate unbeliever, who takes his unbelief and therefore God seriously, becomes a witness to God. For it is a challenge to a religion that has become detestable to God because it has become a routine, conventional cult of reassurance.

A MUCH-NEEDED WITNESS

The witness of the passionate unbeliever to the seriousness of faith and the all-importance of God is a witness that men have needed at all times, but at no time perhaps more than today. For today, with the boom in religion under way in this country, we are in danger of being stifled by a heavy blanket of conventional religiosity as superficial and shoddy as anything known in history. Everybody is religious, and religion is everywhere; but it is a religion that is little more than a celebration of the values of our culture, and a way of achieving "peace of mind" and the "power of positive thinking" in a situation where it is rather "divine discontent" and an unblinking confrontation of the hard facts of life that are required. Contemporary American religiosity is converting God into a great cosmic public utility which we find useful in advancing our purposes as individuals and as a nation. We have appointed God to his place in our scheme of things, and we are sure that since we are "religious" he will not fail us in the duties we have assigned to him. Having settled that little detail, we can go on to the things that really count, the things that John Wesley was wont to describe as the "pride and desire of life," in other words, the things through which we can display to all the world our success and superiority. No wonder that over half of the American people who say they regard religion as a "very important thing" also readily admit that their religious beliefs have little or nothing to do with their ideas on economics or politics or other concerns of everyday life. Our lives we fashion on other grounds and other principles, and then we look to God, if we look to him at all, to certify our values and guarantee their success.

A CHALLENGE TO COMPLACENCY

It is here that the unbeliever utters his word of denial as a challenge to our complacency. Are we really so sure of God as we like to believe? Note that here the unbeliever with his questioning, and the prophet with his words of judgment and wrath, join in shattering the false securities we have built up in the name of religion. It is indeed sometimes not easy to tell them apart, the prophet and the unbeliever. That great Christian thinker Søren Kierkegaard, to whom we owe so much of contemporary religious philosophy, ended his brief and stormy life with a series of writings which he called *Attack Upon Christendom*. By "Christendom" Kierkegaard meant the established, conventional Christianity of his time. What he found so repulsive in it was the all-pervading, though unconscious, hypocrisy in which it was involved: the Christian faith in all its ultimacy was indeed affirmed, but life continued to be lived on the comfortable level of human self-sufficiency. Whatever else he could tolerate, this was one thing Kierkegaard could not stand, and he lashed out at it with all the scorn and fury at his command. No wonder so many of the scandalized churchmen of his time put him down as an atheist, a madman, or both! How could one claim to be religious and yet say such horrible things about religion!

If Kierkegaard is the God-possessed prophet who speaks words that make him sound like an atheist, Freud, like Nietzsche, is the atheist who speaks words that have their prophetic ring. Freud, as we all know, was hostile to religion; but then much of what he took for religion was sham and deserved his hostility. Above all, Freud hated sham. He had a truly Kierkegaardian contempt for those who were trying to win favor for religion by presenting it under false colors so as to deprive it of its "scandal" and challenge. In the midst of one of his diatribes against religion, he breaks out with these impassioned words: "One would like to count oneself among the believers so as to be able to admonish the philosophers, who try to preserve the God of religion by substituting for him an impersonal, shadowy, abstract principle, and say to them: 'Thou shalt not take the name of the Lord thy God in vain!' " In these words Freud the atheist stands at the verge of the faith he denied; and we who espouse this faith can recognize in him, despite himself, a witness to the God of Truth whom we serve.

OBSESSED WITH GOD

Yes, the God-obsessed God affirmer and God-obsessed God denier have something in common that we do not always estimate at its true worth. Both insist on ruthlessly tearing away the false securities we build up in the name of religion and forcing us to confront God and his absolute demand face to face—the prophet out of the passion of faith, the unbeliever out of the passion of doubt, but both out of the passion of infinite concern. It is this infinite concern that is at the heart of the matter. Where that is present, even though in negative form, there is nearness to God; where that is absent, nothing remains.

I do not want to disparage the importance of right belief in the life of faith. It is both central and indispensable, for right belief in matters of faith is essentially a right understanding of one's existence and a right direction to one's life. Nor do I want to minimize the gross errors in matters of belief committed by Nietzsche, Freud, and the other unbelievers of whom I have spoken. Nietzsche's views on Christianity were perverse and often incoherent; Freud's views on religion were something of which not even his most devoted disciples are particularly proud. We need not mince words: Freud's philosophical outlook was shallow and crude, his understanding of the Jewish and Christian religions embarrassingly superficial, and his venture into the formal critique of religion a lamentable blunder. The explicit teachings of these men as they deal with religion are often dangerously misleading and have misled many fine minds. This we cannot overlook or excuse. And yet—for there is a "yet"—and yet it is not the last word. Luther was surely not unaware that the teachings of those who "hate and deny" God were false and blasphemous (he even uses this very word "blasphemous"); yet he also understood that for all their grievous error, they were performing a service on behalf of the truth and the God of Truth: they were denouncing spiritual sham and calling to spiritual authenticity, even if the true nature of this authenticity was hidden from them. Because this was what they were doing, Luther was bold enough to assert that they were "near and dear" to God.

Luther was a great man of God and a great theologian. He saw the perils of false belief, but he also saw the perils of conventional religion. He had the courage to state the paradoxes of faith in opposition to conventional piety with the whole force of his being. Speaking thus, Luther spoke in a great tradition, stretching all the way from the prophets of Israel to the so-called "religious existentialists" of today. And just as Luther dared to say that "nobody in this life is nearer to God than those who hate and deny him," so today we should have the courage to consider the possibility that unreligious, even antireligious poets, novelists, and philosophers may have more to say to us about the deepest problems of faith than those who drone out the pious platitudes of conventional religion, or those who try to convert these platitudes into a cheery, self-serving gospel of "peace of mind" and "positive thinking." There is a deeper and more genuine understanding of the religious dimension of life, it seems to me, in an "existentialist" novel such as *The Plague* or *The Fall* by Albert Camus than in all the exhortations of the professional purveyors of the gospel of reassurance put together. But was not Camus an atheist? Perhaps, but he was an atheist concerned—one might almost say obsessed—with the ultimate problems of human life and therefore with God, though it is a God he did not know; while the conventional representatives of religion seem to be concerned mainly with "being religious," which almost leaves God out of the picture.

It is this concern that is decisive one way or the other. The one unforgivable sin, let me remind you, is lukewarmness, mediocrity, taking God for granted. The man of faith, in his passionate concern with the ultimate, is sometimes less distant from Luther's "God denier" than he is from the conventional believer, precisely because the former is passionately concerned with the ultimate and the latter is not. Luther understood this very well; so did the eighteenth-century Jewish teacher, Nahman of Bratslav. One day a man came to Rabbi Nahman defiantly yet anxiously proclaiming that he did not believe in God. "So," said Rabbi Nahman, "you don't believe in God; why get so excited about it? If God does not exist, it can't be very important, can it?" "But, Rabbi," the unbeliever expostulated, "how can you talk that way? It *is* important; it's the most important thing in the world." "Then, my son," said Rabbi Nahman, "you need not despair: though far from God, you are near to him." Martin Luther and Nahman of Bratslav: they understood the meaning of faith.

Will Herberg wrote the following essay for a book published in honor of Carl Michalson, his professorial colleague at Drew University, whose teaching career was abruptly terminated, at the very peak of his creative influence, by a tragic airplane accident. The book, prepared under the direction of the World Methodist Council and edited by Dow Kirkpatrick, appeared in 1966 with the title *The Finality of Christ* (Abingdon Press). Herberg's contribution to the symposium summarizes and supplements his understanding of the relationship between Christian and Jew expressed earlier in the essay "Judaism and Christianity: Their Unity and Difference" (included in this volume).

5

A JEW LOOKS AT JESUS

"Who do you say that I am?" Jesus asked his disciples (Matt. 16:15), and this question, which led to Peter's confession of faith, still remains a crucial question, for the Jew no less than for the gentile, today no less than nineteen hundred years ago. It is this question I should like to discuss here. Speaking as a Jew, from out of what I take to be the authentic tradition of Jewish faith, what can I say about Jesus, the man of Nazareth whom Peter hailed as the Christ?

I

Jesus was, first of all, a great and incomparable moral teacher. Of that there cannot be, and indeed never has been, any doubt. His exhortations and discourses stand unrivaled in the ethical literature of mankind. Men of all cultures and religions have paid tribute to the inexhaustible truth and power of his moral teaching. The Sermon on the Mount is known wherever men anywhere have concerned themselves with the moral life, and nowhere has it failed to stir the imagination and raise the heart to the self-giving love which Jesus preached. By the common testimony of mankind, this Jewish rabbi from Nazareth nineteen hundred years ago reached the high-water mark of moral vision and ethical teaching.

But if that were all there was to it, there would be no

question to ask and no problem to discuss. For, as a moral teacher, Jesus stands merely as one among many, one of the rabbis of Judaism, entirely in the line of rabbinical tradition. Scholars, both Jewish and non-Jewish, have shown beyond the shadow of a doubt that all his moral teachings, even the most exalted, have their sources and parallels in the contemporary religious literature of the Jews, from whom he sprang and among whom he taught. It is not enough to point to the consummate synthesis that this teacher of genius achieved in his teaching. This may be granted, but it is not simply, or even primarily, as a moral teacher that Jesus confronts us as a problem and a challenge. As a moral teacher, he is a Jewish rabbi of great power and insight, drawing upon the traditional wisdom of his people. That is a great deal, but it is not enough to answer the question we are asking. We must look further.

Jesus was, on the next level, in the line of the prophets of Israel. If the prophet is the God-possessed man standing over against the community to which he belongs, bringing to bear upon it the word of the Lord in judgment and promise, then Jesus of Nazareth was a prophet in Israel, in the succession of Amos, Hosea, Isaiah, and Jeremiah. His denunciations of the corruptions and idolatries of the age, his call to repentance, his promise of divine grace for those of a broken heart and and a contrite spirit, his proclamation of the new age to come as judgment and fulfillment, follows, as it was meant to follow, the pattern of the great prophets. There is, indeed, something new because of the new situation; but this newness, this speaking out of and to the condition of the time, is precisely what characterizes the living word of prophecy. Jesus, the rabbinic teacher, is also among the prophets of Israel, with clear affinities to the great prophets of the past

But again, if that were all there was to it, there would be no question to ask and no problem to discuss, for again, neither as prophet nor as moral teacher is Jesus anything more than one among many. It is not here that his uniqueness, if unique-

ness there be, is to be discovered. Jesus' prophetic proclama-
tions follow the prophetic word of his predecessors; his denunciations of the self-righteous "scribes and Pharisees" can be
abundantly paralleled in the literature of rabbinic self-criticism;
the promise he held out of divine mercy for the repentant
sinner was a promise which every contemporary Jew could
understand even if he could not prevail upon himself to take
hold of it. No, not here can we find the answer to our question
—we must look still further.

II

The Jesus that confronts us as a problem is the Jesus whom
Peter confessed as the Christ and whom the Fourth Gospel
represents as declaring: "I am the way . . .; no one comes to
the Father, but by me" (John 14:6). What can a Jew make of
this confession and this claim?

It seems to me obvious that this claim and this confession
have no meaning outside the context of the faith of Israel, as
defined in the Hebrew Bible, in which Judaism and Christianity alike are grounded. The persistent attempt through the
centuries to throw out the Old Testament and replace it with
some other so-called "preparation for the gospel," such as
Greek philosophy, Hindu mysticism, or modern science, is
inevitably and inescapably, however unwittingly, an attempt to
destroy the biblical substance of the Christian faith, and to
convert Christianity into a pagan salvation cult. Christian faith
is biblical and Hebraic, or it is nothing at all.

Viewing it from the biblical-Hebraic standpoint, and in the
light of a biblically defined understanding of God's redemptive
purpose, what can a Jew say of the Christian church and the
Christ it proclaims? It is hard to avoid the conviction that
Christianity emerges, in God's plan of redemption, to open the
covenant of Israel to the "nations of the world." In biblical
faith it is in and through membership in the covenanted people

of God that—humanly speaking—man has his standing with God and can avail himself of God's grace for redemption. "The individual Israelite," Alan Richardson has pointed out, "approaches God in virtue of his membership in the holy people. . . . In the whole of the Bible, in the Old Testament as well as the New, there is no such thing as a private personal relation between an individual and God apart from this membership in the covenant folk."[1] Man's relation to God is essentially responsive; it is God's call, expressed in the grace of election, that gives man the possibility—*from his side*—of entering into personal relations with God. (Modern existentialism, in its very welcome emphasis on personal confrontation, has tended to forget that such confrontation is, humanly speaking, possible only *within*, and on the basis of, the covenant.) In the biblical view people outside the covenant, properly called gentiles, cannot—apart from the uncovenanted grace of God—of themselves find their way to God or meet him in personal encounter. In our modern intellectualistic, and therefore inadequate, terminology this is equivalent to saying that only the religion of Israel brings men to God; other, pagan religions, the "religions of the world," lead men away from him.

The covenant of Israel is understood by the prophets, and perhaps much earlier, as the covenant of a redeemed and redeeming community; the purpose it defines is a universal purpose, and the people it brings into being are an instrument of God for the redemption of mankind. All are to be gathered into the covenant and, within the covenant, restored to a right relation to God. It is in this context that the Jew finds it possible to understand the providential role of the Christian church, and the church to understand the never-failing providential function of Jewry. Through Christ God's covenant with Israel is—in the fullness of time—opened to all mankind. As the one by whom and through whom the covenant of Israel is opened to mankind, Christ appears in early Christian thinking as, quite literally, an incarnate or one-man Israel. Through union in faith with him the gentile believer, the pagan of yesterday, becomes part of Israel; he therefore comes under the covenant, and thereby becomes heir to the promise of God to Israel. "If you are Christ's," Paul says, "then you are Abraham's offspring, heirs according to the promise" (Gal. 3:29). "That the blessing of Abraham might come on the gentiles through Jesus Christ"; that is how the apostle describes this aspect of Christ's redemptive work (Gal. 3:14, KJV). He admonishes recent gentile converts:

> Remember that you were at that time separated from Christ, alienated from the commonwealth of Israel, and strangers to the covenants of promise. . . . But now in Christ Jesus you who once were far off have been brought near . . . so [that] you are no longer strangers and sojourners, but you are fellow citizens with the saints and members of the household of God. (Eph. 2:12–19.)

Solomon Grayzel, a modern Jewish writer, has—I think quite correctly—put what he takes to be Paul's meaning in these words: "He so broadened the term 'Jew' as to include in it . . . all those who transformed their lives by being faithful Christians."

Attempting to understand what has happened in terms of the divine purpose, the Jew can see Christ as the one in whom God was, and is, acting for the redemption of the peoples. Through Christ a new covenant community is created—the church, the "Body of Christ." Through Christ, Israel's redemptive history becomes the redemptive history of the pagan-turned-Christian, who becomes in effect an Israelite. "Through Jesus Christ," H. Richard Niebuhr points out, "Christians of all races recognize the Hebrews as their fathers. . . . All that has happened to that strange and wandering people of God becomes part of their own past."[2]

Christian faith thus brings into being and defines a new covenant; but it is new not in the sense of supplanting the old,

but in the sense of extending and enlarging it, very much as
we speak of the new world side by side with the old. For with
the emergence of Christianity the election and vocation of
Israel are not annulled, nor does the church supersede the
people of the "old covenant." The notion that it does, not only
renders unintelligible the survival of Jewry these nineteen hundred years; it is itself a manifestation of that spiritual pride, the
pride of supersession, that goes a long way toward corrupting
the meaning and power of the gospel that is proclaimed. The
election of Israel remains, and its vocation remains, though it
assumes a very different form in the Christian world from that
which it possessed in the pre-Christian.

It is in terms of this conception of the double covenant that
the Jew can see Jesus on the level of his uniqueness. He is
indeed the way—the way by and through which the peoples
of the world may enter the covenant of Israel and come to serve
the God of Israel, who is the Creator of the universe and the
Lord of all being. "Israel," Franz Rosenzweig, the great Jewish
religious philosopher, has said, "can bring the world to God
only through Christianity."[3] And this "Christianity" is, of
course, the extension into history of the Jesus whom Peter
hailed as the Christ.

But there is also the other side of the medal. "Christianity,"
Rosenzweig continues, "could not long remain a force for
redemption without Israel in its midst,"[4] and what that means
can best be seen in the words of Paul Tillich, who speaks from
the Christian commitment:

> It is important that there always be Judaism. It is the corrective
> against the paganism that goes along with Christianity. . . . The
> Church is always in danger of adoring the gods of space in
> which she is ruling. . . . The Church is always in danger of losing
> her prophetic spirit. . . . Therefore, the prophetic spirit included
> in the tradition of the Synagogue is needed so long as the
> gods of space are in power, and that means to the end of his-
> tory.[5]

Against all idolatries, Judaism proclaims: "Hear, O Israel, the Lord is our God, the Lord alone"; and this is a word which the church as well as the world—and the church because it is so immersed in the world—never ceases to need. Judaism's witness to the living God, which it is compelled to bear by its divine calling as that is expressed in history, is a witness that cannot end until all things are brought to the end of judgment and fulfillment.

Yes, each needs the other: Judaism needs Christianity, and Christianity needs Judaism. The vocation of both can be defined in common terms: to bear witness to the living God amidst the idolatries of the world. But, since the emergence of the church, and through the emergence of the church, this vocation has, as it were, been split into two parts. The Jew fulfills his vocation by "staying with God," "giving the world no rest so long as the world has not God"—to recall Jacques Maritain's unforgettable phrase.[6] The Christian can fulfill his vocation only by "going out" to conquer the world for God. The Jew's vocation is to "stand," the Christian's to "go out" —both in the same cause of the kingdom of God. Judaism and Christianity thus represent one faith expressed in two religions —Judaism facing inward to the Jews, and Christianity facing outward to the gentiles, who, through it, are brought to the God, and under the covenant, of Israel, and therefore cease to be gentiles in the proper sense of the term. This is the unity of Judaism and Christianity, and this is why a Jew is able to see and acknowledge Jesus in his uniqueness as the way to the Father.

I know that what I say here will not satisfy those who are Christians, although they will, I hope, recognize its truth so far as it goes. And, indeed, it should not satisfy the Christian, since to the Christian, Jesus as the Christ must necessarily mean much more than he can possibly mean to the Jew. For the Jew sees Jesus as emerging from Israel and going forth; he sees him from the rear, as it were. The Christian, on the other hand, precisely because he is a Christian, will see Christ as coming toward him, in the fullness of divine grace, to claim, to judge, and to save; he meets him as Paul met him on the road to Damascus or as Peter outside Rome, face to face in confrontation. Yet this difference of perspective should not blind us to the fact that it is the same reality we see. And indeed—here again I refer to Franz Rosenzweig—the two religions relate to the same truth, being equal representations of it—equal before God.[7] With God, truth is one; but for men it is irreducibly split, since the truth as men see it is confessional and conditioned by one's community of faith. This is not a vicious relativism, nor does it assert for one moment that all religions are equally valid or equally true. On the contrary, as Rosenzweig puts it, man is either a pagan or a Jew or Christian.[8] The pagan, as pagan, is outside the scope of the covenant—that is what being a pagan means—though God, in his mercy, may, of course, reach out to him. Jew and Christian, on the other hand, has each his assigned position, defined in the covenant that relates him to God. Their positions, their "standpoints," being different, their views of the one truth and the one reality will be different—although both will be views of the same truth and the same reality, just as two people standing in the same room but in different corners will see the room in different perspectives and therefore somewhat differently. Each will be loyal to the truth if he speaks out the truth as he sees it, though recognizing that his truth is never quite identical with the full truth of God. This approach does not derogate from the "finality" of either Judaism or Christianity, if that is properly understood; it merely prevents our making an idol of either; both are seen as instruments in the redemptive purpose of God, though each in a different way.

In short, each—the Jew on his part and the Christian on his —sees the truth as it is to be apprehended from his perspective, defined by his covenant and his vocation. Each must stand by his truth and confess it, recognizing that insofar as he does so in integrity and wholeness of heart, he remains faithful to the God whose truth it is. Naturally, since the two see the same reality in somewhat different ways, each may see an aspect of the truth hidden to the other, and even interpret the same truth differently. But perhaps that is part of God's purpose in placing the Jew and Christian on different sectors of the fighting front of the Kingdom, so that each may bear not only the common witness to God, but also a witness against the perils, inadequacies, and temptations of the other. The witness of Christianity against the legalistic, moralistic tendencies in Judaism is a witness for which the Jew must always be grateful. And the Christian, too, it seems to me, ought to see the value of the Jewish word in this dialogue. The Christian who tends to be impatient with the Jew for refusing to see in Jesus the fulfillment and completion of God's redemptive work might pause a moment to consider whether this Jewish "obstinacy" was not itself important as an indispensable reminder of the very incompleteness of this completion, of a redemption which may indeed have come but is nevertheless yet to come. The heart of each, Jew and Christian alike, may ache, perhaps, that the other is not in his camp, seeing things his way and fighting side by side with him on his sector of the front; but he ought also to recognize that though the other fights on a different sector, he is also fighting the same battle for the same God, and that it is perhaps by the providence of God that they are thus separated.

III

This, then, is how a Jew may see Jesus and the faith and church built upon the confession of him as the Christ. I realize how difficult it is for one to communicate what he has to say on this matter. "Christ," Franz Kafka, the Jew, once exclaimed, "is an abyss filled with light; one must close one's eyes if one is not to fall into it."[9] And yet speak one must. In Jesus

—not merely Jesus the moral teacher, or Jesus the prophetic voice, but also the Jesus whom Christians confess the Christ —Jew and Christian find their unity . . . and their difference. In answering the question "Who do you say that I am?" Jew and Christian stand separated, yet united. The unity far transcends the separation, however real that may be, for the two are united in their common allegiance to the living God and in their common expectation of, and longing for, the One who is to come: for the Christian, the One who came and is to come again, for the Jew the One who is promised to Israel; but for both the same Promised One. In this one faith and hope, Jew and Christian—to recall Paul Tillich's words—stand united until the end of time in the struggle for the Lord of history against the pagan and idolatrous powers that threaten to overwhelm us on every side.

NOTES

1. Alan Richardson, "Instrument of God," *Interpretation*, Vol. III (1949), p. 278.

2. H. Richard Niebuhr, *The Meaning of Revelation* (The Macmillan Company, 1946), pp. 115–116.

3. Nahum N. Glatzer, ed., *Franz Rosenzweig: His Life and Thought*, (Schocken Books, 1953), p. 341.

4. *Ibid.*

5. Quoted in A. Roy Eckardt, *Christianity and the Children of Israel* (King's Crown Press, 1948), pp. 146–147.

6. Jacques Maritain, *A Christian Looks at the Jewish Question* (Longmans, Green & Company, Inc., 1939), p. 29.

7. Glatzer, *op. cit.*, p. 341.

8. *Ibid.*

9. Gustav Janouch, *Conversations with Kafka* (Frederick A. Praeger, Inc., Publishers, 1953), p. 93.

Will Herberg wrote the following sermon, strikingly Christian in content and expression, for a Communion service on June 5, 1961, at the request of members of the graduating class of the Theological School of Drew University. The unusual request was both an expression of affection and esteem for Herberg, and an appreciative tribute to his ability to understand and interpret the Christian faith while maintaining his identity as a Jew. The editor's Introduction to this volume elaborates both on the circumstances leading up to this occasion and on the significance of the sermon in the context of Herberg's theology.

6

THE INCARNATE WORD

A Communion Service Homily

Members of the Graduating Class:

You are about to participate in Holy Communion for the last time as members of the seminary community, and you ought to consider, very seriously, what it is you are about to do and what it is that is about to happen. For it is no ordinary thing that you are about to do and that is about to happen; it is the supreme miracle of the Christian life.

Remember that as you receive the bread and wine in Holy Communion it is the Incarnate Word, fully, really, and truly, that you are receiving—the very same Incarnate Word that died on the cross, was raised the third day, and was exalted to the right hand of the Father. The Incarnate Word comes in the proclamation and the preaching; but it comes likewise in the consecrated bread and wine. The preaching is an ever-renewed commentary on the sacrament; the sacrament is an ever-renewed enactment of the preaching. The Word preached and the Word enacted are one; and they are offered to you in the same way for the same purpose through the incredible goodness of God.

As you receive the Incarnate Word in proclamation and sacrament, in gospel and Holy Communion, you receive once again the new life implanted in you by the grace of God in Christ when he chose you to bring you out of the world into his church. For the life of the Christian is a supernatural life, empowered with resources that are only God's to give. When you receive the Incarnate Word in proclamation and sacrament, you receive those resources of grace without which your life would be as nothing. Let then your life show forth the grace God has conferred upon you this day and every day: you have received the gift, priceless beyond measure; see that you now use it wisely and responsibly.

As you receive the Incarnate Word in proclamation and sacrament, remember that you who receive it are a sinner—a justified sinner, perhaps, but a sinner nevertheless. The new life implanted in you is implanted in a soil in which the old leaven is still working. Your faith is a faith against the background of unfaith; your obedience an obedience against the background of disobedience; your life is a life against the background of death. The final victory has not yet been won! and until it is, there can be no final security. The certitude of grace must not be confused with the self-assurance of sanctity. The Incarnate Word in proclamation and sacrament comes as a word of forgiveness before it comes as a word of renewal, or rather it comes as a word of renewal precisely because it comes as a word of forgiveness.

As you receive the Incarnate Word in proclamation and sacrament you are being confirmed anew as a member of the Body of Christ which is his church. You are being received into a community infinitely more splendid than any community of this world, for it is a community where you stand with the patriarchs, the prophets, the apostles, and the saints of all times and places. Never let the divisions, perversities, and shortcomings of the institutional church blind you to the splendor and glory of the church founded upon the Incarnate Word. You have been, or will be, ordained ministers of the church which is the Body of Christ, and you will be working within the institutional church which is both its implementation and its perversion. Your life will therefore be a life of tension, very frequently a life of frustration and heartbreak. But this ought not to dismay you, for the church in which, through the goodness of God, you have your being, is fixed on everlasting foundations which nothing can undermine or destroy. Not the outcome, which is certain, but the quality of your life and work in the church, ought to be your proper concern; and it is this concern which ought to be both heightened and sustained by your reintegration into the Body of Christ through Holy Communion.

As you receive the Incarnate Word in proclamation and sacrament, remember too that the kingship of Christ is not restricted to the visible confines of his church. In a very real sense, all mankind, the entire cosmos, is in the church, for they are within the scope of God's redemptive activity. Every human being anywhere is your fellow church member, even though his membership in the Church of Christ still remains merely latent and implicit. The communion which you enter into through receiving the Incarnate Word in proclamation and sacrament is communion with all men and women everywhere. The woes of all mankind are your woes; the injustices that afflict men anywhere are injustices inflicted upon you. As you enter the community which is the Church of Christ—and you enter it anew every time you receive the Incarnate Word in Holy Communion—you undertake the responsibility never to rest so long as there is evil in the world—which there always is! The Church of Christ, to which you have been admitted by the grace of God, is not a rest home for the weary; it is rather the Church Militant, commissioned and empowered to wage unceasing war in the cause of Christ against the demonic powers of the world.

Members of the graduating class! As you present yourself for Holy Communion this morning for the last time in the seminary community, remember these things. Remember that in Holy Communion, God is performing an incredible miracle of grace for you, giving you new life, giving you new power, giving you new community with all mankind in Christ. Be sure, as you receive the Incarnate Word in Holy Communion, that you are in the proper disposition of heart to receive it—repentant, steadfast in the intention of faith, single-minded in loyalty and love—for there is no greater sacrilege than to come forward to Holy Communion in defiance and hardness of heart.

Members of the graduating class! In Holy Communion, you receive the Incarnate Word of God: God, in his incredible goodness, is making himself available to you in Christ. Realize the immensity of the goodness of God; realize too your own unworthiness and receive God's gracious gift of himself in humility and gratitude. Remember: because God makes himself available to you in Christ, you do not have disposal over him; you are at his disposal, to will and to do. As you receive the bread and wine in Holy Communion, never forget that you are receiving the Incarnate Word, fully, really, and truly; but never forget, either, that awful word of warning, which clergymen, perhaps, need more than anyone else: "Woe unto the man so possessed that he thinks he possesses God!"

May Almighty God make the words I have spoken serve his glorious purpose. Amen.

Part Two

THE UNDERSTANDING OF FAITH

In January, 1955, Will Herberg lectured to pastors in a continuing education seminar held at the Theological School of Drew University on the special field of theology known as "hermeneutics" (from the Greek verb meaning "to interpret," derived from *Hermes,* the name of the messenger of the gods known for his science, eloquence, and cunning). In his lecture, Herberg traced the study of hermeneutics from its origins to the modern period, with special consideration of the philosopher Wilhelm Dilthey. Finally, Herberg considered the position of the New Testament theologian Rudolf Bultmann, whose views on hermeneutics were vigorously discussed in the 1960's and with whom Herberg violently disagreed, even though he shared some of his existentialist interests. The following essay is based on notes taken during Herberg's lecture by the editor, who was the host for the occasion. The notes were subsequently reviewed and approved by Herberg for use in seminary classes. However, the reader should be reminded that here Herberg's thought has been cast through the prism of another, albeit sympathetic, mind.

7

HERMENEUTICS

The Mode of Interpretation

To begin with, let us give a brief definition of the subject: *Hermeneutics is the disciplined procedure for understanding man through his works.* In other words, hermeneutics is an inquiry into the meaning of an artifact. What does it "want" to say? Here the French idiom is helpful: *Que veut dire cela?* When we ascertain what a thing "wants to say," we understand. If a text is in a foreign language, it must be translated, though translation itself is not the hermeneutical problem per se. Translation is, at least in part, a matter of philology and linguistics. But the problem of *understanding* arises even when no linguistic translation is necessary.

I

Hermeneutics as a self-conscious discipline began with Plato. He read the received Greek texts, especially Homer and Hesiod, in his native Greek; but he was troubled about these texts. He could not solve his problem by throwing them out, for they had become staples of Greek education. To him, however, these texts *seemed* to say things unworthy of the gods. He questioned whether what they seemed to say was what they really meant. Thus arose the hermeneutical question: What does the text *really* mean? What does it want to say?

Generally speaking, the ancient Greeks found two ways of overcoming this difficulty. First, the Stoics developed the approach known as *euhemerism*—after the Greek philosopher, Euhemerus, who lived in the fourth century B.C. According to this view, the gods of mythology were deifications of dead heroes; hence, mythology is based on traditional accounts of real people and real historical events. The second approach was *allegory*. According to this view, a story speaks in a hidden manner of timeless principles of metaphysics or of ethics. Philo of Alexandria exploited this method of interpretation to show that the Bible really sets forth Platonic philosophy. For instance, when the paradise story speaks of Adam and Eve as counterparts, surely Adam must be spirit (mind) and Eve bodily passion!

Alexandrian Christians adopted the allegorical approach in order to deal with troublesome aspects of Christian scripture, especially the Old Testament. Thus arose the school of Alexandria, represented by Origen and others, in opposition to the school of Antioch (Chrysostom and others). The latter stressed the method of typology and insisted on the literal meaning of a text.

The allegorical school developed the doctrine of "multiple meanings" in a text. This, however, was only an elaboration of the primary distinction between what the text seems to say and what it really says—that is, the "literal" and the "higher" meaning. According to this view, there were at least four levels of meaning: (1) literal; (2) allegorical (moral and spiritual); (3) tropological (figurative); and (4) anagogical (mystical).

Typology, on the other hand, is a historical mode of understanding. It rests on the belief that a crucial event has occurred for which there are anticipations (seen in retrospect), and from which flows an outcome. An illustration from American history is the Revolutionary War—the crucial event. Yet, in typological perspective, this event was anticipated much earlier when an episode was enacted in the time of a New England governor,

Edmund Andros. At that time there was already a dramatic tension between colonial aspirations and the agents of James II.[1] Similarly, the scriptural interpreter starts from a crucial event (e.g., the crucifixion) and, in retrospect, sees foreshadowing, anticipatory events.

Jerome became critical of allegory and was more sympathetic with typology. Allegory, he said, is all right for preachers, but not for theologians. By the High Middle Ages, however, typology was virtually forgotten. Allegory had taken over. It was during the period of the Reformation that typology was revived, especially under the leadership of the early Luther and of Calvin.

II

We now leap across a great chasm of time to Wilhelm Dilthey (1833–1911), a philosopher of culture whose influence was not felt strongly until around 1940.[2]

The key concept in Dilthey's philosophy is the word *Geist*, which is inadequately rendered into English as "mind," "spirit," "intention." This term was a direct inheritance from the philosopher Hegel.[3] Hegel, in turn, assumed the meaning of *Geist* received from G. B. Vico (1668–1744), namely, human creativity including concretions of such creativity—in other words, "man and his works." Dilthey was the first modern philosopher to develop the science of hermeneutics, although his ideas were anticipated by the theologian Schleiermacher.

Hermeneutics, as we have seen, is the search for meaning, the effort to understand. But, according to Dilthey, only human beings can be understood. Only human works have meaning *(Bedeutung)*, for man and his works are *Geist.* Nature we can *explain* by subsuming a phenomenon under a "law"; but the *Geistesleben* ("the life of the Spirit") we can *understand.* This distinction presupposes that between human beings there is affinity, whereas between man and nature there is alienation. Therefore we can see (understand) the assassination of Julius Caesar from the inside, so to speak; but we cannot understand nature. Only God can see the planets from the outside (Vico) and can understand them. In other words, nonhuman occurrences have no *meaning*. It may be added that creation does not pertain to a natural sphere which may be "explained" (science). Insofar as creation is a subject to be understood by human beings, it is the beginning of history; but creation *ex nihilo*, the beginning of all things, reaches beyond human explanation or understanding. Only God, the Creator, has the wisdom to understand creation (see Job 38:2–7).

Dilthey described three "concretions" of *Geist:* (a) human actions, which are concrete, but fleeting; (b) human concepts, which are enduring but abstract; and (c) life expressions *(Lebensäusserungen),* which represent a synthesis of the previous two, for they are both concrete and enduring. The interpreter (hermeneuticist) is interested primarily in the latter, that is, in *expressions*—of a text, a poem, a painting, a piece of music.

The *first principle* of Dilthey's hermeneutic is *Ahnung,* which may be translated as divination or insight. To illustrate: we see a young man tearing his hair, wildly gesticulating, etc., and we say that he is distracted, angry, maybe out of his mind. This judgment is not a psychological inference; nor is it, in the strict sense, empathy, a term that properly refers to the projection of human feelings upon nature (e.g., "the sky is weeping"). Rather, such a judgment rests upon *Ahnung,* or divination. It is re-living *(Nacherleben)* or, to use the terminology of the American sociologist C. H. Cooley, it is "dramatic re-living." This is actually the way we understand a play; and it is the way we understand any "life expression."

Frequently the criticism is made that understanding is "subjective," but this rests upon a confusion of terms. The word "objective" presupposes a subject-object relation, as in science:

the subject views or explains a nonhuman object. The word "subjective" properly refers to the attitude of the subject, the ego. But Dilthey's hermeneutic deals with another dimension: the communication of meaning from an author to an interpreter, or interpersonal communication. This is neither "objective" nor "subjective" but rather, as someone has put it, "transjective," that is, communication *across,* from one person to another. This is what Dilthey meant by his aphorism that understanding is "a rediscovery of the I in the Thou" *(Das Verstehen ist ein Wiederfinden des Ich im Du).*

Understanding involves grasping the meaning of the whole. Dilthey is emphatic in saying that *Bedeutung* (meaning) is not a matter of grasping "the relation between an expression and what it expresses" but of seeing the relation between the whole and the part. As one grasps the pattern *(Gestalt),* he understands the part. This is true in the case of a novel or a play: at some point the pattern begins to appear, and then the part is understandable.

This brings us to the *second principle* of Dilthey's hermeneutic: namely, *Ahnung,* or divination, is not unregulated or arbitrary but is controlled by "shared meanings." These meanings can be universal, or they can be culturally conditioned. To take an example of the former: grief is a universal human experience. We can enter into the experience of the loss of a friend or relative because this is a shared meaning which pertains to human life itself. But the universal experience, of course, is always culturally conditioned, that is, the experience takes the form of certain ways of expressing grief: mourning rites, funeral customs (e.g., some dress in black, others in white). Yet because we share the universal human meaning of grief we can understand the culturally conditioned expression.

It is true, of course, that there is always the possibility of misunderstanding or of misinterpreting the meaning which is expressed. Is a particular gesture, for instance, a sign of anger or of madness? Understanding involves a constant checking, rechecking, and disciplined study of expressions. And specifically in the field of literary criticism, it demands a rigorous and careful attention to the text.

III

Recent theological discussions of hermeneutics have stressed "pre-understanding" *(Vorverständnis)*, a theme that was anticipated by Dilthey. Pre-understanding implies that we can get *answers*—from a text or other source of meaning—only if we ask certain prior *questions*.[4]

According to Dilthey, one can come to the text with the following kinds of questions:

    a. What does this document, as a concretion of the author, say about the author's *Geist?*

    b. What does this document, as a concretion of a time "then and there" have to say to an inquiring *Geist* "here and now"?

    c. What does this document, as a concretion of *Geist* in a particular man, have to say to generic man?

Dilthey maintains that a hermeneutical understanding is always a *historical* understanding. Man is a historical being; therefore it can be said that, properly, "I am the story of my life." Understanding, then, does not come through introspection or "rummaging about in one's self," but through a history. There are fundamentally three types of personal knowledge, that is, ways of knowing persons:

    a. Through the interpretation of one's own life, that is, *autobiography.* In this case, one will have to rely on documents, diaries, mementos, etc., as well as personal memories which, however, must be critically checked.

    b. Through the understanding of another human being, that is, *biography.* This involves the same procedure as above, except for the reliance on subjective memories.

c. Through the movement of objective *Geist,* that is, the writing of history, *historiography.*

Thus, hermeneutics becomes for Dilthey a subtle interpretation of history, for he believes that the essence of anything (meaningful) is historical. "Man is there not to be but to act."

The question arises as to how human beings may know God since, by definition, God is not a historical being. Dilthey was not concerned directly with this question; hence it is proper to retreat behind Dilthey to Vico, upon whom he depended. Both Vico and Croce qualified man's freedom to act (i.e., to be) by two conditions. First, man is limited from below (nature). Natural factors such as soil, climate, and heredity enter into human history as conditioning realities, even though as natural "objects" they cannot be "understood" in themselves. And, secondly, man is limited from above. In this case, however, the Limiting Power is known only by revelation.

Something more must be added to this discussion, however. How do we know God? The answer is that we know God precisely in the same way that we know other persons, that is, historically. The theme of the Bible is that God discloses himself in a "shared history," remembered and confessed by the believing community—whether the "Israel" of the Old Testament or the "New Israel" of the New Testament. That is what *Heilsgeschichte* means.

IV

Let us turn now to the New Testament theologian Rudolf Bultmann, one of the leading figures in recent hermeneutical discussions. Remember that in the first instance—that is, in the case of Plato—hermeneutics arose out of a felt difficulty. This is true likewise in the case of Bultmann. For him the New Testament presents two major problems.[5]

First of all, Bultmann maintains that the New Testament presents the Christian gospel in terms of an unscientific world picture, namely, the so-called three-storied view of the universe. This statement, however, immediately invites criticism, for Bultmann presupposes a scientific view of the universe which scientists have long since abandoned! Scientists today would not think of the universe as a closed system of laws. Furthermore, ancient Christian thinkers did not hold the three-storied view of the universe naively. Even Paul knew that the world is round—a truth to which Greek science had already attained.

Secondly, and even more seriously, Bultmann as a Lutheran was disturbed by the quite un-Lutheran tendency of modern theology to make faith dependent upon objective, factual evidence. To him this is the modern form of justification by works. In this regard, Bultmann joins forces with the philosophy of phenomenology as advocated by Edmund Husserl.[6] Raising the question "How can we know things?" Husserl insists that such knowledge comes through the fulfillment of two conditions: first, we must eliminate *feelings*, for such subjectivity is not in the thing; and second, we must eliminate *facticity*. Facticity is a concern of the physicist but not of the philosopher who wants to grasp the thing conceptually, that is, in terms of its intentionality. Thus Bultmann declares that the modern concern for historical fact, for instance, the fact of the resurrection, is motivated by the desire to prove one's faith by giving it historical grounding.

Bultmann modifies the conception of pre-understanding that was introduced by Dilthey. Like Dilthey, Bultmann asserts that one does not come to the text without presuppositions; rather, one comes with the purpose of interrogating the text. But for Bultmann the question addressed to the text is always a question about existence—specifically, the structure of existence. Everywhere the Bible is really talking about human existence. So once again the grand distinction is made between what the text seems to say and its real meaning.

According to Bultmann, the New Testament speaks only to

the one who comes asking about "authentic existence." The questioner must be willing to stake his whole being on the question and its answer. The new self-understanding that is received is called "the new being." The point is that only those who are existentially committed can understand.

This view, however, is inadequate for biblical hermeneutics. Admittedly, one comes to the text with presuppositions, but these need not be existentialist. It is sufficient to say, in agreement with Dilthey: I am a human being and, because of affinity with other human beings, can understand expressions of their life. We could adduce many illustrations of interpreters who, though not sharing a particular religious or philosophical stance, have been able to put themselves into another viewpoint imaginatively and have given first-rate interpretation.

When interpreting the Bible today, the expositor assumes only that this literature deals with "shared meanings" which are universal, such as guilt, anxiety in the face of death, longing for salvation (wholeness), etc. Even the question of God is not alien to man in the modern world, for "natural man" is polytheistic, that is, he makes and worships a hierarchy of gods. Here it is appropriate to recall Luther's remark that what a man loves and relies on in his heart, that is his god. Thus man's restless polytheism is, at depth, a longing for the God beyond the gods.

NOTES

1. [Sir Edmund Andros (1637–1714) was one of the ablest English colonial governors in seventeenth-century America, thoroughly loyal to the Crown and therefore unpopular with the colonists. His jurisdiction included the Dominion of New England. When the news of the overthrow of James II arrived in Boston, the colonists summarily deposed and arrested him.— EDITOR]

2. See, for instance, H. A. Hodges, *Wilhelm Dilthey: An Introduction*

(London: Routledge & Kegan Paul, Ltd., 1944); *Pattern and Meaning in History: Thoughts on History and Society*, edited with an introduction by H. P. Rickman (London: Allen & Unwin, Ltd., 1961; Harper Torchbooks, 1962).

3. [See Herberg's essay "Hegel and His Influence on Biblical Theology," included in this volume.—EDITOR]

4. Rudolf Bultmann has given special emphasis to "pre-understanding." His view is expressed, for instance, in his essay "The Significance of the Old Testament for the Christian Faith," in *The Old Testament and Christian Faith*, ed. by Bernhard W. Anderson (Harper & Row, Publishers, Inc., 1963; Herder & Herder, Inc., 1969), pp. 8–35.

5. Bultmann's famous essay "The New Testament and Mythology," which touched off a great debate when it appeared during the Second World War, is available in *Kerygma and Myth*, ed. by Hans Werner Bartsch (S.P.C.K., 1953; Harper Torchbooks, 1961), along with the responses of critics.

6. [Edmund Husserl (1859–1938) is regarded as "the father of phenomenology," a type of philosophy that has had a powerful influence in recent years. Husserl's method, which attempts to grasp the meaning of "the intentionally given" in its purity, apart from scientific or theological interpretations, is discussed, for instance, by Quentin Lauer, *The Triumph of Subjectivity* (Fordham University Press, 1958).—EDITOR]

Will Herberg once expressed the view that today the major philosophical alternatives are German idealism (especially Hegelianism) and some form of existentialism. He pointed out that Søren Kierkegaard, a classical exponent of existentialism, could not escape Hegel, but had to fight against him; and that in the twentieth century, biblical scholars such as Julius Wellhausen, Hermann Gunkel, Martin Noth, and Gerhard von Rad have been more influenced by Hegel than they realized. The following essay, which discusses Hegel's influence on biblical interpretation, was presented as a public address at Princeton Theological Seminary in the fall of 1969 under the auspices of a graduate seminar in biblical theology. The taped lecture was transcribed and edited by Ruth A. Anderson, a philosophy major at Williams College, who has maintained insofar as possible the oral style of presentation.

8

HEGEL
AND HIS INFLUENCE
ON BIBLICAL THEOLOGY

It is my purpose in this address to attempt to define and assess the influence of Hegel and Hegelian thought upon biblical studies in the nineteenth and twentieth centuries. This is a task of enormous difficulty. In the first place, in the case of Hegel, no part or aspect of his thought can be understood without understanding something of his system as a whole. It will therefore be necessary to sketch in the outlines of the Hegelian system and the dominant motifs of his thought before proceeding to our subject itself. In the second place, the Hegelian ideas have become part of our own thinking, the thinking of nineteenth- and twentieth-century Western man. Unless we make a supreme effort to get outside of ourselves intellectually and critically, we shall be completely unaware of these influences. Such ideas as "evolution," "patterns of culture," and "creative mythopoeia" (or mythmaking) are quite definitely Hegelian—with a look back at J. G. Herder (1744–1803), and further back, perhaps, at G. B. Vico (1668–1744). But it was Hegel (1770–1831) who recovered Vico from his long submergence in obscurity, and it was through Hegel that Herder's "folk-idea" took hold. It requires a strong intellectual effort to disengage these ideas and examine them; but that is just what I propose to do here.

I

I shall deal first, then, with the overall Hegelian system.
Quite accurately, the Hegelian system is called "dialectical
idealism," and each of these two words has its important reference. What does "idealism" mean? Idealism takes the position
that *ultimate reality is of the nature of thought.* In fact, it
becomes very difficult to distinguish "thought" from what is
"not-thought," as will become apparent in the ensuing discussion. What does "dialectical" mean? It means that *both
thought and reality* (and reality is ultimately of the nature of
thought) *have a dynamic movement through internal contradiction and resolution of these contradictions.*

With this understanding of dialectical idealism, I want to
sketch the structure of the Hegelian system. It is thoroughly
well constructed, and thoroughly comprehensible, in spite of
the fact that many people say that they cannot understand a
word of it (a claim which reflects not on Hegel, but on their
own posture—they know in advance they won't understand a
word of it, therefore, they don't understand a word of it!). The
dialectic takes place through *thesis, antithesis,* and *synthesis.*
Now, these are Greek-derived words; in fact, they are almost
exactly the Greek words. There are Latin-derived words, too,
which mean exactly the same: *position, opposition,* and *composition.* Hegel begins with pure Thought (or pure Reason, as he
sometimes expresses it), and calls this "Idea-in-itself." The
Idea-in-itself, through its internal dynamic, pours over into its
antithesis; that is, the Idea-in-itself (*Idee-an-sich*) becomes the
"Idea-outside-itself" *(Idee-ausser-sich).* "Outside itself" *(ausser
sich)* is a pun in German; in English, we say a man is "beside
himself"—meaning either very angry, or even mad, insane—
in German, *ausser sich* is used in this sense. So, the Idea
externalizes itself, *alienates* itself, becomes the Idea-*outside*-
itself. The Idea-outside-itself is Nature—you will see why as I
explain further. The reality of Nature is the rationality of it.

But this rationality is hidden in an alien form. Look at a tree, or a mountain, or a cow, for example—the reality of each is the rationality of it, but the rationality is hidden in an alien, empirical form. Therefore, Hegel speaks of Nature as the Idea-outside-itself, *ausser sich*. The study of the Idea-in-itself is called "Logic"; the study of the Idea-outside-itself is called "philosophy of Nature."

Now comes the synthesis. As we have seen, there is the thesis, and the antithesis, and thus a kind of contradiction. Contrary to the usual vulgar belief, Hegel is not fond of contradiction. In Hegelian thought, there is a pressure to *overcome* this contradiction on a higher level, in a synthesis. The thesis and antithesis, facing each other in contradiction, *press* for resolution on a higher level, that is to say, in synthesis, or composition. Now consider: where does one have both the Idea-in-itself (pure Thought or Rationality) and the Idea-outside-itself (Nature)? Where do these two meet in synthesis? Where can we find both united? The answer is, in *Man*. Man is, first of all, the rationality of thought; on the other hand, he is also part of nature. In Man, there is rationality of thought, now united with nature—Hegel calls this union *Geist*. *Geist* sounds like the English "ghost" or "spirit," but it is not that at all. The German word *Geist* cannot be adequately translated into English. The nearest thing I can think of is what the anthropologists call "man and his works." *Geist* is man and his works, man creating and the created works—Hegel calls this the "Idea-*returned*-to-itself." In summary, then, there is the Idea-in-itself; the Idea externalized, alienated, outside itself; and the synthesis, the Idea-returned-to-itself in *Geist*.

We are interested in the third element in this dialectical triad: the Idea-returned-to-itself in *Geist*. Here, too, there is a dialectical development. *Geist* is usually translated as "Mind." If one understood "Mind" in the broadest possible sense, this would not be so bad, but one must not think of it in its narrower sense. I will use "Mind" for *Geist* from this point on.

As Hegel sees it, there is, first, "subjective Mind," or "Mind-subjective"—in other words, mind in the usual sense in which we think of it (in its subjectivity). Then this Mind-subjective externalizes itself and becomes "objective Mind." Objective Mind is the realm of history and institutions. Notice that history takes place in the realm of *objective*, not subjective, Mind. Institutions also—preeminently the state, economic institutions, and so on—are in the realm of objective Mind. I shall develop this in a moment. The synthesis of subjective Mind and objective Mind (for remember, there is a dialectical development within Mind, or *Geist*, itself) is "absolute Mind." Here we shall be concerned only with objective Mind and absolute Mind.

Let me go back for a moment to objective Mind. The first manifestation of objective Mind is the *family*, which is characterized by immediacy, feeling, and kinship. The antithesis of the family is *civil society*, or *Bürgergesellschaft*—which has been rendered as "bourgeois society" by some ignorant translators who would give a Marxian twist to it. *Civil* society has nothing to do with *bourgeois* society. Civil society consists of institutions that people form for utilitarian purposes. Nobody ever joins a family; one is born into it: membership in a family is immediate, and is based on feeling and kinship. Civil society, on the other hand, is mediated through organizations that have been set up on the basis of utility—labor unions, for instance, or farmers' organizations.

There is family, on the one hand, and civil society, on the other. The synthesis of these two is the "State." But this is "state" in the European or Continental sense, not in the American or British sense. Britons and Americans have no equivalent word for what the Continentals—especially the Germans—mean by this term. The word "state" in "the United States" means either a subdivision of a nation, or else government, but neither of these is Hegel's meaning. To Hegel, the State is a synthesis of family and civil society. The

State, like the family, is immediate, based on feeling (patriotism) and on kinship (the "folk"—in German, *Volk*); but it is also like civil society—it is an organization, an institution, and so on. From this bare sketch, one can see the basic structure of the dialectical movement, which, according to Hegel, underlies the dynamics of *every* particular state.

We come now to absolute *Geist* (Mind). The Hegelian account could be said to present a long odyssey, one that begins with the Idea-in-itself and ends up with *Geist,* and finally absolute *Geist.* At the outset, there is sheer, empty logic; at the end, there is absolute *Geist,* which is laden with an entire history of dialectical experience. Absolute *Geist* exists in three forms, each of which expresses the Absolute: art, religion, and philosophy. In art, the Absolute is expressed in sensory materials (color, sound, etc.). There is a *tension* between what is expressed (the Absolute), and how it is expressed (through the medium of sensory materials). On a level above this is religion. Here it is still the Absolute that is expressed, but now it is expressed in *Vorstellung* (representation)—by which Hegel means myths, images, stories, and so on—rather than in sensory materials. There is still another level beyond that— namely, *philosophy*—where, again, the Absolute is expressed (as in art and religion), but through the medium of *Begriff* (concept). At this level, in other words, there is no longer any tension, as there is between the Absolute and sensory material, and between the Absolute and *Vorstellung* (representation); the Absolute *is* concept, and it is expressed in concept. There is complete homogeneity.

Of course, it must be remembered that art, religion, and philosophy have their own long, dialectical histories. The dialectical history of philosophy ends with the Hegelian philosophy. The Hegelian philosophy is *the Absolute become conscious of itself in and through the human mind.* You will notice that art, religion, and philosophy all express the same thing— the Absolute; but they do so in less and less inadequate forms.

Art is inadequate to express the Absolute. Religion is also inadequate, though less so. In philosophy, the Absolute is expressed in perfectly adequate form. In other words, what we have here in Hegel is a demythologization of religion. What is expressed in religion *mythologically*—using one of Bultmann's various definitions of "myth"—is expressed in philosophy conceptually. Hegel, like all great philosophers as far back as Plato, saw the demythologization of religion as one of his primary tasks. I hope nobody believes that Bultmann invented demythologization: the great philosophers have always been doing that and have far outdone him.

II

So far I have presented, in the very briefest form, a conspectus, a synoptic view, of the Hegelian system. I proceed now to a discussion of Hegel's view of history. Much time could be spent discussing the Hegelian view of history—and profitably; I do not know anyone who has ever seen more deeply and profoundly into the problems of historical movement than Hegel. Hegel sees history in terms of the operation of the *Volk*, which I shall translate somewhat artificially as "Folk" for lack of any adequate English equivalent. "Folk" in English sounds "folksy," as in, "I wrote a letter to my folks"—an impossible usage in German. The Folk—an ethnic, national, cultural group—is the agent of history. It is the real, concrete, corporate entity of men. It manifests itself in the *Volksgeist*—translated inadequately, "the spirit of a nation," but really meaning *"the inner structure of the Folk."*

The State, to Hegel, is *the Folk organized on the highest level.* In this sense, it is like the great *polis* [city]—society organized on the highest level. It is the supreme embodiment and expression of the *Volksgeist* (that is, the spirit of a nation, or internal structure of the Folk). One can see how remote this meaning of "state" is from the American or British meaning.

The State is the vehicle, or agent, of history. To put this in another way, history is the *unfolding* of the infolded Idea in and through the State. Here Hegel uses the term *Entwicklung* in the German, which is usually translated as "evolution," but which means "unwinding" or "unfolding" (I will explain this concept further shortly). According to Hegel, the *Volksidee*—the core Idea of the Folk that is manifested in the *Volksgeist*—unfolds itself in history. Every Folk has its "Folk-Idea" which unfolds itself in the history of that Folk, proceeding dialectically in tension and conflict. But these *Völker*—in English, "folks," an odd word—do not proceed helter-skelter; they proceed under the direction of the *Weltgeist,* the "World Spirit." The *Weltgeist* is the comprehensive and immanent director of the *Volksgeiste* (plural), and is an important concept in the Hegelian system.

Let me outline certain basic Hegelian motifs: first, *development.* Development—or evolution—is a concept that we use constantly, where appropriate and where inappropriate (mostly the latter). But one must realize that "development" is a *new* word in its evolutionary sense, dating from the eighteenth century. The word "evolution" was used in the seventeenth century for military formations and tactics, and is still used in that sense today, though this usage is very archaic. In the eighteenth century, the terms "development" and "evolution" were at first used by botanists and biologists who held a theory of preformation: they saw the whole plant or animal as preformed in the nucleus, and the whole subsequent *development* of the organism as the *unfolding* of this preformed nucleus. Hegel was the *first* to use "development" (unfolding) in the philosophical and historical sense. That seems incredible. What would one do if the words "development" and "evolution" were taken away? One would be struck dumb! Yet each expresses a special concept that was unknown until Hegel. To repeat, then, the first Hegelian motif is development *(Entwicklung),* the unfolding of an infolded Idea (where "infolded" is the correlative of "unfolded"). In the Folk there is the infolded Idea; the history of the Folk unfolds that Idea.

The second basic Hegelian motif is *process*. Process, in a certain sense, is also a Hegelian concept, believe it or not! I can explain the term best by saying that, for Hegel, it is not origins, beginnings (as for the Greeks), and not ends (as for the Hebrews [*eschata*]), but the *process*, the dialectical movement, that is central. I doubt if this emphasis is to be found anywhere at all before the beginning of the nineteenth century with Hegel.

The third basic motif is what I call *"Folk-imagination"*— in the German, *Vorstellung* (literally, "representation"). Hegel (and Herder before him) saw myth, symbol, and imaginative elaboration *not* as ignorance, not as imposture, but as the unconscious creation of the Folk mind—or perhaps I should say, as the not-deliberate creation of the Folk mind, for I do not mean "unconscious" in the Freudian sense. This is very influential in biblical studies, as will be seen when I discuss D. F. Strauss and F. C. Baur.

Dialectic is the fourth basic idea. By dialectic, I mean the antithetical struggle of tendencies, of opposites. I will discuss this further when I come to the early Germans Strauss and Baur.

Finally, the fifth basic motif is *Reason*—true rationality, coming through all the welter of the strange and incoherent complexities of history. Just as the Idea externalizes itself or alienates itself into Nature, where it is lost in the incoherence and irrationality of Nature, so the Idea permeates and loses itself in the complexities of history.

One explanation should be made before I continue. I said that the first of the Hegelian motifs is "unfolding." However, we use the word "unfolding" in many senses. Bernhard W. Anderson has written a little book, *The Unfolding Drama of the Bible*,[1] but he uses "unfolding" in a sense that is not Hegelian. To a Hegelian, "unfolding" means the unwinding of a preformed Idea; to Anderson, it means dramatic elaboration through time—a different thing. When we say, "The plot of this drama, of this novel, unfolds itself," we are not referring to a Hegelian preformed idea elaborating itself; we mean that it moves through time dramatically. One must be careful about these words; they become so pervasive in our thinking that we can shift their meanings without even knowing it.

III

With this brief introduction, let us move on to the variations of Hegelian themes in biblical studies. First, I shall give an example from Hegel himself. He presents a dialectic movement: the *thesis* is paganism, which he regards as immediacy and feeling; the *antithesis* is Judaism, which he considers externalization and law; the *synthesis* of both of these is Christianity. I am not vouching for the accuracy of this analysis—don't take my word for it! I am merely illustrating Hegel. Take another Hegelian triad: the thesis is God in his deity; the antithesis is man in his otherness; the synthesis is the God-man, the supreme paradigm of perfected mankind. This is how Hegel thought of us, in our relation to biblical history.

A third example of this kind is found in Paul Tillich's theology. According to Tillich, in his elaboration of the doctrine of the Trinity, the thesis (the first Person) is God, the power of being—or, in his words, "the *abyss* of being," where "abyss" means a bottomless well of power. The antithesis (the second Person) is the *logos* of being, or structure of being. The synthesis (the third Person) is the *life* of being, in which power and structure are united. Tillich's thinking is strictly Hegelian here (though it is doubtful if it is Christian).

I shall now proceed to more elaborate examples. I take first a Jewish theologian of the nineteenth century, whom I am sure no one has heard of, Nachman Kachmo (1785–1840), because he illustrates Hegelianism "right out of the horse's mouth," so to speak—immediately. In fact, most of his productive life was in Hegel's lifetime; he survived Hegel by only nine years. The problem he deals with is how to reconcile revelation with historical criticism—an old problem—and in dealing with it he takes up the Hegelian concept of the Folk-Idea. For him, the nation is a cultural, spiritual superorganism, as Hegel suggested. The Idea of the nation is the expression of the *Volksgeist* (spirit of a nation). Every nation has its nuclear Idea: the ancient Greeks had—let us say—beauty (although some people think it was philosophy); the Romans, law; and so on. The *vocation* of a nation (here is a new element) is to actualize the potentialities of the *Volksgeist*—the Folk-Idea, or nuclear Idea of the people. This is called a "principle of plenitude" (fullness); and, according to Hegel (echoed later in Marx), no nation ever disappears from the scene of history until it has actualized its potentialities. Once it has actualized its potentialities, it disappears entirely, or it becomes a shadow; like modern Greece (as Hegel would view it), or modern Italy, it no longer has any vocation. Now, as I pointed out, Kachmo sees history as successive actualizations of different national Ideas, one after the other. After an Idea has been actualized in its fullness (plenitude), it passes off the stage of history. But Israel is not like other nations. The Ideas of other nations are partial, limited, sooner or later to be exhausted, Kachmo says; whereas Israel (the Jewish national Idea) is the eternal spirit, *never* to be exhausted. The Torah of Israel is the literary embodiment of the Jewish national Idea *(Volksidee)*. Kachmo, therefore, maintains that it is possible to see the movement of Jewish thought through history, and yet to have an unchanging, enduring kernel of revelation.

Note that there is a basic shift here: from divine activity to immanent, indwelling Idea. What operates in Jewish history, according to Kachmo, is the indwelling Idea—not divine activity, as the Bible tells us ("the Living God," "the God who acts," and so forth). Furthermore, there is a shift from the positive religion of Israel to the Jewish Idea. Now, we speak frequently of "the German idea," "the Jewish idea," or other ideas, without knowing where these expressions come from—they do not mean much to us. But to Kachmo, such an expression referred to the Hegelian nuclear reality of a nation. It is no longer the positive religion of Israel; now it is the Jewish Idea. Martin Buber uses the same terminology in his early writings—all derived from Hegel, and before him, suggested by Herder.

Turning now to Protestant biblical scholars, I will take up first David Friedrich Strauss (1808–1874). His basic contention was that the New Testament stories represent the mythopoeic (mythmaking) projection of the Folk-imagination. Now this may seem a platitude to some, but it is not platitude at all. Before Strauss and Hegel, rationalists of the eighteenth century, such as Heinrich Paulus, who examined critically the stories in the New Testament, could only explain them as impostures—that is, they supposed that somebody had devised a deliberate scheme of falsification. But Hegel opened up a new possibility: the view that the whole community can project its mythmaking without any element of imposture being involved, since such projection is the legitimate, creative, mythmaking faculty of the Folk. Recall that the second level of absolute Mind (after art) is religion, which expresses the Absolute in *Vorstellung*—mythology, images, and so on. This manner of expression is not primitive. Hegel insisted that *Vorstellung* is the abiding way in which all but a few philosophers think of the Absolute.

Strauss developed this with extraordinary depth. It is not merely that the Folk—by which he means the early Christian community—elaborates a mythological corpus of stories coming from its core Idea without *imposture*, without any intention of inventing stories; but that these stories, developed mythologically from the Folk-Idea, have *symbolic truth*. The Folk myth is not an invention, an inferior kind of knowledge, or anything of that sort—it bears the essential, spiritual truth. Only philosophy can uncover and elicit the *real* truth behind religious *Vorstellung* (and that is the highest reach of philosophy). Otherwise, religious *Vorstellung*, in the elaboration of the community myths, most adequately tells the real truth. Strauss' *Leben Jesu* (Life of Jesus), written in 1835, was translated in 1846 by George Eliot (the pseudonym used by the English writer Mary Ann Evans—a brilliant woman). In a letter to a friend of hers, Mrs. Peter Taylor, written in 1863, George Eliot remarks that "we can never have a satisfactory basis for the history of the man Jesus; but, that negation does not affect the picture of the Christ, either in its historical influence, or in its great symbolic meaning." This statement anticipates Martin Kähler and the whole school of "the Jesus of History and the Christ of Faith." Eliot points out that, although we can know very little about the historical Jesus, that does not preclude knowing him through his historical influence (see "the Christ of Faith," in Martin Kähler's celebrated essay).[2] But *more* than that, she speaks of what Martin Kähler did not speak of: the great symbolic meaning of the life of Jesus. We can know nothing about the life of Jesus, yet the elaboration of his life by the early community in its mythopoeic faculty tells the symbolic meaning. This view is strictly Hegelian. Indeed, according to Strauss, if one interprets these myths literally, one stultifies them, makes them stupid. If taken for factual truth, the myths become "crude" and "crass falsifications," as he put it. If anyone thinks that this mythological and symbolic business was developed by the ultramodern theologians, he is greatly mistaken; it has its roots in early Hegelian thought. One can see how Hegelian ideas molded Strauss' investigations into the New Testament.

I take now another one of the early, celebrated Germans: Ferdinand Christian Baur (1792–1860). He emphasizes a different aspect of Hegelian thought altogether. Anyone who has heard of Baur has heard of *Tendenzkritik*—criticism by bare tendencies. One usage of the word "tendency" has been adopted in English from the German *Tendenzroman*—a novel with a thesis, or in other words, a novel that is moving in the direction of a certain tendency. Baur used the term to mean this, but he also meant something much more. A *Tendenz* is a special interest bias, an inclination, a partial concern, a one-sidedness. But Baur did not mean simply that a biblical writer exhibited such one-sidedness; he meant, furthermore, that such one-sidedness was *not* a mere psychological matter, not an emotional or intellectual inadequacy. Rather, in line with Hegelian thought, he saw it as an inherent and necessary operation of the dialectic of Being and Thought. The nature of Being, and hence the nature of Thought, is always to move through one-sidedness. There is one-sidedness, other-sidedness, and synthesis, as I shall illustrate presently. The truth, he says, emerges in a synthesis of *Tendenzen* (plural).

Baur's scholarly writings develop the following antitheses: first, Jesus versus the Jewish Messiah tradition; second—and more important than any other—Paul versus a Judaizing element; and third, the Old Catholic Church *(altkatholische Kirche)* versus the Gnostic heresy.[3] Now, try to understand how radically different Baur's idea is. In the past, up through the eighteenth century, writers on these matters saw an original orthodoxy, and various heresies challenging this orthodoxy. But Baur insists that in the beginning (in the original antithesis) *both* elements of the antithesis are orthodox—*both* derive from the earlier Christian tradition. Then, later, they come into conflict, and are resolved. Resolution is a new stage of orthodoxy. Thus orthodoxy is *created* by the antithetical struggle of tendencies *(Tendenzen)*. One can see how thoroughly Hegelian that view is.

This *Tendenzkritik* uncovers a hidden dialectic: the struggle of particular group interests, or intellectual interests, or spiritual interests. It sees the constitution of orthodoxy as a synthesis, that is, as the resolution of this *Tendenz* conflict.

This resolution, according to Baur, is in line with immanent teleology. Within the Christian movement there is an indwelling drive to actualize its own potentialities, and the resolution of the conflict of *Tendenzen* is in line with this indwelling drive.[4]

In a debased and bastard form, the Hegelian *Entwicklung* becomes the superficial idea of progressive development, as found, for instance, in Harry Emerson Fosdick's *A Guide for the Understanding of the Bible* (1938). I doubt if Fosdick knew anything of Hegel, except his name. But one does not have to *know* Hegel; by 1938, people had absorbed the Hegelian teaching through the atmosphere. (One has to breathe, doesn't one, intellectually? One breathes in Hegel!) Notice Fosdick's debased form of the dialectic and of the development *(Entwicklung)*. He finds six lines of *progressive* development, each beginning at a low level and moving up to higher and higher levels. The movement is in a spiritualizing and individualizing direction. It is sufficient here to mention only some of the six lines of developmental movement—for instance, from particularism to universalism, from corporate consciousness to moral individualism, from priestly ritual to prophetic spirituality, from the externality of law to the spirituality of love.

I will take one of these as an example to show the superficiality of this kind of argument: namely, the movement from corporate consciousness to moral individualism. Fosdick points out, rightly, that in the literary prophets there is the saying in various forms, "The fathers have eaten sour grapes, and the children's teeth are set on edge." But according to Ezekiel, this must be said no longer, for ". . . the soul that sins shall die" (see Ezek. 18:4). Now, Fosdick interprets this as a denial of corporate responsibility and the attainment of a higher level in the progression toward moral individualism. But the prophets would not have shared such an interpretation. They did not see this as an advance, but as a kind of historical disaster. In the early days, the Hebraic community had had its *shalom*—its integrity or wholeness—and the individual saw the meaning of his life and his destiny within the community. In modern terms, there was solidarity of sin, and there was solidarity of grace. But in the time of the prophet Ezekiel, the *shalom* in the community was broken up; the individual could not stand on the community, but rather had to stand on his own feet. Therefore, an individualizing tendency emerged. This tendency was regarded as an aspect of the destruction—hopefully temporary—of the *shalom* of the community. The early Christians, furthermore, insisted on recovering their corporate existence. Contrary to vulgar Protestant notions, the New Testament is not an individualizing document, but just the reverse —it speaks of "a kingdom of priests," "a holy people," and so forth (see I Peter 3:9). This should not need further elaboration. But one can see what has happened in this case: the profound insight that Hegel had (and Strauss and Baur too, even though they were mistaken in many ways) is now gone, *verflacht* (flattened out). Nevertheless, Fosdick's views *derive* from Hegelian thought, and because of his influence, the debased *Entwicklung* (development, unfolding) has been seen in America in terms of a Deweyan progressivism. I am sure that Fosdick was more influenced by John Dewey than by Georg Friedrich Wilhelm Hegel.

Next let us consider Julius Wellhausen (1844–1918)—a well-known and a great scholar, with a truly profound understanding of the Old Testament and biblical materials. If one dismisses Wellhausen, for any sort of reason, one is making a great mistake. What aspects of Hegelian thought do we find in Wellhausen? Hegelian thought is many-faceted, like a diamond, and thinkers influenced by Hegel, for the most part, deal with only one facet or a group of associated facets. In Wellhausen we find, first of all, the Hegelian motif of *Gestalt*. Hegel, you will recall, introduced the concept of the *Volksgeist* —a nuclear idea, elaborating itself in all aspects of the culture. Hegel was one of the first (with Herder preceding him) to see that what we call the culture of a group is not a random aggregation of items but a coherent *Gestalt* (configuration or pattern). One cannot take one element of the culture of a group and replace it with something else without changing all the other elements of the configuration. This motif of *Gestalt* is one of the earliest of Hegelian ideas and, as can be readily seen, is not particularly theological. When the British made strong efforts to replace primitive Egyptian technology with modern technology, many of them had the notion that they could simply improve the technology of the Egyptians without affecting the rest of the culture in any way. But they couldn't —the *whole* culture was changed. Modern cultural anthropologists (such as Ruth Benedict) speak of a "pattern of culture." Though they may not have heard much of Hegel, they are repeating the Hegelian idea, word for word: the *Gestalt* of culture, translated into American English, means the "pattern" of culture. Wellhausen understood this concept very well. He deals throughout his work with patterns of culture, and is very sensitive to modifications occurring in one element of a culture that are brought about by a change in other elements.

The second motif that is strong in Wellhausen is *development*, the unfolding of the infolded idea. This aspect of his thought is fairly well known. The third motif that should be mentioned is *dialectic*—the antithetical struggle. This is not as marked in Wellhausen as in Baur, for example; but it is there. Finally, I want to emphasize again Wellhausen's undoubted achievements, despite the substantial supersession, or perhaps I should say, the completion of source criticism by form criticism today.

I go on now to Gerhard von Rad and Walther Eichrodt, theologians of our own time. Von Rad, the younger man, was born in 1901. His main thesis is stream of development—not *what* is developing, or *where* it is going, but the endless process of development itself. More specifically, he advocates development without formative event, and religious tradition without a historical religious center. He is not alone in this: Martin Buber also saw the Old Testament as a religious movement without a center—or rather, as he says, as a religious movement with a "movable center" (by which, however, he does not mean a historical center at all, but an existential one).[5]

Over against this, Walther Eichrodt takes a position which stresses the historical course of the integral nuclear community, and the community as the bearer of this tradition (in Von Rad, one gets the impression that the tradition moves itself). In Eichrodt's account, the community is an integral core organized around a historical formative event. The unity it provides arises not out of an idea, as those more influenced by Hegel suggest, but out of the faith of the community—a faith that is oriented toward historical events.

I come now to James Barr, the youngest of all those considered here (b. 1924). Barr has at least three important works: *Semantics of Biblical Language* (1961), *Biblical Words for Time* (1962), and—the most important—*Old and New in Interpretation* (1964), a study of the two Testaments. In the case of Barr, all desirable events in Israel's history are dissolved in a process stream called "tradition." (He carries out the incomplete "process" logic of Von Rad entirely on his own.) "Tradition," in his usage, means tradition apart from the historical community which is the bearer of that tradition, and apart from the formative events by which the community is constituted. I think in this case there is more Deweyan influence than Hegelian. Knowing the Scottish intellectual tradition, I find it hard to believe that a Scottish biblical scholar, such as Barr, was much influenced by Hegelian thought (or by the thought of Baur, either).

Let me now conclude. I want to stress that I have the highest possible regard for Hegel and his thought. The incredible extent of his knowledge, the breadth, penetration, and depth of his thinking, his unparalleled capacity for system-building—

these constitute one of the chief glories of the Western mind. However, his influence on biblical studies has not been an unequivocally happy one. Due to the weight and all-pervasiveness of his influence, direct and indirect, the Hegelian concepts and categories have been so effectively imposed on our thinking from the outside, so to speak, that it seems practically impossible to escape them now. We all more or less operate with these concepts and categories, in spite of the fact that at many points they are at odds with the primary biblical materials themselves. I have made an effort here to elicit and uncover some of the Hegelian influences on biblical studies, and to view them from a certain distance. I do not suppose that my remarks have been at all exhaustive—I know they have not. They have been hardly more than suggestive. But, for what they are, I recommend them to you for your attention.

NOTES

1. Bernhard W. Anderson, *The Unfolding Drama of the Bible: Eight Studies Introducing the Bible as a Whole*, 2d ed. (Association Press, 1971).

2. Martin Kähler, *Der sogennante historische Jesus und der geschichtliche, biblische Christus*, 2d ed. (Munich: Chr. Kaiser Verlag, 1956). English translation by Carl E. Braaten, *The So-called Historical Jesus and the Historic, Biblical Christ* (Fortress Press, 1954).

3. See Ferdinand Christian Baur, "Die Christuspartei in der Korinthischen Gemeinde," *Tübinger Zeitschrift für Theologie*, Vol. 4 (1831), pp. 61 ff.; *Paul, the Apostle of Jesus Christ*, ed. by E. Zeller and tr. by A. Menzies (London: Williams and Norgate, 1876 [German 1st ed., 1845]); *Die sogenannten Pastoralbriefe des apostels Paulus* (Stuttgart: Cotta, 1835).

4. A recent work by Samuel Laeuchli, *The Serpent and the Dove: Five Essays on Early Christianity* (Abingdon Press, 1966), undertakes to discuss the entire early history of Christianity in this manner, showing how orthodoxy emerges at various stages. A very interesting and revealing book.

5. In a similar manner, Bultmann discovers the *Heilsgeschehen*, or saving event, as occurring whenever the *kerygma* is proclaimed to a person and is received in faith. Thus he too sees a movable center.

Again and again Will Herberg has said in private conversations that he regards this little essay with special satisfaction. The semantic clarification is, as he puts it, a "useful preliminary" to fruitful discussion and, some would add, a "necessary preliminary" to faith seeking understanding, if faith is truly to be expressed in historical terms. It should be noticed that, in Herberg's judgment, *all* of the nuances of the term "historical" are important in theological discussion. For the biblical theologian, however, the question is: Which meaning has the ascendancy? As suggested in the Introduction to this volume, Herberg seems to stress the fourth meaning, but not to the exclusion of the others, especially the theological concern for historical "facticity."

The following essay was published in *The Christian Scholar*, Vol. XLVII (1964).

9

FIVE MEANINGS
OF THE WORD "HISTORICAL"

It has been well said[1] that the most characteristic feature of theological thinking through the decades of this century has been its *historical* orientation. Every significant type of theology to emerge in this period has proclaimed itself to be anchored in the conviction of man's historicity. Sometimes explicitly, more usually by implication, man's reality has been held to be his history; and this insight has on occasion been extended to all reality as such. All the more disturbing, therefore, is the confusion that seems to engulf this key concept. Terms like "history," "historical," etc., are used in a variety of ways, some close to ordinary language, others very far from it. This variety of usage and meaning is not always recognized, which is particularly unfortunate since the various meanings are in fact interconnected, and none of them can be properly understood without an adequate grasp of the rest.

I suggest that there are at least five distinct meanings or uses of the term "historical." Let me enumerate them with some comment and illustration.

1. In its first and most obvious sense, "historical" means *factual,* what has actually happened. We say that it is historical, or a historical fact, that Washington crossed the Delaware on December 26, 1776, but that it is probably not historical fact that he stayed up all night praying at Valley Forge. Of course, philosophical questions, difficult ones, too, immediately

arise: What, or where, is "the past"? How is knowledge of "the past" possible? and so on. But the ordinary usage is undisputed, and we all somehow know what is meant. In this sense, the historical is opposed to the fictitious, the fabulous, the mythical, the legendary, and the like. The historical is past facticity.

2. But we sometimes oppose the historical not so much to the fictitious, the legendary, or the mythical, as to the timeless and the eternal. The propositions of economics or sociology (some say) are historical truths, while those of physics or mathematics are not. Here historical means "enacting itself temporally"; perhaps *historiform*, if I may coin the term, would be appropriate. The opposition here is to the kind of timeless eternity possessed, or supposed to be possessed, by abstract concepts, eternal verities, and the like. In this sense, we can speak of Judaism or Christianity as historical religions, and of Buddhism (at least the more rigorous Theravada Buddhism) as nonhistorical: the former requires presentation as a story, a recital, of the doings of God and men; the latter is a communication of eternal truths about reality, human life, and deliverance from evil.

3. A third usage of the term is found in such expressions as a "historic" act, event, occasion, etc. (For this, in English, we tend to reserve the form "historic" rather than "historical," although the latter is not unknown.) What we mean here is something we deem to be *especially influential* on the future course of events. In this sense, historic is opposed to the unimportant, the insignificant, the trivial, on the one side, and to the "merely factual," on the other.

In this sense, too, the term has been extraordinarily influential in modern theology. It is at the heart of the momentous distinction between the "historical Jesus" *(der historische Jesus)* and the "Christ of history" *(der geschichtliche Christus).* This is precisely the distinction emphasized by Martin Kähler in his epoch-making work *Der sogennante historische Jesus und der geschichtliche, biblische Christus,* which appeared in 1892.

Besinnen wir uns! [Kähler appeals] Was ist denn eigentlich eine geschichtliche Grösse? . . . Eben der Urheber und Träger seiner bleibenden Fortwirkung. Als Wirkungsfähiger greift der Mensch in den Gang der Dinge ein; was er dann ist, das wirkt, dadurch wirkt er.[2]

("Let us stop and think! What, then, really is a historical magnitude? . . . Precisely the originator and bearer of its [own] continuous influence. As one who is able to act, man intervenes in the course of events; what he then is, that is what acts, and that through which he acts.")

And E. Wolf, restating Kähler's thesis, in his foreword to his recent edition of Kähler's work, writes:

Der in der Geschichte wirksame Christus ist der von den Aposteln als der Gekreuzigte und Auferstandene verkundete, und nicht ein "historischer" Jesus, den erst unsere wissenschaftliche Technik mühsam hinter den Urkunden neu entdecken müsste.[3]

("The Christ who is effective in history is he who is proclaimed by the apostles as the crucified and resurrected one, and not a 'historical' Jesus who must first be painstakingly discovered anew behind the documents by our scientific technique.")

Kähler's point has been much misunderstood, but these passages ought to make it clear. Note also that, in recent German theological and philosophical writing, the attempt has been made to reserve the term *"historisch"* for historical in the sense of past facticity, and *"geschichtlich"* for historical in senses that go beyond, or even ignore, the element of facticity.

4. The last two are the more nearly "existential" usages. As opposed to those ontologists who see human being as constituted by a fixed and determinate nature, there are the thinkers who insist that *man's being is "essentially" constituted by his history.* Reinhold Niebuhr is perhaps the best-known champion of the historicity of man in this sense and, on this level,

he apparently sees his greatest difference with the ontologism of Paul Tillich. Niebuhr declares:

> The human person and man's society are by nature historical, ... [and] the ultimate truth about life must be mediated historically.[4] ... The human community is defined in a dramatic-historical pattern, just as is the individual.[5]

In a real sense, so the historicists of this brand would contend, a human person is his personal history: he is constituted by it, and it alone defines his uniqueness, his "personness." And, by extension, this is felt to be true of human communities as well, particularly of *Gemeinschaften*, which are seen as historical rather than as purely organic entities. To these thinkers, it is this historicity of man that constitutes his "essence"—that is, his capacity to transcend indeterminately all fixed structures of being, even of his own being.

5. The fifth, and final, meaning of the term "historical" follows from the fourth; it is, in fact, bound to it in a Janus-head fashion—one aspect looking backward, the other forward. For, if the human person is constituted by his history, he is constituted by his doings and sufferings, decisions and actions: and precisely here lies the element of freedom. But that means that as the self stands in the "moment" facing the future, it is called upon to choose, decide, venture, and act. In so doing, it (in a measure at least) constitutes and reconstitutes itself. Its historicity consists not only, and perhaps not primarily, in its being constituted by its history, but in its *existential self-constituting in the face of the future of possibility*.[6] Man's "nature," insofar as he has one, is, so to speak, radically *open-ended*: it is forever being made and remade by choice, decision, and action, which is what constitutes man's historicity. It is this that is expressed in the familiar formula, "existence precedes essence," a translation, probably unwitting, of the late medieval saying familiar in certain "voluntarist" circles, *Esse sequitur agere* (reversing the Thomistic *Agere sequitur esse*). Rudolf

Bultmann may be called upon to illustrate the latter meaning, as Niebuhr the former.

Historicity [concludes Bultmann] now gains the meaning of responsibility over against the future, which is, at the same time, responsibility over against the heritage of the past in the face of the future. Every moment is the *now* of responsibility, of decision.[7]

And so we have run the full gamut: beginning with the historical as *past facticity*, we have arrived at the historical as *future possibility*. And each of the meanings or usages traversed is not only legitimate and proper in its place; it is quite indispensable. The five are, moreover, closely connected; this connection is particularly obvious in the last two, although it should be clear also for the other three, and for the five as a whole.

My purpose has been to clarify uses and meanings, and to show relevance to theological and philosophical discourse. This seems to me a useful preliminary to fruitful discussion and controversy.

NOTES

1. See Carl Michalson, "Fifty Years of Theology in Retrospect: An Evaluation," *Journal of Bible and Religion*, Vol. XXVIII (1960), pp. 215–221.

2. Martin Kähler, *Der sogennante historische Jesus und der geschichtliche, biblische Christus*, ed. by E. Wolf, 2d ed. (Munich: Chr. Kaiser Verlag, 1956), p. 37. [English translation by Carl E. Braaten, *The So-called Historical Jesus and the Historic, Biblical Christ* (Fortress Press, 1954).—Editor]

3. Kähler, *op. cit.*, p. 8.

4. Reinhold Niebuhr, "Religious Education," *Religious Education*, Vol. XLVIII (Nov.-Dec., 1953), p. 373.

5. Reinhold Niebuhr, *The Self and the Dramas of History* (Charles Scribner's Sons, 1955), p. 49.

6. For a profound inquiry into the metaphysical problems involved in

existential self-constituting and self-creating, see Emil L. Fackenheim, *Metaphysics and Historicity* (Marquette University Press, 1961).

7. Rudolf Bultmann, *History and Eschatology* (Edinburgh University Press, 1957), p. 143.

During a luncheon conversation in the fall of 1975, Will Herberg said that the problem of the relation between history and myth was at the frontier of his thinking. It had long been his intention to publish an essay on various meanings of the word "mythical" which would be a companion to his "Five Meanings of the Word 'Historical'" (included in this volume). As early as 1969 he produced an outline on "Some Variant Meanings of the Word 'Myth,'" which was circulated in mimeographed form for class use. The following essay, based on notes taken during private conversations about the outline and supplementary notes from Herberg himself, conveys some of his thinking on the subject, although the editor assumes responsibility for its composition. The result may appear somewhat disjointed and not characteristic of Herberg's vigorous thought, but every effort has been made to paraphrase his ideas faithfully and, wherever possible, to incorporate his own language.

10

SOME VARIANT MEANINGS
OF THE WORD "MYTH"

The Semantic Problem[1]

A prerequisite for fruitful theological and philosophical discourse is clarification of the uses and meanings of the terms of discussion. Two key concepts are "history" ("historical") and "myth" ("mythical"). In my essay "Five Meanings of the Word 'Historical' " [included in this volume], the nuances of the first term were considered. There it was shown that the word "historical" has at least five major usages which, in some way, are interrelated but are nonetheless quite different. Beginning with the ordinary sense of the term as something that actually happened in the past, as opposed to myth, legend, or fairy tale, it ends up with a meaning in which the "historical" abjures all *pastness* and comes to mean "openness to the *future* of possibility and decision." According to the latter view, made familiar by Heidegger, Bultmann, and their followers, to be *datierbar* ("datable") is a degradation of authentic *Geschichte*. The dismissal of the question of what actually happened as having any theological significance has led some scholars to reinstate the term "myth," and to speak of "the myth of history" or of "history as myth." Thus, confusion about the word "historical" is further compounded.

This semantic confusion is illustrated in W. Taylor Stevenson's *History as Myth: The Import for Contemporary Theology* (1969). Interestingly, Stevenson begins from the premise that the difficulties into which so much of Western theology has fallen have come from the failure to recognize that "the understanding of the historical nature of reality is *the* distinguishing characteristic of our time." He observes that the distinction between *Historie* (ordinary history that is open to investigation) and *Geschichte* (interpreted history) does not succeed in restoring history to its proper centrality, even when *Geschichte* is understood under its theological aspect as *Heilsgeschichte* (salvation history); and he proposes, instead, to consider history as "basically a mythic way of perceiving the world." "The myth of history," he says, "shares in what we take to be the formal characteristics of all myths." For this "myth" gives to participants in the community their "true history"; it portrays certain originating events which are not demonstrably true in a strict historical sense but which call for decision on the part of those who accept them; and, finally, it provides a set of linguistic images which enable people to apprehend the true story of reality, and thus to understand man, nature, and God in "historical" terms.

Thus, we arrive at the paradox that the only way to take history seriously is to consider it as myth. Stevenson, however, has failed to measure the full range of ambiguity in the word "historical" and even more in the word "mythical." Having attempted to clarify the various usages of the word "historical," we must now do the same in regard to the word "mythical." The following discussion attempts to enumerate the variant usages of the term "myth" ("mythical") and to give some illustration of each.

DEFINITIONS[2]

Popular

1. **A fantastic story with no substance in fact.** This usage of the word expresses the popular notion of myth as unreality,

as expressed in the statement, "That's only a myth." A person who thinks mythically is living in an unreal world, the realm of fantasy.

History of Religions (Religionsgeschichte)

2. **Legends (including world pictures) deeply embedded in tradition, but unsubstantiated, or unsubstantiatable in fact—especially stories about the intermingled doings of gods and men.** Thus we speak about Greek mythology or Canaanite mythology: the stories of the loves and exploits of the gods and the goddesses who live in the celestial realm (Mount Olympus) and who from time to time intervene in human affairs. Such stories presuppose a three-storied picture of the universe: heaven, earth, and underearth (Hades, Sheol).

Religio-Theological

3. **Speaking of the *Jenseits* (the Beyond) in terms of images, concepts, and categories drawn from the *Diesseits* (the Here and Now), in particular the protological and the eschatological presented as history.** An excellent illustration of the theological use of the term "myth" is found in Reinhold Niebuhr's essay "As Deceivers, Yet True."[3] The Christian religion, so Niebuhr says, uses stories and historical symbols of the temporal world deceptively to point to the dimension of the Transcendent, the Beyond—just as an artist, in painting a portrait, falsifies physiognomic details in order to catch a moment in the time and space of personality which transcends two-dimensional limitations. Thus the story of the Beginning in Gen., chs. 1 to 3 or the portrayal of the End in the book of Revelation are not intended to be historically accurate presentations. The language of temporal experience is used "deceptively" in order to state what is

"true." "Every Christian myth, in one way or another," says Niebuhr, "expresses both the meaningfulness and the incompleteness of the temporal world, both the majesty of God and his relation to the world."[4]

4. **Narrative articulation of ritual *drōmenon*.** Here the Greek word *drōmenon*, which comes from the ancient Greek mystery religions,[5] is used to indicate a cultic enactment in which ritual, myth, and dogma are inseparably related. Myth is not prior to, and independent from, cultic enactment, but essentially belongs to and functions within the cultic drama. The story is a verbalization of the enacted drama, as in the case of the Babylonian creation myth *Enuma elish*, which was recited during the New Year's festival. The Christian celebration of the Lord's Supper (Eucharist) may be viewed in this light, for it combines three elements: *drōmenon* (the ritual), myth (the New Testament account of the Last Supper), and dogma (transubstantiation).

Religio-Cultural

5. **A transfigured vision of the past, present, and future of the collectivity (nation, folk, community), imaging forth its inner meaning, its mission, and its destiny.** Myth does not apply to individuals, but to a corporate whole, which projects itself imaginatively into its myths or dreams. This is true, for instance, of the American people. They image forth their sense of identity and mission in the Puritans: a New Israel, in a New Wilderness, building a New Zion. Indeed, the United States seal contains the words *"Novus Ordo Seclorum"* (the New Age)! And they speak of "the American dream," essentially mythical language which was used effectively by Martin Luther King in his famous address "I Have a Dream," given from the steps of the Lincoln Memorial. According to this usage, the American myth is not something unreal: it expresses the reality of the people's corporate life.

Depth-Psychological

6. **Archetypal motifs from the deep-unconscious.** This usage is illustrated by the depth psychologist C. J. Jung, for whom symbolic images and myths express the depth level of the human psyche which at times surfaces in the individual through dreams. In this case, mythical representation does not express, say, the identity of a community or a transcendent dimension for which space-time thought categories are inadequate; rather, in Jung's words, the "archetypes" or "primordial images" are "mental forms whose presence cannot be explained by anything in the individual's own life and which seem to be aboriginal, innate, and inherited shapes of the human mind."[6] They are the evidences that individual psychic life is inescapably part of the psyche of archaic man, in all parts of the world and back through time to the very dawn of human consciousness.

Literary-Mythopoeic

7. **Imaginative projection of formative themes in man's life and experience as paradigmatic.** In this usage, myth is an imaginative elaboration of the fundamental problems and tensions of human experience in the form of a story, whether told of an individual or of a corporate entity. Examples within this category are Herman Melville's *Moby Dick* and the theatrical version (though not the book itself) of Cervantes' *Don Quixote*. Such stories have a paradigmatic meaning, in that their truth is not limited by the historical particularities of authorship, time, and place, but speak symbolically to the universal human situation, which is not bounded by time or space. One dimension to which symbolic images and myths speak is expressed in the words "the impossible dream," or in the vision of "the angelic life." Human aspirations and visions are ultimately unrealizable; nevertheless, they are a real and powerful

factor in human experience under the conditions of time and space. Plato gave philosophical expression to this "mythical" theme; it is also expressed in the Greek tragedies in which human hubris (self-inflation) is followed by nemesis (deflation, downfall).

Socio-Political

8. **An articulated vision of collective aims and aspirations projected as fulfilled and realized.** This usage of the word "myth" is related to number 5 discussed above (cf. "the American dream"); but it differs in the sense that the interest is definitely political and the myth is projected imaginatively toward the realization of a political goal. The following three examples illustrate this category: (a) Georges Sorel's *General Strike,* in which the French writer portrays his vision of the consummation of history in the form of a general strike and the new society emerging from it. (b) Karl Marx' vision of the classless society. According to the Marxist "myth," the ideal society or utopia will emerge at the consummation of the historical process, understood as an economic or class struggle between those who possess the means of economic power and those who are dispossessed. (c) The Nazi myth, as espoused by Adolf Hitler's understanding of "the Third *Reich.*" According to this mythical view, history moves inexorably toward a political goal: the First Reich (the Hohenstaufens), the Second Reich (the Hohenzollerns), and the final Third Reich (Hitler).

9. **Transfigured elaborations of the lives and deeds of charismatic figures, historical or taken as historical.** We are all aware of how figures of the past, who possessed a charisma, are "glamorized" in the remembrance of later generations and thus become "mythical" figures. This happened, to some degree, in the case of David, whose faults were largely forgotten or ignored by later generations so that eventually he came to

represent the ideal king (even the prototype of the Messiah). The same transfiguration, however, has taken place in the case of other historical figures in Western civilization. Take, for example, King Arthur. While he may actually have been a king in pre-Saxon Britain, his historical character was irrelevant to future generations who acclaimed him as "the once and future king." Likewise Frederick Barbarosa, whatever his actual role in his lifetime, was later remembered for the perfection of his responsibility and hence as the one who would bring history to its beatific conclusion. Similarly, Napoleon Bonaparte has been glamorized in popular remembrance; and, in the American tradition, the figures of George Washington and Abraham Lincoln have been transfigured. In all of these cases, and others that could be mentioned, creative figures of the past have become mythical expressions of a people's historical vision.

Existential

10. **Dramatic presentation of human existence in the face of Being—of God, man, and the world.** This usage of the word "myth" has been illuminated by existentialist thinkers who are indebted to the philosophy of Martin Heidegger. At one level, *Dasein* (existence or "being there") is existence caught between authenticity and inauthenticity. To exist is to be cast into this struggle which, in traditional terms, is like the struggle of the soul caught between the good and evil angels. But at another level, the whole question of language—whether spoken or written—is at stake in our understanding of myth. Heidegger attempts "to reinstate the poetic function of language as found in man's elemental experience in the face of Being. He maintains that it is the poets who understand most profoundly the way language functions—not as a tool of man under his control, but as a window, so to speak, through which Being unveils itself and man lives in relation to Being. Accordingly, he cites the lines of Hölderin:

Full of merit, and yet poetically, dwells
Man on this earth.

Man 'poeticizes himself' through language, so that language becomes an act, an event."[7] Thus myth belongs to ontology, the philosophy of Being.

Myth and Mythmaking[8]

We live in a historical situation in which, consciously or unconsciously, our minds are dominated by the scientific way of thinking. Along with a clarification of the variant meanings of the word "myth," it is thus appropriate to delineate the difference between "scientific" and "mythical" thinking.

Scientific thinking (or "languaging") is abstract and classificatory. Its "symbols" are carefully constructed to be precise and exact, with no ambiguity, no overtones (hence mathematics is the ideal model). This type of thinking builds up a para-world of scientific entities, which are conceptual constructs, precisely related. It is *nomothetic*—that is, it sets forth "laws." The purpose is to construct mathematical or quasi-mathematical formulas which, upon the application of appropriate translation rules, enable the scientist to predict and control empirical phenomena. In the words of Victor F. Lenzen, professor emeritus of the philosophy of science at the University of California in Berkeley:

> Science is limited to the kind of knowledge it furnishes. Natural laws express regularities of relations between events in an abstract scheme, the determinateness of which results from idealization. Indeed, it may be argued that the conceptual schemes of science are the products of thought only, and not constituents of reality.[9]

Mythopoeic (mythmaking) thinking, on the other hand, is concrete and dramatic. Its elements have the appropriate ambiguity of the dramatic. It is characteristically *historiform,* since its purpose is to express, by imaginative projection in vivid dramatic form, deep-lying and perennial motifs in human life and thought in the face of God, man, and the world. Ernst Cassirer has expressed the difference between the two kinds of thinking:

> Nature, in its empirical or scientific sense, may be defined as "the existence of things as far as determined by general laws." [Kant, *Prolegomena to Every Future Metaphysic*, sec. 14]. Such a "nature" does not exist for myths. The world of myth is a dramatic world—a world of actions, of forces, of conflicting powers.[10]

The predominance of "scientific" thinking in our culture has led to the disparagement of myth, as in the popular notion, that myth is only a "fantastic story"—a view which was anticipated in the sixth century B.C. when Xenophanes expressed his "contempt for myth" in a scathing attack against Homer and Hesiod for foisting on mankind the scandalous tales of the gods. However, the theologian should not share in this "contempt for myth," for myth, in the variant uses of the word, deals with human existence and therefore in a broad sense with history rather than nature. The question is whether the word "myth," in any of its nuances, can be conscripted to serve in the understanding of the scriptures of the Bible, both Old Testament and New Testament, which are at once so thoroughly historical and so thoroughly dramatic.[11]

NOTES

1. In this section the editor has drawn freely on Herberg's review of the book by W. Taylor Stevenson that appeared in *Interpretation*, Vol. XXIII (1969), pp. 497–499.

2. Definitions in boldface type are from Herberg's original outline. The

illustrations are also his, though elaborated by the editor on the basis of conversations with Herberg.

3. Reinhold Niebuhr, *Beyond Tragedy: Essays on the Christian Interpretation of History* (Charles Scribner's Sons, 1937), pp. 3–24.

4. *Ibid.*, p. 7.

5. In the mystery religions, a distinction was made between *legomena*, the words said, and *drōmena*, the actions performed.

6. See *Man and His Symbols*, conceived and edited by Carl G. Jung (London: Aldus Books, Ltd., 1964). Quotation from p. 67 of Jung's lead essay.

7. Quotation from Bernhard W. Anderson, "Myth and the Biblical Tradition," *Theology Today*, Vol. XXVII (1970), pp. 46–47.

8. Apart from the first paragraph, this section is based on Herberg's written notes that accompanied his outline of the definitions.

9. Victor F. Lenzen, "Philosophy of Science," in *Twentieth Century Philosophy* (Philosophical Library, Inc., 1943), pp. 131–132.

10. Ernst Cassirer, *An Essay on Man* (Yale University Press, 1944), pp. 76–77.

11. The editor has composed the concluding paragraph on the basis of personal conversations with Will Herberg. These conversations are also reflected in the editor's essay "Myth and the Biblical Tradition" (see n. 7), which begins by referring to Herberg's analysis of the variant meanings of the word "myth."

The following essay attempts to show the limitations of natural science in order to make room for the possibility of the I-Thou relationship of faith, as expressed in prayer. In a conversation about this essay at a luncheon meeting in 1968, Will Herberg recalled the story told by the philosopher A. N. Whitehead about a certain man who went fishing with a net. The fisherman went out to catch marine life with a net which had meshes one-inch square and, not surprisingly, caught only fish larger than one inch. But the fisherman, of course, could not justifiably conclude from this that there was no *smaller* marine life!

This essay was published in the October, 1948–January, 1949 issue of *Conservative Judaism*. Reprinted by permission of the Rabbinical Assembly.

11

ON PETITIONARY PRAYER

One form of petitionary prayer asks for divine intervention in the course of "physical" events—the curing of an illness, for example. The prayer may be on one's own behalf or on behalf of another. Is such prayer vain, superstitious, meaningless, or objectionable on other grounds? Most "modern-minded" people have already answered this question in the affirmative, but I think it can stand reexamination.

THE "SCIENTIFIC" ARGUMENT

Divine intervention in response to this kind of prayer would obviously be miraculous in the most familiar meaning of the term—that is, it would be a "supernatural intervention in the course of nature." One argument against this type of prayer is that "science shows that miracles *can't* happen" and that such prayer is therefore superstitious.

This argument rests on a complete misunderstanding of the nature of science. Science, as procedure, is a technique for devising formulas of functional relation ("laws") for the prediction and control of phenomena; science, as system, is an organized structure of propositions embodying or expressing these formulas. Aside from the general assumption of the objectivity of the "external world," the entire enterprise of science depends upon one central assumption: the assumption of the *uniformity of nature.* This assumption makes possible the so-called "inductive inference" from past to future—that is, it entitles us to affirm as probable that a functional relation ("law") found to hold regularly in the past will hold in the future. But—and this is crucial—this is an assumption: a methodological postulate that is *neither proved nor provable* by science for the reason that science cannot start "proving" anything unless and until it is assumed. It cannot be validated by experience because any attempt to use experience to validate something must make use of this very rule. To use a principle to prove itself is obviously improper.[1]

The postulate of the "uniformity of nature," in other words, is literally a *postulate*—that is, an assumption unproved and necessarily incapable of proof. It is assumed in order to make the enterprise of science possible. Therefore every scientific statement, or "law," properly bears the form: *Assuming the unbroken uniformity of nature,* such and such will (probably) be the case. Since the "unbroken uniformity of nature" is assumed, a rupture in the "uniformity of nature" is excluded —*by assumption.* Within the purview of science "miracles don't happen," simply because the question science asks and answers is: What can be expected to occur—*assuming that "miracles don't happen"?*

Once we understand what science really is—and I have described it in its own terms, as its best practitioners and philosophers understand it—it becomes obvious that science does not assert that "miracles are impossible." Science cannot and does not make *any* assertion about miracles, because the term "miracle"—an event outside the uniform course of nature—simply has no meaning in the scientific universe of discourse. In science, no matter what the event, *if it is properly authenticated* (that is, if by the canons of scientific observation it must be admitted that the event has really occurred) it has exactly the same standing as any other. Of course, an event may run counter to all hitherto formulated scientific "laws," but, to the scientist *as scientist,* that means not that the "uni-formity of nature" has been broken, but that the existing "laws" are inadequate and must be revised to take account of the new fact.[2] Saying that "science knows nothing of miracles" is, at bottom, merely saying that, *on the level of science,* every event must be taken (assumed) to be part of the causal con-tinuum (order of nature). To convert this *methodological pos-tulate,* which defines the enterprise of science, into a *meta-physical principle,* which is revelatory of the structure of reality, is utterly illegitimate.

Hence there is no scientific objection to miracles; but, by the same token, there can be no scientific validation of miracles. Science simply has nothing to say about it. To repeat: no matter how extraordinary an event may be, science *must* take it as a "natural" event, simply because that is how science operates. The statement that "science knows nothing of mira-cles" is indicative of the nature of science rather than of the nature of things.

The "scientific" argument against "physical" petitionary prayer is therefore no argument at all. It is just a misunder-standing of the nature of science.

Theological Considerations

Hebraic faith posits an absolute, transcendent God, opera-tive in life and history, with whom man can establish a genuine I-Thou relation. From this religious standpoint, the problem of "physical" petitionary prayer is primarily a theological one. The absoluteness and the transcendence of God obviously im-ply the relativity and conditionedness of everything that is not God, and hence of the physical universe. In a literal sense, *every* event is ultimately dependent upon the will of God.

The personality of God in the I-Thou relation implies that God hears and answers prayer. To exclude the physical universe *in principle* from the field of God's responsive action means quite simply to affirm the ultimate unconditionedness of the physical universe and its independence of God. That would mean then not one God but two gods, coeval and each limiting the other.If, on the other hand, it is asserted that God's withdrawal of responsive action from the physical universe is really a self-limitation, it must then be recognized that this withdrawal is never final—in other words, that it is always possible that, *in this particular case*, God may take responsive action in the course of physical events.

To say that there is no point in asking God for any benefits, physical or otherwise, because God already knows what we want, is not a valid objection. Without going into the question of divine omniscience in general, it may be asserted that human freedom implies that a genuine act of will on the part of man is intrinsically unknowable until it takes place, because, literally, *there is nothing to know* until that happens. Prayer, if it is to have serious religious meaning, cannot be simply a therapeutic outpouring of the feelings but must be a genuine address to God—or, more accurately, a genuine I-Thou dialogue with God.

The only serious consideration that can be raised against "physical" petitionary prayer is essentially religio-ethical: that it is sheer folly and presumption to expect God to "change the order of nature" for our particular benefit, especially when we cannot know the consequences such change might have for others or even for ourselves. It is this consideration that has influenced devout souls through the ages to avoid "physical" petitionary prayer, no matter how acute their distress.[3]

While this argument is fundamentally a serious one, it seems to me that it can never be *finally* decisive. For most people, religion loses much of its significance if it is not possible—despite everything—to speak to God about one's deepest woes, even when these woes are "merely" physical. If God is truly Father, then there is *nothing* that can be excluded from the divine-human dialogue of prayer. But all prayer must bear the proviso, explicit or implicit, of humble submission to the divine will.[4] This is indeed the final reach of prayer, that includes all other forms yet does not render them superfluous.

NOTES

1. "The principle [of induction] itself cannot, of course, without circularity, be inferred from observed uniformities, since it is required to justify any such inference. . . . Induction . . . is incapable of being inferred either from experience or from other logical principles, and . . . without this principle science is impossible" (Bertrand Russell, *A History of Western Philosophy* [Simon & Schuster, Inc., 1945], p. 674). "In other words, the order of nature cannot be justified by the mere observation of nature" (A. N. Whitehead, *Science and the Modern World* [The Macmillan Company, 1926], p. 75).

2. Note that *no* conceivable event could *ever* lead the scientist to say that the "uniformity of nature" has been ruptured. This indicates that the principle is not empirical in nature.

3. It should be noted that this consideration may be raised not merely against "physical" petitionary prayer but against *any* kind of prayer that is concrete and particular in its terms.

4. Compare the saying of R. Judah the Prince given in *Aboth de-Rabbi Nathan* (version B, ch. 32, p. 71, ed. by Schechter): "If thou hast done His will as though it were thy will, thou hast not yet done His will as though it were His will. But if thou hast done His will as though it were *not* thy will, then hast thou done His will as though it were His will."

Although Will Herberg emphasizes the dramatic character of the Bible and man's existential involvement in the *Heilsgeschichte*, he objects strenuously to any interpretation that would reduce the biblical story to mere story, with no basis in actual, factual events. In his judgment, "objective facticity" pertains fundamentally to "the historicity of faith." The following essay was originally presented as theses to the members of his seminar, "The Problem of History," at Drew University in January, 1972. He accompanied the written theses with a note to the class which said in part: "Despite the considerable time devoted to the subject of Christianity as a historical religion, not all important aspects of this matter could be adequately dealt with in class. To sharpen the line of argument and help bring it to a focus, I have formulated the problem of historicity and objective facticity as it affects the New Testament account of the resurrection and the ascension."

12

OBJECTIVE FACTICITY AND THE HISTORICITY OF FAITH

A New Version
of the Doctrine of Two Truths

Thesis 1

In Acts 1:9–11, I Cor. 15:4–7, and elsewhere, the New Testament writers bring forward evidence of the facticity of the resurrection and the ascension—the ocular testimony of those who (so it is alleged) witnessed these occurrences.
  a. The evidence brought forward is of the same kind as is ordinarily adduced for any occurrence, that is, eyewitness accounts.
  b. The evidence brought forward for the ascension seems to be, if anything, even stronger than what is adduced for the resurrection.

Thesis 2

Paul and the author of The Acts of the Apostles clearly present this evidence to substantiate the objective facticity of the resurrection and the ascension.

This prompts a *query:* What becomes of Bultmann's contention that it is theologically illegitimate to adduce facticity in support of an affirmation of faith?

Thesis 3

From the point of view of the professional historian, the evidence adduced by Paul and the author of Acts is not strong enough at any point.
  a. In the first place, the evidence is indirect. Paul in particular does not say that *he* saw the occurrence in its facticity. What he says is that others have seen it; and this he presumably knows through eyewitnesses reporting to him or through hearsay.
  b. Secondly, the kind of occurrences in question require for the certification of their facticity incontrovertible evidence. These are the kinds of occurrences that are extremely improbable (in terms of current scientific knowledge), and the more improbable the alleged occurrence, the stronger the evidence required to certify its objective facticity.

Thesis 4

There are two major alternatives, each of which contains a spectrum of possibilities.
  a. From the point of view of *objective historical criticism*, the possibilities would seem to be:
    1. Paul and the author of Acts were misled by alleged eyewitness accounts.
    2. Paul was deliberately concocting a story for its "propaganda" (religious) effect.
    3. Paul and the others were victims of a faith-induced hypnotic vision.
    4. Paul was a neurotic (psychotic) and suffered from delusions.
    5. The New Testament accounts belong to a rapidly burgeoning mythological creation.

b. From the point of view of *the Christian faith,* there are
the following possibilities:

   1. The historicity (not the facticity) of the resurrection
and the ascension are affirmed as *belief.*

   2. The historicity of these occurrences is affirmed be-
cause they are integral to the Christian sacred story
(Heilsgeschichte), which is the authentic form of
Christian faith.

   3. Belief in these (and other like) occurrences is certified
by divine revelation conveyed through scripture and
the church.

Thesis 5

These major alternatives present, in effect, another and
more valid version of the doctrine of the "double truth."

In the more familiar form, the doctrine of Two Truths, as
developed in the thirteenth century by the so-called Latin
Averroists (e.g., Siger de Brabant, 1235–1280), held that it is
possible for a proposition to be true theologically and yet not
to be true philosophically, and vice versa. (There is some ambiguity in the meaning of "not true." It might mean not proved
or provable as true; or it might mean provable to be not true.)
Thus, creation of the world *ex nihilo* is a proposition held to
be true theologically; but philosophy (reason) has either insisted on the eternity of the world or on the futility of any
attempt to prove *creation ex nihilo.* Aquinas combated the
doctrine of Two Truths in this form, conceding, however, that
reason was indeed incapable of proving creation *ex nihilo,*
which depends for its validity on revelation, not on reason; yet
he insisted that if reason could not prove the theological doctrine, neither was reason in a position to disprove it.

The modern problem of objective facticity has raised the
doctrine of Two Truths in another, perhaps less objectionable,
form:

a. There is the objective-factual truth attested by historical scholarship: Truth is what can be established and supported by objective historical science. This may be called "objective facticity."
b. There is the truth of the biblical-Christian faith: Truth is what is divinely revealed through scripture and the church as integral to the Christian sacred history. This may be called "historicity within the structure of faith."

It is quite conceivable for something to be an essential belief of faith and yet not to be factually warranted by objective historical scholarship. Such scholarship, like any other scientific discipline, is intrinsically incapable of disproving, or of proving, any of the beliefs of faith, no matter how improbable it might have to judge them, when regarded simply as "natural" occurrences.

We thus reach a new and, I think, a more tenable, version of the doctrine of Two Truths.

In the turbulent 1960's a theological movement that proclaimed the "death of God" gained wide public attention through the news and television media. To call it a "theological movement" sounds paradoxical; but it was certainly a type of theological discussion that was carried on by Christian theologians and in a broad sense within the church, even though many churchgoers were not affected by it. Although the "death of God" movement has died, many of the issues are still alive. Indeed, the philosophy known as "phenomenology," which provided the impetus for the movement, is now widely influential in other ways. In the following essay Will Herberg, with his characteristic clarity and vigor, discusses what the movement was all about, starting with its philosophical premises. His essay properly belongs in this section, for one of his concerns was to explicate the meaning of faith in the face of a philosophical challenge and, in particular, to make room for the Jewish and Christian witness to the presence of God in history.

The essay that follows appeared in three installments in *The National Review,* Vol. XVIII, August 9, August 23, and September 6, 1966, and is reprinted by permission.

13

THE "DEATH OF GOD" THEOLOGY
—AND THE LIVING GOD
OF THE BIBLE

THE PHILOSOPHY BEHIND IT

In all the "death of God" excitement, let us be clear about two things: first, the "death of God" talk does not constitute a "new theology," or even a new direction in theology, despite all the irresponsible hullabaloo manufactured by the mass media; and secondly, however strange it may sound, the "death of God" propagandists are not atheists, but Christians, and Christian theologians to boot. It is easy, and sometimes useful, to expose the incoherencies, the inconsistencies, and the absurdities of their doctrine. But they are not schizophrenics or buffoons; they are, or at least they believe themselves to be, serious Christian thinkers, trying to say something significant. What is it they are trying to say?

How can Christian thinkers speak of the "death of God"? Note, they are not saying, "There is no God" or "God does not exist," as is the way of the conventional atheist. They are saying, in effect, that once God was "alive," now he is "dead." What can they possibly mean?

The underlying philosophy of these "death of God" theologians—and indeed, of many contemporary theologians who are not of their school—is what has come to be known as phenomenology. It is not easy to make clear just what phenomenology is, so many and so different are the varieties of thought that go under that label. By and large, I should say, the phenomenological enterprise may be described as the effort to grasp and display the essential features of what is as it appears; anything that is, is really and truly what it appears as being, without having any prefabricated system or theory imposed on it to find out what it "really" is. A phenomenology of religion—for example, one such as Rudolf Otto undertakes, in part at least, in *The Idea of the Holy*—strives to discern and describe what it is to be religious for those who are religious.[1] This approach requires the methodological "bracketing out" of two kinds of questions: questions about facticity and questions about psychology. Really to understand what it means to be religious, it is necessary to put aside, for the time being, the question, "Are these beliefs 'factually true'?" and the question, "How have they come to feel, or believe, or act this way?" In other contexts, these questions might be interesting and important; but they are not relevant, and indeed can only prove confusing, to the effort to understand religion as it is—that is, as it appears (the "phenomenon of religion").

Now, if in phenomenological analysis we "bracket out" facticity and psychology, what do we have? Meaning! The entity, the being, the what-is, becomes its meaning. Let me illustrate this conclusion with an example from another field.

Let us say that I am writing a monograph, "Toward the Understanding of the Meaning of Graham Greene's *The Heart of the Matter.*" What would be the difference if I spoke of it as "Toward an Understanding of Graham Greene's *The Heart of the Matter,*" omitting "the Meaning of"? Nothing, no difference. Why? Because, for the reader, the novel and the meaning of the novel are identical. Not for the printer, of course, or for the old-paper dealer: they have other interests and concerns that do not involve the meaning of the book. But for the reader as reader, the novel is its meaning, and nothing but its meaning. That is how the reader "sees" the novel. This, the phenomenologists say, is how we human beings "see" anything that enters into the sphere of human spirit (*Geist* in the Hegelian sense).

So here we are. The being of anything in the sphere of human spirit is its meaning. It is as it means, what it means —exactly as a novel *qua* novel is as it means, what it means. Admittedly, it is not easy to grasp this strange way of seeing things, so remote from, and yet so near to, our "naive" outlook. But it is the premise of much of contemporary theologizing.

All this underlies the thinking of the "death of God" theologians, though not all of them clearly understand it or are able to relate it to their enterprise. But this is not the only occasion on which we have to try to understand people better than they understand themselves, if we are to understand them at all.

Now the "death of God" theologians, and many others as well, systematically extend the phenomenological approach, the phenomenological "bracketing out," the phenomenological identification of being and meaning, to religion and Christianity. Religion, Christianity, God are—for the believer, or for anyone who wants to understand the believer—their meaning. They are as and what they mean. If you think of God as having being apart from meaning, then you must be thinking of God as a kind of supernatural object "out there," and this (we are told) implies that talking about God is indulging in a strange kind of superphysics unknown to science; it is to commit the cardinal sin of "objectivism" (in philosophy) or "supernaturalism" (in theology). No; to assert that "God is," or "God lives," is to assert that God has meaning and relevance, and that the being of God is his meaning and relevance, and nothing else. Many, if not most, contemporary theologians would agree with this, to some extent at least, and many have stated it explicitly with a good deal of sophistication.

What is so special about the "death of God" theologians is

their loud and rather strident insistence that whatever meaning and relevance God may once have had he has now lost this meaning and relevance for modern man. Modern man (they assert) no longer asks the question about meaning, nor can he understand it when it is asked. Therefore, by the "meaning" formula I have described, it must be said that God is "dead," and that he has ceased to "be." At one time, God was "alive," because he had meaning and relevance in a fundamental sense; now, with his meaning and relevance fundamentally gone, it must be said that God is "dead."

Such is the meaning of the "death of God" gospel. There is no agreement among the "death of God" people as to just when God and faith in God first lost their meaning and relevance, that is, when God "died." And there is a great difference, too, as to what conclusions to draw. The classical response to fundamental loss of meaning is despair, radical despair. But such is the residual strength of our American pietistic, evangelical tradition that, in some cases, it has exorcised away the existential despair and replaced it with a happy-happy Jesus cult. Jesus—removed from the Trinity, of course—has become the object of a sentimental cult as a kind of exemplary Superman. H. Richard Niebuhr, who saw this trend emerging many years ago, called it a "unitarianism of the Second Person"—that is, a unitarianism of Christ, which breaks the Trinity just as surely as does the more conventional unitarianism of the First Person. It is worthwhile to note this, but it is not serious enough to merit extended discussion.

The collapse of ultimate meaning in the modern world, at least in the modern Western world, has been a recurrent theme in the philosophy and theology of recent decades. The documentation of the American "death of God" writers is generally shallow, scrappy, and journalistic. Here again, we must try to do better by them than they seem to be doing by themselves, if we are to understand whatever is worth understanding in their thinking.

Secularization and the Collapse of Meaning

Thus far I have endeavored to explain the philosophy underlying the so-called "death of God" theology. In its essentials, the basic position of this way of thinking may be formulated in two propositions: (1) In line with the phenomenological approach, it is asserted that God's being is his meaning and relevance, that God is as and what he means. This approach, in one way or another, is shared by many vanguard theologians of the day. (2) Whatever meaning and relevance God may once have had, such meaning and relevance (we are told) has collapsed in the modern world, where man has become irretrievably secular. God has lost his *meaning;* he has therefore lost his *being.* Where God once "lived," he is now "dead."

The documentation intended to display the radical loss of religious meaning in the contemporary world, draining it of all sense of the divine, and therefore depriving God of his being, is—so far as the "death of God" theologians are concerned— usually rather superficial, sometimes little more than pseudo-sociological journalism. Yet there is a strong and impressive intellectual tradition upon which they could draw, and upon which they actually have drawn in part. Let us examine some aspects of this tradition for a better understanding of the current "death of God" thinking.

We begin with Friedrich Nietzsche, from whom the phrase "death of God" actually derives, so far as we use it today. In many ways, Nietzsche was a conventional nineteenth-century atheist—but not in the passages in which he speaks of the "death of God," where he has something very different to say. Here are Nietzsche's unforgettable words:

> Have you not heard of that madman who lit a lantern in the bright morning hours, ran to the market place, and cried out incessantly: "I am looking for God! I am looking for God!" As

many of those who did not believe in God were standing together there, he excited considerable laughter. Have you lost
him then? said one. Did he lose his way like a child? said
another. Or is he hiding? Is he afraid of us? Has he gone on a
voyage? Or emigrated? Thus they shouted and laughed. The
madman sprang into their midst, and pierced them with his
glance. "Where has God gone?" he cried. "I shall tell you. We
have killed him—you and I. We are all his murderers . . . God
is dead. God remains dead. And we have killed him. How shall
we, the murderers of all murderers, console ourselves? That
which was holiest and mightiest of all that the world has yet
possessed has bled to death under our knives—who will wipe
his blood off us? With what water could we purify ourselves? . . ." It has been related further that, on that same day,
the madman entered divers churches, and there sang a requiem
aeternam Deo. Led out and quieted, he is said to have retorted
each time: "What are these churches now if not tombs and
sepulchers of God?"[2]

Despite all the misty visions of the Superman with which
this "announcement" of the "death of God" is usually linked,
there can be no doubt about the mood in which Nietzsche
made this proclamation. Radical despair, bitter indignation!
They, these men of the modern world, these "murderers of all
murderers," have killed the "holiest and mightiest of all that
the world has yet possessed"! The "death of God" (perhaps we
had better say, the *murdering* of God) is the "darkening of the
world" *(Weltverdüsterung);* it is the "desolation of the world"
(Weltverwüsterung). The proclamation of the "death of God"
was for Nietzsche, at least, a bitter outcry in his radical expo-
sure of the degenerate world of his time.

Where the atheist Nietzsche projects indignation and despair, the Protestant theologian Dietrich Bonhoeffer finds
much to be satisfied with in this new modern world. It is
difficult to comment on Bonhoeffer's thought as a whole, since
he was not afforded the opportunity of developing it and giving
it integral shape and form: he was executed in 1945, at the age

of thirty-nine, for his part in the last conspiracy against Hitler. Yet there are at least three aspects of his teaching that we can see as directly relevant to our inquiry.

The first is Bonhoeffer's teaching about the "world come of age."[3] The modern world, through its technological power and all-pervading secularity, has now at long last achieved maturity *("die mündig gewordene Welt");* it is self-confident and self-sufficient; it no longer needs God to fill in the gaps in its knowledge and power. The typical man of this "world come of age" is "religionless." He needs no religion: he is autonomous, he "stands on his own feet," he is no longer dependent upon anything beyond himself. Bonhoeffer not only describes the modern world in these terms; he basically affirms this kind of world, because it has, at least, freed God of the degradation of being "used" to make up for human shortcomings, as is the way of "religious" people, he says. In any case, Bonhoeffer's picture of the thoroughgoing secularization of the modern world has, naturally enough, been much utilized by the "death of God" theologians.

Here I must make a critical aside. The notion that, at last, in our time, the world has achieved maturity and "come of age" is, in Bonhoeffer, only too obviously a remnant of the eighteenth-century Enlightenment. As a matter of fact, almost every age we know of has made this claim, and every succeeding age has rejected the claim with a kind of amused contempt, insisting, of course, that *it,* and not any previous age, was the age of the world's maturity. And so it goes; the whole business is a pitiful illusion, an aspect of utopian thinking. The world will never "come of age" within history, just as it will never achieve perfection within history. Nor is our present-day world, or modern man, "religionless" in Bonhoeffer's sense. "Religionless" man, or "religionless" culture, is an impossibility, as both theologians and anthropologists agree. Man is intrinsically *homo religiosus;* religion is a functional prerequisite of society. Man may abandon the *Christian* faith, he may lose his *Chris-*

tian consciousness, but that only means that the spiritual void
will be filled with a legion of modern idolatries, some of them
almost too weird to describe. The kind of autonomous "religionless man" Bonhoeffer talks about, bearing a strange resemblance to Nietzsche's autonomous Superman, is a veritable
monster who never was, and never can be.

But there is a third element in Bonhoeffer's teaching that
seems to me to be more serious and more impressive. It is what
I would call the teaching about "God-commanded godlessness." Here is what Bonhoeffer says:

> Honesty demands that we recognize that we must live in the
> world as if there were no God. . . . God himself drives us to this
> realization. God makes us know that we must live as men who
> can get along without him. . . . We stand continually in the
> presence of God, who makes us live in the world without the
> God-hypothesis.[4]

Something, but only something, of what Bonhoeffer means
here may be communicated by a well-known Hasidic tale. A
Hasidic rabbi (we are told) was once assailed by a devout
follower who was always asking questions. "Rabbi," he in-
quired, "you say that everything God makes is good; why, then,
did he make atheism?" The rabbi reflected a little, and replied:
"So that, when someone in need comes to you, appealing for
help, you won't tell him, 'Go; God will help you; don't you
believe in God?' You help him yourself, as if there were no
God. At that moment, be an atheist!"

It should be clear why Bonhoeffer, with his teaching about
the "secularized world," "religionless man," and "God-commanded godlessness," has become a primary source for the
"death of God" school.

But perhaps the most profound contemporary source is that
great philosopher Martin Heidegger. Heidegger, in a really
significant way, harks back to Nietzsche.

Heidegger, for decades now, has been describing this modern age as an age of dry rot, a wasteland, a meager, bleak, impoverished, sterile age, an age of enfeeblement. It is an age marked by the triumph of technologization and mass society. It is an age in which life is being systematically devitalized by being mechanized; an age in which the human person is being systematically dehumanized by being converted into a faceless unit in a vast anonymous system; an age in which personal authenticity is forever being swallowed up in *das Man*— the anonymous, depersonalized "they" ("they say . . . ," "that's what they're doing, or wearing, or believing . . ."). From this kind of world, the "gods have fled"; we have driven out the gods, we have left no place for the divine. What can we do but wait for the return of the gods, wait resolutely, wait without manufacturing idols to console us and fill the void? "This is a time of the gods who are coming," Heidegger says. "It is a time which stands in the no-longer of the gods departed and the not-yet of the gods coming." In such a situation, it is impossible to talk significantly of God and the divine. The only thing to do is to keep silent; any talking about God and the divine in such circumstances could only result in distortion, even blasphemy. This is the mood magnificently expressed by Heidegger's beloved poet, J. C. F. Hölderlin (1770–1843):

> Oft must we keep silent;
> We lack holy names.
> The heart may beat and break,
> Yet speech remains unsaid.
>
> . . . .
> But alas! our generation walks in the night,
> Dwells in hell, without the divine.

The current "death of God" theology obviously owes much to Heidegger, but unfortunately, with one or two exceptions, it has "superficialized" what it has taken over in the process of taking it over. There is very little of Heidegger's profundity, as there is very little of Nietzsche's radical indignation and despair, in American "death of God" writing.

Nietzsche, Bonhoeffer, Heidegger: much of whatever appeal
the current "death of God" theology may have comes from the
brilliant and profound critique of the modern world elaborated
by these Continental thinkers and pressed into service, not
always very happily, by the so-called new theologians. In certain circles, the "death of God" theologians certainly do have
an appeal. But does their theology have any enduring value, or
even any value at all?

What Is Wrong with It?

We have now come to the point where exposition must give
way to criticism. We now have some notion of what the "death
of God" theology is all about, and what its main sources and
ideas are. But how shall we appraise it as a whole—how shall
we assess it, what shall we say is right and wrong with it?

There is no point in denying that the "death of God" theology has its strong points. The phenomenological approach
appeals by its sophistication and the extraordinary light it casts
upon the structure and reality of manifestations of spirit.
Equally impressive is the radical criticism of the modern world
that forms such an important part of most of the "death of
God" thinking. The combination of the two, apparently making it possible to be a Christian without God, often proves
irresistible.

But considering it soberly, I think it must be said that the
"death of God" theology is wrong—fundamentally wrong, and
wrong in every one of the ways it presents itself. Let me
elaborate and substantiate this judgment.

I do not mean merely that the "death of God" theology in
its various forms is grossly heretical. Of course it is. But who
cares? For heresy to mean anything, there must be orthodoxy,
as there is not today, even among Catholics. Today, people
eagerly vaunt themselves as heretics, hoping that they will

thereby prove interesting; for what does a heretic mean today but an original mind, a man who thinks for himself and spurns creeds and dogmas? No; if we are going to fault the "death of God" theology, it cannot be on the ground that we find it heretical. We must judge it in its own terms.

The entire "death of God" system, as we have seen, rests on the phenomenological approach, according to which, to understand anything that pertains to spirit (in the Hegelian sense of *Geist*), we must "bracket out" questions of facticity or psychology, and try to grasp meaning. Being is meaning. Anything in this realm of spirit is as and what it means. If we want to understand, say, a certain North African religion, or the novel *David Copperfield*, we must put aside such questions as "Did these things which North African believers say happened, really (that is, factually) happen?" or "Did David Copperfield really (that is, factually) exist?" These questions are irrelevant. What we should be trying to do is to elicit the structure of meaning of the religion or the novel. The being of the religion, to the believer, or to anyone who wants to understand the believer, is its meaning, and nothing else. Apply this approach to Christianity and you must conclude that the being or reality of the Christian religion is its meaning, without regard to any claims of facticity. The way is now open to a "death of God" Christianity.

But the "death of God" theologians are too hasty, and therefore their argument becomes superficial. In the ancient world, there were many cults of the dying-and-reviving god (Attis, Adonis, Osiris, *et al.*) who recurrently went through the cycle, so close to the cycle of nature, of being done to death by the dark powers and coming up alive again to the jubilation of his worshipers. And to many in the ancient world it looked as though the new Christian cult of the crucified and resurrected Lord was but another example of the same thing. But the Christians vehemently rejected this notion. Their story, they insisted, was not one of those "myths" of periodical recurrence, without locus in time or history; their story, they insisted, had actually happened, and had happened once and for all. Their salvation-event actually took place in recent history: it had its well-defined location in ordinary time and space. He who does not understand this—that the claim to historical facticity is at the very heart of Christianity, the way it is not in the various pagan salvation cults—does not in fact understand what Christianity is all about.

If we are to employ the phenomenological approach here at all, we must come to realize that the meaning of the Christian religion is not only the story of the life, death, and resurrection of Jesus the Christ but also the insistence that all this happened "under Pontius Pilate," that is, in the context of ordinary factual history. That is part of the meaning, and therefore part of the being, or essence, of Christianity.

Let me give an illustration to make my point clear. In its structure of meaning, apparently, a work of history cannot be told apart from a historical novel. This may lead some to claim that the two—historical novel and work of history—are identical; that it makes no difference which it is. But those who say this are obviously wrong. The very meaning of a work of history includes the claim that the story told is factual, that it actually happened in time and place. Even the most inaccurate historical work must make this claim; otherwise, it would not be what we call a historical work, a "factualized story." So with Christianity: it must claim historical factuality for the story it tells and for the characters in the story; that is part of its meaning and, therefore, of its being.

The phenomenological approach of many contemporary theologians, who ignore the claim to facticity as part of the meaning of Christianity—who, in fact, see Christianity as though it were like a novel rather than like a work of history —is clearly superficial and inadequate. With a deeper understanding of what Christianity means, they would see that it is not possible to say that, because (allegedly) God has lost his meaning or relevance for the modern world, God has "died."

Once we recognize the claim to facticity as essential to the Christian faith, it becomes possible, even necessary, to claim reality and meaning for God, even though the modern world may have lost the sense of his reality and meaning. The philosophical ground is thus taken from under the "death of God" theology; whatever else it may claim, it cannot claim to be Christian—that is, to grasp within itself the meaning of Christianity. And yet that is the claim of these theologians. In the context of a true understanding of the Christian faith, however, it is possible, with Martin Buber, to say that "the eclipse of the sun is something that occurs between the sun and ourselves, not in the sun itself."[5]

If its inadequate phenomenological analysis of Christianity undermines its philosophical foundations, the analysis of the modern world given by the "death of God" theology is even more misleading. This analysis can be given in one word: "secular." Now this word "secular" is one of the most ambiguous words in our intellectual vocabulary; like "nature" or "history," it is subject to many meanings, which are often difficult to distinguish even through the context. But, if we use the term now in the way it is most often used in the "death of God" literature—that is, in the Bonhoefferian sense of autonomous self-sufficiency, with man "standing on his own feet," having no need of what is beyond—then we can say with assurance that a really "secular" man, or a really "secular" society, does not exist, has never existed, and never can exist. By virtue of the human way of being, man (as I have already pointed out) is *homo religiosus,* and religion is a functional prerequisite of society. "Man must worship something," Dostoevsky once pointed out with profound insight. "If he does not worship God, he will worship an idol made of wood, or of gold, or of ideas." Modern man may be losing his Christian consciousness, but he cannot lose his religiousness, which is a mark of his human being. As a perceptive observer of the religious scene in England has noted, we must beware . . . of the traps set by people enamored of such terms as "secularization." Those who talk about secularization are generally either humanists or existentialist theologians. Whatever we are, we are not a secular society, particularly if by that omnibus adjective we mean that "average thinking" is tending toward the norms of natural and social science. . . . I challenge the notion of secularization, especially if it means any increase in generalized (religious) scepticism. . . . Our society remains imbued with every type of superstition and every type of metaphysic. . . .[6]

The analysis of the "modern world" (this term itself could stand criticism) presented by most of the "death of God" theologians (and, I am afraid, by Bonhoeffer too) is abstract, doctrinaire, and quite unreal. A theology which makes this kind of analysis of the modern world an essential part of itself is seriously faulted by that very fact itself. The "death of God" theology, while claiming to illumine the Christian's position in an allegedly "religionless" world, has not shown much capacity for dealing with the problem of the Christian in a world run mad with the grossest idolatries and the most lurid false faiths.

I think I have indicated why I must regard the "death of God" theology as fundamentally wrong: its very foundations, intellectually, will not stand critical analysis. In the United States, however, there is another interesting feature which should not be ignored. Having eliminated God (to their own satisfaction) by denying him any meaning in the contemporary world, what do you think the "death of God" theologians do? Abjure Christianity, or throw aside religion as an outworn husk? Oh, no! After all, some of them are professors of theology and religion, or even ecclesiastics themselves. They throw God out, but keep on with religion, even with Christianity. Breathing a sigh of relief at the elimination of so unsecular and unscientific a being as God, they fall back upon a fervid pietistic cult of the Jesus, a Jesus obviously torn out of the Trinity, and converted into an exemplary image of the religious superman. God may be abandoned, but religion, Christian religion, never! A Christianity of no real content but religiosity: how strangely akin to the mass religion of Americans, as sociologists and theologians have been describing it in recent years. These vanguard theologians may have escaped, or so they think, the snares of traditional belief and "objectifying" philosophy; but apparently they have willingly yielded to the blandishments of American religion, with its sentimental and optimistic pietism and its empty religiosity. After all, we're all Americans, aren't we?

I am an American, too, so I don't want to end on a negative. There is some good in everything, our sages teach us. And, indeed, the "death of God" theology, for all its self-destroying errors and dubious religiosity, does have something significant to say: it challenges us to bethink ourselves about what we really mean when we say that we "believe in" God, or insist (if we do) that God is not "dead"; and it compels us to reflect upon the kind of world into which we are thrown. More directly, it demands of us that we reflect upon how we can serve God in a world so radically "God-eclipsing." And, for that, for that alone, we ought to be appropriately grateful.

NOTES

1. [Rudolf Otto's monumental work *Das Heilige* was first published in 1917 and within a decade passed through no less than fourteen editions, during the course of which it was revised and expanded. The English translation was made by John W. Harvey under the title *The Idea of the Holy: An Inquiry Into the Non-Rational Factor in the Idea of the Divine and Its Relation to the Rational*, rev. ed. (London: Oxford, 1929).—EDITOR]

2. Friedrich Nietzsche, *Die fröhliche Wissenschaft* (Chemnitz: E. Schmeitzner, 1882); Eng. tr. by Thomas Common *et al.*, *The Joyful Wisdom* (Edinburgh: T. N. Foulis, 1910).

3. [On the theology of Bonhoeffer, see for instance John D. Godsey, *The*

Theology of Dietrich Bonhoeffer (The Westminster Press, 1960).—EDITOR]

4. [Herberg has apparently given his own translation here. The quotation is taken from Bonhoeffer's letter to Eberhard Bethge of July 16, 1944; see Dietrich Bonhoeffer, *Letters and Papers from Prison,* ed. by Eberhard Bethge and tr. by Reginald Fuller *et al.,* enlarged ed. (London: SCM Press, Ltd., 1971), p. 360.—EDITOR]

5. See Martin Buber, *Eclipse of God: Studies in the Relation Between Religion and Philosophy* (Harper & Brothers, 1952).

6. David Martin, "The Unknown Gods of the English," *Listener* (London), May 12, 1966.

Part Three

THE WITNESS OF FAITH IN THE WORLD

The following essay presents the arresting thesis that the Communist view of history is essentially a secularized form of the biblical-Christian view. Will Herberg's ability to interpret both views sympathetically and incisively reflects his own struggles, in which his earlier devotion to "the Marxist faith" was shattered by historical events and, largely under the influence of Reinhold Niebuhr, he was "converted" to the prophetic biblical faith (Herberg's autobiographical testimony is cited in the Introduction). It is apparent from this essay, one of Herberg's earliest (1943), that already in an early period he was interested in "mythological thinking" or "myth-making" which, as he says, "arises out of the very necessities of social action."

This essay is copyright by The Antioch Review, Inc. First published in *The Antioch Review,* Vol. III, No. 1 (1943), it is reprinted by permission.

14

THE CHRISTIAN MYTHOLOGY
OF SOCIALISM

The essentially religious nature of Socialism (or Communism) is widely recognized. It plainly exhibits all the earmarks of organized religion. It is a faith, emotional and mystical. It has its dogma, creed, and scripture; its theology and apologetics; its orthodoxies, schisms, and heresies; its mythology, hagiography, and cult. It serves all the vital social and psychological functions of religion. And its authoritarian, hierarchical forms of organization find a close counterpart in many ecclesiastical structures. So much is well known and fairly obvious.

But the parallel goes deeper: it reaches down to what might be called the religious scheme of human destiny. The orthodox Socialist scheme of salvation (emancipation) exhibits the most startling likeness to the traditional Judeo-Christian scheme, and the analogy covers not merely the general outline but the entire pattern and many important details as well. This inner similarity seems at least as significant as the more familiar resemblance in external feature and function.

I

Both Christianity and Socialism have their "doctrine of first and last things." The Judeo-Christian drama of human destiny and salvation takes place in three acts; so does the Socialist. And the three acts of the one are like those of the other in some essential respects.

Both dramas proceed in three phases that may be described as follows: (1) a primitive state of harmony, justice, and happiness; (2) an intermediate stage (in which mankind generally still finds itself) of conflict, injustice, and misery; and (3) a final or ultimate state of regained harmony, justice, and happiness forever and ever. Anyone familiar with the Judeo-Christian and Socialist schemes will recognize how well and how completely they fall into this triadic pattern. Let us examine these three phases in some detail.

1. *Primal Innocence.* In the traditional Judeo-Christian drama, the curtain rises on man's estate of primal innocence and perfection in Eden. It is the Christian version of the "state of nature" of seventeenth- and eighteenth-century rationalism and the "golden age" of classical antiquity. In this state, of course, freedom, virtue, and harmony reign supreme; happiness is universal; private property, coercive government, and strife are unknown. It is Paradise indeed.

The exact counterpart in the Socialist scheme is the so-called Primitive Communism that orthodox Marxism posits as the initial stage of human social development everywhere. This Primitive Communism, still another version of the "state of nature" and the "golden age," is a veritable social paradise—harmonious, truly democratic, bound together by tribal solidarity, free from exploitation of man by man, free from classes, private property, and government. Except that one is described in anthropological terms and the other in theological, Christianity's Eden and Socialism's Primitive Communism can hardly be told apart.

2. *The Fallen State.* Man sinned and was driven from Eden. Private property and emerging class divisions brought Primitive Communism to an end. In both cases, man fell and entered upon his fallen state. In traditional Christian theology, the necessity for private property, class inequalities, and coercive government—institutions utterly unknown in Paradise—is traced to the sinful nature of man after the Fall. In Socialist doctrine, these institutions are themselves manifestations of

man's lapse from Primitive Communism. In one case, it is the spiritual self-alienation of man; in the other, his social self-alienation—the self-alienation of society.

It is of interest to note that both Christian and Socialist theologians have always had some difficulty in accounting for the Fall. How could man, in the perfection of his goodness, succumb to temptation? How could private property and class society emerge from the bosom of Primitive Communism and tribal solidarity? The wide variety of answers advanced by the one group of theologians or the other are of little direct interest in this connection; what is of significance is the similarity of the problem.

3. *Regained Innocence.* In the end, man is redeemed. Mankind, transfigured, is restored to primal innocence, or rather elevated to a new innocence. Happiness, harmony, virtue, and perfection again prevail. Man's spiritual self-alienation is overcome. It is the Kingdom of Heaven, "Paradise Regained."

The third and final stage in the Socialist scheme of salvation is the stage of Communism. (Here the term is used to represent not a movement but a type of social order.) Under Communism, mankind is restored to primitive social virtue but on a "higher" level. Private property, social classes, and coercive government are done away with. The new stage marks the end of the social self-alienation of man; it is the social innocence of Primitive Communism regained.

The parallel extends to the conception of human nature, which at first sight may seem widely different in the Christian and Socialist systems. But the difference is due primarily to differing frames of reference. The traditional Christian doctrine regards human nature as deeply tainted with evil and corruption *in its fallen state,* but as having been pure and good in Paradise, and, with Paradise regained, destined to become so again in the future state of grace in the Kingdom. Socialism, too, looks upon human nature as debased and corrupted *in class society,* but holds it to have been very noble indeed in the original state of Primitive Communism and bound to become so again in the future Communist society. In both systems, human nature was originally good, became evil through the Fall, and will be restored to goodness and virtue in the future state. Both sets of theologians, Christian and Socialist alike, are therefore realistic, pessimistic, even cynical about human nature as it is, but boundlessly optimistic and utopian about human nature as it will be "after the revolution," when strictly speaking it will no longer be mere human nature. In Socialism, however, the "revolution" is conceived as within history; in Christianity, as at the end and outside of history.

With the coming of the Kingdom of Heaven, an end is put to the spiritual adventures and history of mankind; with the inauguration of Communism, an end is put to its social history. Both are ultimate stages in which time is annihilated, and final perfection is realized.

It cannot have escaped the reader that these three phases of man's life, destiny, and salvation fall into the familiar triadic pattern of the Hegelian dialectic:

1. Thesis: Paradise—Primitive Communism
2. Antithesis (Negation): The Sinful World (Fallen State) —Class Society
3. Synthesis (Negation of the Negation): Kingdom of Heaven—Communism

The triadic pattern is quite explicit in Marxian theory, which, of course, swears by the Dialectic. It is equally pertinent to the Christian theme, as certain keen Hegelian theologians, including Hegel himself, have noted.

The Kingdom of Heaven (Communism) marks the end of man's spiritual (social) adventures and history. But the Kingdom of Heaven is itself ushered in by the most tremendous event in history—a great apocalyptic catastrophe in which the Son of God appears leading the legions of Light against the hosts of Darkness. The ultimate denouement, the triumph of the Kingdom of Heaven, comes only after a titanic final struggle with the forces of the Antichrist, who will have reached the summit of his power and glory on the very eve of his annihilating defeat. (The Jewish apocalypses follow a somewhat similar pattern.)

Just so in the orthodox Socialist apocalypse. The new social order of Communism is to be ushered in through a sudden, cataclysmic proletarian revolution marking the culmination of a gigantic final struggle with the forces of capitalist reaction, which, in the form of fascism or its equivalent (Engels spoke of Bonapartism), will have reached their highest point in this last stage. " 'Tis the final conflict . . ." could well serve as the hymn of struggle and victory for both.

The dreadful chaos, confusion, portents, wars, and disasters marking the reign of the Antichrist just before the great culmination, as described in the visions of the biblical and apocryphal writers of apocalypses, are faithfully duplicated in the accounts to be found in the apocalyptical writings by Socialist revolutionaries of the horrors of fascism, war, imperialism, and the "imminent collapse of capitalism."

All this is the orthodox or "classic" version. But just as "reformist" Socialism, following bourgeois liberalism, attempts to reduce the cataclysmic social revolution to a slow, gradual accumulation of social reforms, so does "liberal" Christianity, taking its cue from secular modernism, attempt to reduce the grand catastrophe that ushers in the Kingdom of Heaven to a steady, gradual advance of mankind toward moral and spiritual perfection. The dogma of Progress through the "inevitability of gradualism" lies at the root of both types of "revisionism."

Returning now to the orthodox version, perhaps the most curious similarity relates to the so-called "transitional stage." We know that, according to orthodox Marxism, the final installation of Communism is preceded by a transitional period of indefinite length, the "dictatorship of the proletariat," during which the victorious proletariat (in actual fact, the Party) holds sway. Is it possible to miss the parallel between this doctrine and Christian millenarianism, according to which a thousand years of rule on earth by Christ and his saints must supervene as a transitional and preparatory period before the final and ultimate inauguration of the Kingdom of Heaven?

We may pursue the analogy further with results quite as instructive. The Kingdom of Heaven, in its power and glory, is prefigured in this sinful world in the Chosen People, the Saving Remnant, the Saints, the Church; just so is the Communist social order of the future prefigured in this capitalistic world in the class-conscious proletariat, the Socialists (or Communists), the Party. In popular Christian theology, the world is the scene of an unceasing, all-pervading struggle between the forces of good and evil, of God and the Devil—a struggle which permeates all spheres of life; in popular Socialist doctrine, society is the scene of a similar struggle between proletariat and bourgeoisie, a struggle that likewise permeates all spheres of life. One struggle culminates in, and is resolved by, the Last Judgment; the other culminates in, and is resolved by, the Proletarian Revolution. The conflict is not merely in the world as such but in each and every Christian soul, a conflict between the Flesh and the Spirit, between the "old" and the "new" man; so does a conflict rage in the breast of every worker between bourgeois and proletarian influences, between the "old" and the "new" order. The individual struggle is merged into the universal in both cases. And in both cases, the "new" man (regenerate man, class-conscious Socialist), though of course *in* this world, is not really *of* it but of the new order to come.

It is through spiritual suffering that the Christian soul wins the gift of grace and becomes a member of the Communion of Saints and a bearer of the Kingdom of Heaven. It is through material, economic, and social suffering that the worker achieves to class (or Socialist) consciousness and becomes a bearer of the Communist society of the future. In the great prophetic vision, Israel (or the Messiah), despised, rejected, crushed, is the Suffering Servant of the Lord, and thereby the instrument of the ultimate salvation of mankind. In Socialism, the proletariat, exploited, despised, oppressed, is the Suffering Servant of History (or Progress) and thereby the instrument of the ultimate emancipation of mankind. Both gospels are passionately Messianic, and "the poor shall inherit the earth" is the promise of both.

The familiar Christian doctrine that men must die on the sinful human level in order to live again on the divine level, the level of grace and salvation, finds its counterpart in the well-known Socialist doctrine that the proletariat must dissolve itself as a class of bourgeois society in order to rise to the higher social level of nonclass producers in Communist society. The predestinarian and free-will schools of historic Christianity are mirrored in the deterministic and voluntaristic tendencies in traditional Marxism. Divine Providence in the theodicy of the one becomes the Dialectic in that of the other. Even the transcendence of the Law of Justice on a lower level by the Law of Love on a higher is duplicated in Socialist theology in the transcendence of the earlier stage of Communist society with its "equal wages for equal work" by the final stage with its "from each according to his abilities, to each according to his needs." Just as Christian theologians stress that grace cannot be achieved through mere human effort but must come from above, so do both Kautsky and Lenin insist that Socialist consciousness cannot be achieved by the proletariat through its own efforts but most come to it from the outside. These suggestive parallels could be extended indefinitely. Plainly, they point to something fundamental.

II

The problem of interpreting these results presents considerable difficulty. There seem to be two main aspects: the basic affinity between the Christian and Socialist patterns; and the role of myth and myth-making in social movements. Some remarks on these questions may be ventured.

Whatever other factors may be involved, the similarity of conception must be due, in large part at least, to the tendency of West European thought to follow the fundamental patterns marked out by the Judeo-Christian tradition. Until the close of the Middle Ages, European culture was almost entirely Christian. The breakup of medieval civilization did indeed destroy the unity of European culture, but it by no means eradicated its basically Christian character. The significant philosophies and ideologies of modern Western civilization are in the last analysis derived from this source. There is little difficulty in interpreting Spinoza, Descartes (in his metaphysics), Kant (in his ethics), Hegel, Rousseau, and other outstanding modern thinkers in this light. Nor is it hard to detect the Christian doctrine of man and society, shorn of its supernaturalism, in the social philosophies of the last three centuries. Socialism reflects another side of this process.

Christianity, both in its Hebraic and its Greek aspects, has ploughed deep into the collective consciousness of the West and has marked out patterns that condition the form of cultural expression to this very day. It has very largely molded even our customary vocabulary of philosophic and social thought. When the Socialist thinks of the ideal society of the future, he almost invariably thinks of it as the Promised Land or as the Kingdom of Heaven and often speaks of it in those very terms. He thinks of "his" class as the Chosen People, of his party as the Church Militant. In denouncing social and economic abuses, he "naturally" falls into the pattern of the Hebrew prophets calling down divine judgment upon an evil generation. So profound and ubiquitous is the influence of the Christian heritage, so effectively does it operate at the unconscious levels of the mind, that even those consciously most hostile to it cannot really escape it. It has, in very truth, become second nature to us. It has put its stamp upon all our thinking, especially in ethics and social philosophy.

These considerations are offered without any prejudice to interpretations at a deeper level. It might, for example, be contended that the very nature of reality determines the dialectical-dramatic structure of both Christianity and Socialism, so that the two become at bottom variant mythological transcripts of a single essential reality, saying the same thing in different languages, on different levels of experience and meaning. But such considerations would take us too far from the subject matter of this paper.

The second problem relates to the role of mythological thinking in social movements. Why cannot such movements be content with the bare verifiable facts? Why need they go beyond and resort to mythologizing, as they always seem to do and as we have seen that Socialism unquestionably does?

Mythological thinking, it seems, arises out of the very necessities of action. The transition to action is a process in which mythology—the imaginative filling out and transformation of experience into a dramatic struggle of personalized forces—is necessarily evolved.

Action implies reference to ends, and ends of a far-reaching, enduring character are projected as ideals. These ideals, linked with creed and faith on the intellectual and emotional sides, provide the dynamic of social action. Indeed, it is only in terms of ideal, creed, and faith that sustained social action makes sense and acquires meaning and significance.

Every vital social movement, particularly a movement of large scope and reach, is, in one of its aspects, a religious movement. Its dynamic is rooted in a faith, in an energizing myth and creed.

In the formation of creed and mythology, scientific ideas and facts of experience may well be utilized. But matter-of-fact reality is in itself generally too meager, too unsatisfactory, too uncertain and precarious to serve the purposes of action. Dy-

namic social action requires the certainty and fervor of faith—
"the substance of things hoped for, the evidence of things not
seen"; it requires an assertion of values, a wholeness of view,
a promise of final achievement, a vision of ultimates far beyond
the poor, bare facts. The usable elements of factual experience
are therefore transformed, filled out, elaborated into an appropriate mythology which serves to idealize, rationalize, and justify the aims of action, to dramatize the struggle, to secure the
values, and to guarantee the ultimate triumph of the cause.

Mythological thinking is thus a form of wish-thinking,
which may be regarded as the normal type of thinking that is
not rigidly held down to the rules of logical inference (as it is
in such special fields as science, technology, and certain types
of philosophy). It is apparently impossible to eliminate the
mythological element from the ideology of a social movement
without destroying its sources of power. Mythology is the dyna-
mism of great social movements as it is of great religions.

The word "historicism" has often been used in a pejorative sense, to refer to a narrow and even archaic historical interest. In the following essay, however, Will Herberg uses the term in its most positive sense and restores to it a depth and breadth of theological meaning which enables it to be the touchstone, or criterion, for determining theological authenticity. The essay was the sixth of a series in which notable figures in American life were asked by the editor of *The Christian Century* to indicate changes in their thinking over the previous decade. Herberg's article appeared in that magazine at the end of a decade in which he had become a leading theological voice in America.

15

HISTORICISM AS TOUCHSTONE

A calendar decade is, of course, a merely conventional division of time, and there is no reason why one's mind should have changed more significantly in the period from 1950 to 1959 than in any other comparable period of time. In my case, however, the calendar decade is something more than conventional, since my first theological work of any size, *Judaism and Modern Man: An Interpretation of Jewish Religion*, which I described in the foreword as "in the nature of a confession of faith," was published in 1951, and therefore reflects my thinking at the opening of the decade. Taking this work as the point of reference, I can ask myself the question, How has my thinking changed in the ten years that have elapsed?

It is not easy to answer this question, or rather it is too easy, for with no effort at all I could list an almost endless series of matters on which I hold views today considerably different from those I held a decade ago. But such a list would be pointless; the question goes much deeper. In effect, the question is: Do these many and various changes of mind reflect something fundamental, some way in which my mind has changed that can be taken as an actual change of direction of thought rather than a mere change of opinion? Allowing for all the difficulties of understanding one's own mind, I believe I can say: Yes, there has been such change of direction in my thought, and I feel with some confidence that I can describe what it is.

I

The new direction of my thinking that has emerged in the past decade I myself would define as a new and startling sense of the *all-importance of history*. I do not mean simply that historical developments in the course of the past decade have had a decisive influence in reshaping my thinking; that is true, but only part of the story. Much more important, it seems to me, is the conviction I have reached that nothing can really be understood about man and his enterprises unless it is understood historically; I see this as a direct consequence of the biblical teaching about the nature of ultimate reality ("for the Hebrew, history is that which is real"). This is not a return to "historicism" in the bad sense, for I am not attempting to relativize everything in terms of the "historical situation." Yet it is historicism in another sense, in the sense that (to quote a passage from a mid-decade article by Reinhold Niebuhr which I have never been able to forget) "man's being and human society are by nature historical, and the full truth about human existence can be mediated only historically." This profoundly theological insight—that man's "nature" is his historicity, that a person is, in effect, a self-conscious personal history—I might not have denied at the opening of the decade, but I certainly did not make much of it. Today it has become the very touchstone of my thinking, the starting point of all my reflections on philosophy, theology, and human affairs.

Curiously enough, this historical way of thinking has made me much more hospitable than before to ways of thinking that are very far from historical. When I look through my book of 1951, I am appalled at the cavalier way in which I dealt with philosophy in its relation to faith. The great philosophers are hardly mentioned, and then only to make them serve as a foil to my own theologizing. I still cannot entirely share their conclusions or even their way of dealing with God and man; but a facile dismissal of them has become impossible for me.

If man is indeed a historical being, his thought too is historically elaborated, and one must take with the utmost seriousness
the continuing conversation through the ages about the "highest things" that the history of philosophy reveals to us. Plato,
Aristotle, Thomas Aquinas, and Maimonides speak to us today
just as contemporaneously as do Heidegger, Sartre, or the linguistic analysts, not because they utter eternal truths (though
they may), but because they speak out of the historical reality
that constitutes our own mind and culture. I have never been
so convinced that the dialogue between philosophy and theology ought to be resumed and that the "classic" philosophers
have something important to say to us in our theological concerns as I am today—precisely because of my new historicism.

II

Very much the same shift has taken place in my thinking
about natural law. I am as aware as ever of the philosophical
and theological difficulties that confront any full-blown doctrine of natural law, but again I can no longer easily write off
as simply an error and a misunderstanding a way of thinking
that has so entered into the historical reality of our thought.
Here my new attitude has been reinforced by the lesson of
recent history. Reviewing carefully the story of the church
struggle in the Hitler decade, I have been struck by the strange
helplessness of German Protestantism in those years to provide
theological grounding for its opposition to Nazi totalitarianism,
even when Protestants were ready to stake their lives on such
opposition. Roman Catholic thinkers, with striking effect,
could condemn the Nazi state as contrary to natural law—
therefore not a legitimate state at all and not entitled to respect
or obedience in conscience. Protestant thinkers, on the other
hand, found great difficulty in giving theological articulation to
their opposition. At first they insisted that what they were
really against was not the National-Socialist state and regime

but its interference with church life. When this position became impossible, they relapsed into some unavowed doctrine of natural law, or else (like Barth) elaborated "christological" doctrines of politics and the state that were obviously ad hoc constructions to bolster beliefs derived from other sources left unexamined.

Whatever the difficulties of the classical natural law position, the difficulties of an out-and-out rejection of it seem to me even greater, and it is not without significance that the Protestant thinkers who have had most to say to the social and political problems of our time, such as Reinhold Niebuhr, Emil Brunner, William Temple, and John C. Bennett, have operated with concepts involving enduring structures of value and meaning not altogether different from natural law. In any case, the grave defects of a purely "situational" ethic ought to be obvious by this time, despite the valuable insights such an ethic contains. A serious rethinking of the natural law tradition is well in order—particularly in view of Jacques Maritain's recent restatement of this tradition in a form that avoids the sterile rationalism with which the natural law teaching has not unjustly been charged.

III

I have also been driven to rethink my social philosophy along the same lines. Like so many others of my generation, I emerged to social consciousness in a largely Marxist context, and this implied an orientation essentially in line with Enlightenment rationalism. Of course, I abandoned every vestige of Marxism long before the opening of the decade, but the political rationalism I had inherited was far too ingrained to be so easily disposed of. I spoke of a "mixed" economy, of the convergence of capitalism and socialism; but through it all I was still thinking of society as some organizational artifact, to be remodeled according to some rational plan. I have now come to regard political rationalism with intense suspicion as one of the deeper sources of the disasters of our time, and to see society and social problems as historical realities calling for historical understanding and action within the historical context. The logic of politics, in other words, now seems to me to be not rational but historical. History defines the possibilities but also sets the limits of political action, and while history may be beguiled, it cannot be coerced.

All this may seem merely abstract and theoretical; yet it has operated as something very concrete and immediate in my own thinking. It has enabled me to see the current desegregation problem, for example, in a very different—and on the whole more hopeful—light than would be possible if one were to go by the rigid principles of the extremists of either side. On the other hand, I am compelled to view the world situation with considerably less optimism than has become fashionable these past few months, for I am convinced that mankind has gotten itself into a historical blind alley in which our freedom of action is drastically reduced and from which every outcome threatens disaster. My social vision is much less grandiose than it once was, but I think that I have today a somewhat better grasp of social reality and a somewhat better understanding of effective social action. There is no better teacher of responsible politics than history; perhaps that is why rationalists of all stripes are so impatient with it.

IV

All this adds up, I suppose, to a well-defined historical conservatism drawing its inspiration from Edmund Burke, who so well understood how to combine natural law with a sense of historical continuity. And indeed, whereas at the opening of the decade I regarded myself as a "liberal," I now think of myself as a "conservative," though I would not want to be identified with what passes for conservatism in contemporary

American politics. A historical conservatism such as I have in mind, precisely because it abjures all rationalistic pretensions, does not easily lend itself to formulation in terms of ideologies or principles; rather, it demands a sense of historical possibility and historical actuality, a feeling for the "grain of history" with which we must act if we are to attain anything both worthwhile and lasting. For this very reason it seems to me to be essentially in accord with Anglo-American constitutional democracy, which needs no ideology because it has a history.

The historical approach also helps to liberate one from historical fetishism. As I have already suggested, I came to social consciousness in a context in which the "social problem" meant the "economic problem," or even more narrowly, the "labor problem." This notion, itself part of a very special historical situation, at the time seemed an eternal truth, and it was very hard to come to the realization that it was no longer valid, at least not for our society and apparently not for Britain and the Scandinavian countries either. Of course, the economic and the labor problems are still with us, and perhaps will always be; but the crucial social problem of today would seem to be no longer how to achieve a larger measure of social justice in a competitive system, but rather how to achieve a degree of personal authenticity amid the massive pressures for conformity and mediocrity exerted by our increasingly other-directed society. It is a social problem that admits of no villains and no programs; one cannot blame the capitalist system and one cannot look to a new social order for salvation. It is a social problem of another kind, a problem of the quality of life, of the creative use of leisure, and of the influence of prefabricated mass-culture in the century of the "common man."

Nothing in the familiar ethics of social justice equips us to understand and deal with this kind of problem. Nor do we seem able to make theological sense of what is perhaps one of the significant moral developments of our time—the turn, so marked in the younger generation, away from the realm of public concern to the realm of the inward, the private, and the domestic. How are we to assess this development: as an abdication of responsibility or as the shift of responsibility to an area where some possibility of personal choice and decision still remains? Nowhere has my mind changed more drastically in the past decade than in the area of my conviction as to what constitutes the major social problem of today; and nowhere do I feel the resources of our theological understanding of society and culture to be more inadequate than in coping with this situation—a situation that has emerged so suddenly in the course of the past two decades.

This new cultural situation has its religious side. When I formulated my theological position a little over ten years ago, I had nothing to say about the religious situation in this country. Of course I was interested in the religious situation and was devoting considerable thought to it, but "merely" as a matter of sociology and history, not really touching my theological concern. Here, too, my mind has changed very drastically. I have come to see the contemporary religious situation in this country as a matter of the most direct theological concern. The great sweep of religion in America during the past two decades has blanketed the nation with a religiosity that is, in effect, a celebration of our culture and the values it embodies. It is a religiosity so thoroughly secularized that there is often no way of telling it apart from what used to go by the names of humanism and secularism; yet institutionally it is identified with the historic religions and speaks in their name. This, it seems to me, is a matter of grave theological concern. I firmly believe that no one can possibly establish his theological existence in contemporary America without clearly defining his position vis-à-vis contemporary American religion, any more than one could possibly establish one's theological existence in Nazi Germany without clearly defining his position vis-à-vis the German religion of the time. The parallel is too close for comfort, but it is a real one and cannot be ignored. In any case,

I could not possibly write a theological work today similar to
the one published in 1951, without including a radical critique
of American religion. Here again theology merges with history
in a way I did not contemplate ten years ago.

These are some of the ways my mind has changed in the past
decade. Or, rather, they are changes in my way of looking at
things more than in the opinions I hold, but they are not for
that reason any less important to me. After all, ways of thinking
about things run considerably deeper than opinions on issues.
And if I inquire, as from my own standpoint I must, about the
larger background of my change of mind, I can only refer to
the change of historical situation. Ten years ago I was still
living in the afterglow of the "situation of the *kairos,*" to use
Tillich's phrase—the time of great expectations. In such a
period, history is at a discount; all interest is concentrated on
the emerging novelty. My writing at the opening of the decade
already expressed a certain degree of disillusionment, but it still
moved in the categories defined by the old orientation. Today
I have become fully aware that the time we are living in is a
"situation of the void" (also Tillich)—a period of crisis in
which the preservation of the historical stabilities and continui-
ties against the incursion of the demonic becomes the primary
concern and responsibility. In such a situation history comes
to be much more real and significant, and the historical dimension of human life and society much more vividly appreciated.
At least I have found this to be the case. I am only too painfully
aware of how precarious my past certainties have turned out to
be; yet I cannot help feeling that in the shift from my theological positivism of a decade ago to the theological historicism of
today, something deeper and more enduring is involved than
a mere change in the cultural climate. Perhaps here, once
more, history may be serving as the vehicle of a theological
insight that transcends the particular historical situation.

In 1955 Will Herberg was invited to join the faculty of Drew University as "Professor of Judaic Studies and Social Philosophy"—a title which Herberg himself helped to formulate with the precedent of Martin Buber in mind. In the ensuing essay, presented as his inaugural address at the matriculation service of the Theological School on October 1, 1958, he sets forth his own understanding of the discipline of social philosophy, relating it both to the situation of man's historicity and to the eschatological perspective of the Judeo-Christian faith.

The essay that follows was published in *The Drew Gateway*, Vol. XXIX (Winter, 1959), and is reprinted by permission.

16

THEOLOGICAL PRESUPPOSITIONS
OF SOCIAL PHILOSOPHY

Martin Buber tells an amusing and instructive story about how he came to be named professor of social philosophy at the Hebrew University twenty years ago. The president of the university, Judah P. Magnes, had invited him to come to Jerusalem and join the faculty, but the question arose: in what capacity, as professor of what? As professor of Jewish theology, as professor of religion, it was first suggested. But no; to that the orthodox element on the faculty, particularly strong in these fields, objected: Buber's views on the Bible and on Jewish religion were too heterodox to make him welcome there. Everybody wanted him on the faculty, but they were at their wits' end as to how to manage it. Finally, someone came up with a brilliant idea: "Let's name him professor of social philosophy!" Obviously, that was just the thing. Since no one had any idea what social philosophy was all about, there could be no objection to his filling that chair and professing that subject. And so social philosophy it was, and social philosophy it has remained.

All good stories limp a little; none ever goes on all fours. Drew University is not afraid of unconventional thinking, and I am no heretic—at least the only heresy I am aware of in myself is the incurable heresy of being a Jew. But even at Drew the question must be asked: What is this thing, "social philosophy," which serves to cover so much ground and to bypass so many problems? It is a question to which I must address myself as I formally initiate my tenure of the professorship to which I have been named.

I

Definitions are not easy to get at. They come rather at the end than at the beginning of serious inquiry, however much they may be presupposed logically. Instead, therefore, of attempting in scholastic fashion to lay down a definition as a point of departure, I will ask the question that seems to me to be much more manageable and much more relevant, the quasi-Kantian question: *Under what conditions does social philosophy, taken seriously, become possible?* It is a question that leads us directly to the heart of the matter.

Running deeper than all differences of philosophy and ideology is the distinction between those men and cultures that interpret ultimate reality and define the meaning of existence in terms of *nature* and those that do so in terms of *history*. The distinction is not a simple one, but it is fundamental. Nature again may be understood in two ways, either as vitality or as rational structure. Understood as vitality, nature becomes the central category of what may properly be called heathen spirituality, a type of spirituality that informs not only the religion of primitive peoples, but also the more "dionysian" forms of vitalism and romanticism that have become such a powerful force in our own culture. Understood as rational structure, however, nature becomes the central category of the "apollonian" logos philosophy which constitutes the mainstream of our intellectual tradition from Plato and Aristotle to the present day. In the one case, nature is power; in the other case, it is reason: in both, however—and here we see their inner unity despite the undeniable and significant differences which separate them—in both cases what is ultimate, and what is ultimately real, is that by which things are what they are, their nature, the *rerum natura.* It is this which is their reality and truth, and it is this to which man must somehow relate himself if he is to be "right" with that in which his being is encompassed. The Greek philosophers, who worshiped the logos, were always uneasily aware of what bound them to the primitive potency of being that was the enemy of the logos. Their whole enterprise might be interpreted as an ever-renewed effort to exorcise this demon of power which shattered all the structures of reason. In this they failed; but their failure constitutes one of the most profound and moving episodes in the intellectual adventure of the human race.

It would be fascinating to pursue this theme, but it would take us too far afield. For our purposes, what is important to recognize is that neither the "dionysian" naturalism of vitality nor the "apollonian" naturalism of rationality provides a real possibility for social philosophy. For whatever else social philosophy is or does, it certainly must take seriously the social forms, institutions, and activities which constitute the human enterprise in history. But for vitalistic naturalism, these social forms, institutions, and activities are either the consecrated forms of the divine, and thus part of the immanent divineness of nature; or they are the dead weight of ossified non-being bearing down upon the surging vitality of life, and so must ever and again be swept aside by the "dionysian" power. In neither case do they become the possible subject matter of a social philosophy which must see them as real, and yet as *humanly* real, and therefore as historical. Vitalistic naturalism knows nothing of history, and therefore can know nothing of genuine social existence which emerges nowhere but in history.

The consecration of social forms expresses itself in the archetypal thinking so characteristic of the nature religions, for in these nature religions the consecrated social forms become both the expression and the vehicle of the divine vitality of nature. We may think of the consecrated forms of Race and Folk if we are seeking for contemporary manifestations. But

much more familiar to us is the other form of vitalistic naturalism, which sees in social structures the enemy of this divine
vitality. This kind of naturalism can be brilliant and profound
in its social criticism, for it clearly perceives all the deadening
hypocrisies, conventionalities, and mediocrities of social institutions, and it hates them with a bitter hatred as enemies of
life. One thinks of Friedrich Nietzsche, the dedicated and
inspired flayer of bourgeois sham and mediocrity; and, on a
much lower level of course, one thinks of George Bernard
Shaw. Both spoke in the name of the Life Force—that is, of
natural vitality divinized—and both denounced existing society for its denial of this god. But neither had any sense of social
reality because neither had any sense of history. Nietzsche,
indeed, came to abhor history, and denounced historicism,
often with telling effect, as the death of vital creativity. It is
no accident that Nietzsche, in his agony, turned to the ancient
doctrine of eternal recurrence as a refuge from what Mircea
Eliade has tellingly called the "terror of history." Archetypal
thinking and eternal recurrence are the two ways in which
vitalistic naturalism meets the challenges of history, and neither makes possible social philosophy properly so-called.

The way of life that finds true reality in rational structure or
logos is not so far from this type of naturalism as one might
imagine. After all, does not Plato himself affirm "all things" to
be "full of gods," and does not Aristotle insist that "the divine
is in the nature of everything"? And do not Plato and Aristotle,
and all their followers, orthodox or heterodox—including the
Stoics, the atomists, and the Epicureans—take refuge in eternal recurrence when they come face to face with history? Yet
there is a difference. It is not in ever-surging vitality and power
that the true nature of things is to be found, but in timeless
being, in the eternal logos, in the intrinsically rational. Man
finds his lodgment in reality by bringing the rationality which
is his true being into union with the rationality that is the being
of Being. It is hardly necessary to belabor the point that from

this view of what constitutes reality, neither the concept nor a philosophy of history, least of all a theology of history, can emerge, and indeed the Greeks had none, for all the noteworthy histories they wrote. What is much more important for us to emphasize is that from this view of what constitutes reality not only no concept of history, but also no real concept of society or social philosophy, can emerge. This seems surprising, perhaps intolerably perverse, since we all know that Plato and Aristotle wrote works on social philosophy which are among our most precious possessions in this field of thought. But so did Thucydides write a great history, which we treasure. The fact of the matter is that for all their magnificent work, Plato and Aristotle could find no more secure lodgment in what they felt to be ultimately real for their social philosophy than Thucydides could find for his history. In both cases, their ontology made it impossible for them to take their social philosophy, any more than their history, with ultimate seriousness.

I say this without any intention of disparaging Plato and Aristotle as social thinkers. Indeed, I never fail to read *The Republic* of the former or the *Ethics* and *Politics* of the latter without renewed admiration, and I can conceive of no course in social philosophy in which they would not enter the discussion with their profound reflections on human life in society. And yet I must say that their ontology—the ontology of nature as eternal logos—makes it impossible for them to take society and social philosophy with ultimate seriousness.

Consider the strange predicament in which Plato and Aristotle find themselves in their thinking about society. Even in Plato's ideal state—the state constructed by Socrates and Glaucon in the light of the archetypal state "stored up in heaven" —even in this ideal state the philosopher is an alien. He has to be pressured—Plato almost says coerced—into playing his indispensable part in governing the polis. The way of life proper to him, his *bios*, is the contemplative life lived in self-sufficiency. Having come out into the light, why should he ever want to return to the cave and its darkness? He returns, but we cannot help recognizing that in doing so he has lost something of the reality and truth he had achieved. "The ultimate conclusion of Plato's ideal," Werner Jaeger, who certainly cannot be accused of any bias against Plato, points out, "was to shun all actual states and to live as a metic *(xenikos bios)*. . . . The solution was not to act, . . . neither to rule nor to be ruled";[1] and this is indeed what the followers of Socrates and Plato were driven to do, by the force of circumstance as well as by the logic of their position. There is nothing in the Platonic picture of ultimate reality that can make life in society real and significant, and there is everything that denies it that status. Plato struggled with this question throughout his life, with no success; and his followers and disciples gave up the struggle entirely—social philosophy is hardly more than peripheral, in the later Platonic tradition, until well into modern times.

It is important to note that this incompatibility between the philosophic way of life and the life of society is not something that concerns the philosopher simply as such. For the philosophic way of life is the "life according to reason," and therefore the *human* way of life; it is the life normative for men insofar as they are truly human. True enough, in the *Republic*, Plato places the vast majority of the members of the polis into positions which have very little to do with the "life according to reason": the Producers are dominated by the "appetitive" impulses, and their virtue is "temperance," or restraint, while the Auxiliaries are endowed with "spirit" and find their appropriate virtue in "courage." In neither case is reason in its true sense implied; the Producers require only their technical skill, and the Auxiliaries mere "right opinion" *(orthe doxa)*. Only the Rulers live the full "life according to reason." But then only the Rulers—that is, the philosophers—are truly human. What Plato seems to be saying, and what his followers say quite explicitly, is that while in any actual society non-philosophers

are obviously necessary—who else would bake the bread and
fight the battles?—they serve their purpose at the expense of
their true humanness, which is their reason *(nous)*. That is why
the life of society is no life for the philosopher, unless per-
chance he finds himself as ruler of an ideal state, and even then
only dubiously. Life in society in any sense in which the sociality is more than merely external is essentially incompatible with
the truly human way which is the "life according to reason."
This is the inescapable conclusion, which engenders not only
its own epistemology and its own ethics, but also its own social
philosophy, even if in the end it turns out to be the negation
of any possible social philosophy. All our appreciation of Plato's
profound reflections about human life in society and his rich
insights into contemporary Greek social life cannot obscure
this conclusion.

Is it very different with Aristotle? True, Aristotle—as Jaeger
emphasizes and reemphasizes—makes a sustained and conscious effort to escape from the Platonic dilemma. But does he
succeed? He certainly knows how to appreciate man's sociality.
It is he, indeed, who defines man as "by nature" a "political
animal" *(phusei politikon zoon)*, that is, a social being; it is he
who subjects man's social existence to a searching analysis, at
once philosophical and empirical; it is he, most important of
all, who—here again I quote Jaeger—strives to replace "Plato's
shattered mythical synthesis of knowledge and life" by a picture of the "life according to reason" that is not at odds with,
but rather requires, life in society. Yet what is the outcome?
After the first nine books of the *Ethics* comes the tenth; and
the tenth is devoted, in large part, to the "contemplative life,"
described in terms that bring us right back to the Platonic
predicament. "For contemplation," Aristotle teaches us, "is
the highest form of activity, since reason is the highest thing
in us, and the objects that come within its range are the highest
things known. . . . Again, self-sufficiency will be found to an
exceptional degree in the exercise of contemplation. The wise

man as much as the just man and everyone else must, of course, have the necessaries of life. But given an adequate supply of these, the just man needs people with and toward whom he may put his justice into operation; and we can say the same thing about the temperate man, the brave man, and so on. But the wise man, however, can contemplate truth quite alone, and the wiser he is, the better he can do it. Doubtless, it helps to have fellow workers, but for all that he is the most self-sufficient of men. . . . Political and military activities, while preeminent among good activities in beauty and grandeur, are full of restlessness and are chosen not for their own sake but with a view to some higher end, whereas the activity of the reason is felt to excel in seriousness, taking as it does the form of contemplation, and not to aim at any end beyond itself. . . . In this activity, we easily recognize self-sufficiency, the possibility of leisure, and such freedom from fatigue as is humanly possible, together with all the other attributes of the highest happiness."[2]

It is impossible to miss the import of this line of argument. For the man who lives the life of true being, the life that actualizes his highest potentiality (reason), and is therefore capable of providing the highest happiness, society as such is not necessary, for this life is self-sufficient and requires no other human beings for its practice. Aristotle, of course, recognizes two things, which are not unrelated: first, that this true life of man is no longer merely human, but divine; and secondly, that actual man must live in a society if he is to have his requirements, moderate though they may be, in any way satisfied. "Such a life," he says, referring to the true life of contemplation, "is too high to be merely human. It is not to be lived by us in our merely human capacity, but by virtue of something divine in us. . . ."[3] But since, for all the element of the divine in us, we nevertheless remain human, we shall, Aristotle does not let us forget, "need the added help of external goods,"[4] which can only be obtained by living in society. But this need is altogether secondary and extrinsic. What is primary and intrinsic is stated by Aristotle with exemplary clarity: "We may apply here the rule already laid down—the rule that what is proper to the nature of a thing is the best and pleasantest for that thing. Since it is reason that is most truly man, it is the life according to reason [the life of the intellect] that is at once best and happiest for man"[5]—and this life is obviously (that is, obviously to Aristotle) self-sufficient and nonsocial.

The point I have been trying to make should now be clear. Aristotle, no more than Plato, can find meaning for social life that is more than merely extrinsic, something to be transcended—or at least relegated to a very subordinate place—in the life that is lived according to a man's highest possibility of being. Clearly with such an ontology and ethic (and here the differences between Plato and Aristotle are merely secondary) no social philosophy in the serious sense of the term can emerge.

II

Let me now repeat my thesis. When reality is understood as *nature*, seen either as vitality or as rational structure, no possibility of social philosophy in the serious sense of the term appears, because from such a standpoint community does not seem to be part of ontological reality and life in society is regarded as falling far short of man's highest possibility of being. Only when reality is understood in some sense as *history* does community receive a secure grounding in reality and social philosophy acquire the significance that alone can entitle it to that name. History, personality, and community belong together. Man as he appears in history is always a person, never a mere organism and never just discarnate reason. Personality in history always appears in the context of community, while history itself, on one level at least, issues forth as the dramatic elaboration of the personal encounters of men in society. Only men can have a history in the true sense of the term, but the men who are thus capable of having a history are men whose highest possibility of being is not achieved apart from or contrary to the social structure of the history of which they are part. Community is not something external to their true humanness, as it cannot help being in Greek thought; it is part of the very substance of their historicity. If one thus sees in history and historical existence the texture of reality for man, social philosophy becomes something that can deal with human being in its full reality, however abstractly its method may force it to view that being.

The understanding of human being as essentially historical, the insistence on the historicity of man, is, of course, characteristically biblical and Hebraic. "For the Hindu," an English writer has noted, "the historical is the illusory; for the Greek, it is the incidental; for the Hebrew, it is that which is real."[6] If today the historical consciousness has come to pervade the thinking of so much of the world, it is a sign of how far and wide the biblical-Hebraic outlook has spread, though often in perverse and distorted, indeed hardly recognizable, forms.

Taking up the question that I placed at the beginning of this discourse, "Under what conditions does social philosophy, taken seriously, become possible?" I should say that at least the first prerequisite for it is: *the essential historicity of man.* Only if, with whatever qualifications, we can say with Reinhold Niebuhr, "The human person and man's society are by nature historical, and the ultimate truth about [human] life must be mediated historically,"[7] can we launch the inquiry known as social philosophy without the peril of having it stultified by the loss of its subject matter—historical man in society.

If what I have been saying is at all true, it means that social philosophy is peculiarly congenial to the outlook defined in biblical faith. But it will have to be a social philosophy largely recast and deriving from sources other than the Platonic-Aristotelian tradition whence so much of our Western social and political thinking is drawn. It will have to be frankly and self-consciously historical, and that means eschatological. For insofar as history is taken seriously—that is, insofar as it is seen as a creative movement leading somewhere—it is eschatologically structured, however obscured that structure may be by overlying ideologies. Historical meaning is always, though often only implicitly, a question of direction and goal. "We make sense of the question as to the essence of history," Jakob Taubes rightly notes, "only if we ask about the *eschaton*. For in the eschaton history overpasses its own bounds and becomes visible to itself."[8] Without an eschaton, history—and that, remember, means human existence—collapses into ultimate meaninglessness, into nothingness.

It may seem strange to think of social philosophy in an eschatological perspective, but this strangeness is the result of the fact that even here we cannot help thinking in naturalistic or rationalistic terms, in terms, that is, of man as a natural organism driven by his vitalities or as a discarnate mind struggling to rise above the encumbrances of history and society. If we take our emphasis on history seriously and define social philosophy in that context, it becomes almost self-evident that any attempt to understand man in society must see both man and society in their historicity, and that means in their eschatological structure.

The Christian social philosopher, insofar as he is Christian in his thinking as well as in his piety, will attempt to see the social phenomena he studies in the perspective defined by the biblical-Christian scheme of redemptive history. He will be ever ready to learn from Plato and Aristotle, from Hegel and Marx, from Vico and Herder, from Toynbee and Spengler, and be grateful for what he can learn; but he will not be able to look at the world with their eyes or to interpret it in their terms. He will see social phenomena, institutions, and activities as emerging out of a historical matrix defined on the one side by the protological act of creation and on the other by the eschatological act of redemption, and permeated through and through by the tension in which it stands between its beginning and its end. The general scheme in the perspective of which the Christian social philosopher will see his material is set forth with extraordinary power and insight by Augustine in *The City of God;* indeed, it is from Augustine, as we observe him dealing with the great social problems of the time—with the State and Empire, with marriage, the family, property, slavery, and war—that we get a glimpse of the authentic Christian social philosopher at work. We may disagree with his conclusions, we may not think much of him as a historian, we may deplore certain extraneous and distracting elements in his thinking; but we cannot doubt that in his social philosophy at least, he was making a sustained effort to think as a Christian, to interpret society, economics, and politics in terms of the Christian understanding of the life of man moving between creation, sin, and redemption.

The overall framework within which Augustine interprets the social phenomena with which he is concerned is the three-phase scheme of redemptive history already current in Jewish thought at the time of Christ and expounded in the teaching of the Tannaim, the rabbinic masters of the age of the Mishnah. N. N. Glatzer formulates this outlook in terms that Augustine could well have used and in fact did use.

> Election, defection, and return [Glatzer writes] are the three great periods in which history is seen as running its course. . . . Election without defection would be an assumption of paradisal historylessness; the fall gives impulse to history. Fall without return, however, would mean history surrendered and planless. Between fall and return, history completes its course.[9]

Creation—for God's great primordial act of election was creation—creation, fall, and return: these are Augustine's primary points of reference, and it is wonderful to watch how consistently he keeps them in mind in his social thinking, and how fruitful this *heilsgeschichtlich* approach turns out to be in dealing with the actual institutions and practices of social and political life. It is this above all—consistency of fundamental outlook and ever-renewed relevance of application—that the Christian social philosopher has to learn from Augustine.

The crucial difficulty lies, of course, in holding the three elements—creation, fall, and redemption—together. Creation without fall is indeed, as Glatzer says, an "assumption of paradisal historylessness": it is substantially this assumption that has vitiated the idealist tradition, religious as well as secular, and has turned it into a sophisticated system of illusionism. On the other hand, seeing man in his fallenness, without seeing that fallenness as a falling away from a primal "rightness" and as destined for a restoration to a final "rightness," leads to Manicheism, and to the kind of cynical de-valuation of life that so shocks us in Machiavelli, with its inevitable consequence of the idolatrization of some proximate good in an effort to revalidate what has been drained of value (I have in mind Machiavelli's divinization of the *patria*, whether Italy or Florence). Emphasis on redemption, dissociated from creation, is no less confusing. It is the perennial vice of gnosticism, it is the first great Christian heresy of Marcionism, and it is (as Michael B. Foster so brilliantly shows in his classic work, *The Political Philosophies of Plato and Hegel*) the vitiating fault of the Hegelian synthesis. Hegel, Foster points out, is "steeped in the Christian teachings of the Trinity, the Incarnation, and the Redemption, . . . but he has failed to assimilate the truth of the Christian doctrine of Creation,"[10] and therefore even what he has appropriated becomes distorted and misleading, as almost every phase of his philosophy of society bears witness. It is here, as at so many other points, that Judaic studies become so important to the Christian theologian and social philosopher, for the emphasis on creation, and on the implications of creation for our life in history, is an emphasis that (as Foster himself notes) runs through Jewish religious thinking from the

Old Testament to Martin Buber.

The Christian social philosopher must live and work in this dialectic tension of creation, fall, and redemption, and learn to recognize the pattern in the distorted and truncated forms in which he finds it in such thinkers as Hegel, Marx, and Condorcet. For the Christian social philosopher, moreover, this tension is redoubled by the specifically Christian direction of his biblical faith, for in his Christian commitment he sees not merely creation, fall, and redemption; he sees a redemption which has already come and yet is to come again. (Something of the same problem, to be sure, emerges within the context of Judaism as the redemption that came with Exodus-Sinai but is yet to come with the Messiah; the emphasis and implications, however, are so different that we are justified, I think, in dealing with this problem as characteristically Christian, and as such I will deal with it.)

We are thus forced back again upon eschatology; there is no escaping it. How we envisage this "already" and "not-yet" will have the most far-reaching consequences for our social philosophy. Neither a thoroughly "futuristic" nor a thoroughly "realized" eschatology will do: the one brushes aside the present actuality as but a kind of suspended animation before the "end"; the other spiritualizes it and converts it into a kind of elaborate sacramental allegory of an achieved divine reality. An exclusively "futuristic" eschatology is impatient with social existence here and now and cannot think it important enough to be worth studying; an exclusively "realized" eschatology, on the other hand, has passed out of time and history into eternity, and thus has virtually arrived as a quasi-Platonistic "de-realization" of the empirical, which is now no more than an emblem of the spiritual. The consequences of the two, from our point of view, are not so very different. Even in the second "dialectical" version of Der Römerbrief (1922), Karl Barth still speaks of social institutions as parables, as "shadow pictures of the outlines of [God]"[11]—how different is that, one may ask, from the Origenistic spirituality of the first edition (1919)?[12]

For a creative social philosophy, the eschatological framework must be genuinely dialectical—the "already" and the "not-yet" held in a tension not to be prematurely resolved one way or the other. I do not want to be compelled to choose; but, if anything, an unequivocally "realized" eschatology would seem to be more dangerous than an unequivocally "futuristic" one, for an unequivocally "realized" eschatology destroys that orientation to the future, that openness to what is to come, without which neither biblical faith nor a Christian social philosophy can have much meaning.[13] At any rate, the dialectic cannot be relaxed; social institutions and activities of actual (that is, fallen) history are to be seen as moving not merely between the poles of creation and redemption, but also between a redemption that has come and a redemption that is yet to come. In this "interim" period, in Augustine's *in hoc interim saeculo*, the drama of contemporary life—and, of course, all life is contemporary—is performed in its endless elaborations.

If we maintain the dialectical tension between creation, fall, and redemption, between a redemption that has come and is nevertheless yet to come, we have the possibility of a social philosophy that is at once realistic and critical, at once capable of grasping the empirical actuality of things and of seeing beyond the given and the empirical. It is made realistic by its recognition of the enduring reality of the created world, and in another sense, by its perception of the pervasive effects of sin upon human life in history. But it is not imprisoned in its realism, for it can look beyond the historical actuality to the eschatological reality, which, on *its* part, is already working in the present. Thus, the man of faith, while *in* the world, and active within it, is never entirely *of* it, since he finds true rightness being only in the eschatological future. The dialectical approach makes it possible to have ideas without falling victim to ideologies, to make discriminate judgments without making these judgments absolute, to detect provisional realizations without claiming to see final fulfillments in history. This dialectical tension disappears in any philosophical or theological outlook that sees the "end" as already in the past with no real future to look to. Nor is the tension better preserved—indeed, it is completely lost—when the eschatological drama is so interpreted that it is no longer a total vision of human destiny but a kind of existentialist allegory of the self's interior life of decision and self-understanding.

So far I have been arguing that social philosophy, in a serious and significant sense, can only emerge out of a historical context in which history itself is eschatologically structured, yet not for that reason drained of its creativity. But is this view of history a real possibility for the Christian who understands himself as living "between the times"? For the Christian, what of real importance can happen in world history now that the Christ has come—at least until his return in power and glory? "Christians," Karl Löwith says, "are not an historical people. . . . In Christianity, the history of salvation is related to the salvation of each single soul, . . . and the contributions of the nations to the Kingdom of God is measured by the number of the elect, not by any corporate achievement or failure. . . ."[14] (Interestingly enough, Franz Rosenzweig spoke of the Jew as standing in the same position, standing *seitenblicklos,* "staring ahead," glancing neither to the right nor to the left, his eyes fixed on the "end.") John Baillie, theologically and temperamentally so far from Löwith, comes to very much the same conclusion. "Have the years of grace," he asks—and by the "years of grace" he means, of course, the years between the first and second coming of Christ—"have the years of grace any interior pattern of their own of a forward-moving kind, or do they form, when regarded qualitatively, a merely static period within the forward movement of the history of salvation?"[15] Baillie's answer, on the basis of what he takes to be New Testament teaching, is that the only historical task that remains for Christians in the "years of grace," if historical it can be called, is to spread the gospel and wait for the end and renewal of all things. Such a view obviously makes social philosophy both unnecessary and impossible; at most, perhaps, it will allow a sociology of the mission enterprise, but even that is dubious.

Is there no way out of this dilemma? Must social philosophy really be given up if one is to remain true to the Christian commitment? I think not. A way out, it seems to me, can be found on the basis of a view in which world history and redemptive history are held together in a dialectical relation which is neither complete identity (as it is for the idealists) nor complete separation (as it seems to be for Löwith and even for Baillie). It is a view in which the "end" of history to which biblical *Heilsgeschichte* points is understood not merely as the successor of the present age, but also in some sense as its fulfillment and completion.

This is the position taken by Reinhold Niebuhr and Emil Brunner, among others. Brunner insists that the "restoration" *(apokatastasis)* which biblical faith envisages for the "end-time" is to be understood as more than a simple return to the beginning. "The end of time and the beginning," he says, "are not the same. . . . Between the two points, the start and the finish, something happens, which *even for God* is real and significant. There is history, an individual and universal human history" (emphasis added).[16] If this is indeed so, if the corporate achievements of mankind do indeed enter into the restored order of things, then history—yes, "secular" history—must be granted genuine importance, and a social philosophy in our sense becomes possible. It is only if we take a view such as this that we can assert with Reinhold Niebuhr that "the *agape* of the kingdom of God is a resource for indeterminate developments . . . in history."[17] But if one does not assert this, history would seem to lose its ultimate meaning, even its substance, and with it any recognizable social philosophy as well, for the two go together. It is another question whether this view is compatible with some of the theologies enjoying currency and influence in the world today.

III

I hope I have done something to delineate some of the conditions under which social philosophy, and in particular, a Christian social philosophy, becomes possible; and in this way perhaps also to indicate what social philosophy, and particularly Christian social philosophy, is like. But if social philosophy bears any resemblance to what I have depicted, the question must arise, How does it differ from theology, and what relation, if any, does it bear to sociology?

In neither direction, I think we will have to recognize, is the distinction absolute; yet it is real and important both ways. Social philosophy does not differ from sociology, as some people think, in that sociology is allegedly purely empirical and unembarrassed with theologico-philosophical presuppositions, while social philosophy admittedly cannot do without such unempirical and "unscientific" encumbrances. The most empirical sociology, as the best sociologists themselves are beginning to recognize,[18] cannot operate without presuppositions— presuppositions about reality, about man and human life— which are quite philosophical and, like it or not, even theological; while social philosophy would lose its value, perhaps even its meaning, if it did not constantly preserve its empirical reference. The difference would seem to me to be rather this: that whereas sociology, even when it becomes aware of them, takes its presuppositions for granted, it is the business of social philosophy—or at least part of its business—to subject these presuppositions themselves to critical examination, and to relate them to the movement of thought, on the one hand, and to the ongoing realities of social life, on the other. Social philosophy is fundamentally philosophy, and like all philosophy it is an implicit theology.

In distinguishing itself from sociology, social philosophy

comes close to theology; but here too the distinction is real and important. The fundamental orientation of social philosophy is philosophical and theological (in the case of Christian social philosophy, explicitly so), but its work is not to elaborate the theological system. It is, rather, to relate its theological position to social reality and social thought—not in order to show its relevance (that is the task of the branch of theology known as apologetics), but in order to make use of the theological teaching for the understanding of its own proper subject matter. Social philosophy, in a way, mediates between theology and sociology; and yet in another way carries on a work beyond the jurisdiction, perhaps even beyond the competence, of both. The social philosopher, as I see him, is one who, consciously taking his stand within the circle of theological presuppositions, strives to illumine and to understand the social life and thought of mankind.

I do not flatter myself that I have answered the question with which I began. In a way, I would not be displeased to leave the question unanswered, so that social philosophy can continue to mean very much what one wants it to mean. But in trying to outline the theological conditions under which social philosophy becomes possible, I have at least given some intimation of the studies I have in mind to pursue as professor of social philosophy. In the pursuance of these studies, and the Judaic studies with which, in my professorship, they are associated, I bespeak the blessing of Almighty God and the aid and assistance of my colleagues at Drew University, theologians and sociologists alike.

NOTES

1. Werner Jaeger, *Aristotle* (Oxford: Clarendon Press, 1948), pp. 281–282.
2. Aristotle, *Nicomachean Ethics,* Bk. X, ch. vii, 1177a–1177b.

3. *Ibid.*, 1177b. See Werner Marx, *The Meaning of Aristotle's Ontology* (The Hague: Nijhoff, 1954), p. 12: "Aristotle shows in the *Nicomachean Ethics* (1177a, 11 ff.) how the activity which is determined by *Nous*—when carried out in the highest possible way *(kat' areten)*—constitutes man's highest possibility-to-be. In fact, it is so high that it is 'not human any more' (*ibid.*, 1177a 27, 28) but 'divine' *(theion).*"

4. Aristotle, *op. cit.*, Bk. X, ch. viii, 1178b.

5. *Ibid.*, ch. vii, 1178a.

6. William Robinson, *Whither Theology?* (London: Lutterworth Press, 1947), p. 76.

7. Reinhold Niebuhr, "Religion and Education," *Religious Education*, Vol. XLVIII, Nov.-Dec., 1953.

8. Jakob Taubes, *Abendländische Eschatologie* (Bern: A. Francke Verlag, 1947), p. 3.

9. Nahum N. Glatzer, *Untersuchungen zur Geschichtslehre der Tannaiten* (Berlin: Schocken Verlag, 1933), pp. 35–36.

10. M. B. Foster, *The Political Philosophies of Plato and Hegel* (Oxford: Clarendon Press, 1935), pp. 138, 203.

11. Karl Barth, *Der Römerbrief*, 2d ed. (Munich: Chr. Kaiser Verlag, 1922), p. 472.

12. Karl Barth, *Der Römerbrief* (Bern: G. A. Bäschlin, 1919); see Hans Urs von Balthasar, *Karl Barth: Darstellung und Deutung seiner Theologie* (Cologne: Verlag Jakob Hegner, 1951), pp. 71–75; tr. by John Drury, *The Theology of Karl Barth* (Holt, Rinehart & Winston, Inc., 1971).

13. It is not without significance that C. H. Dodd, the most effective advocate of "realized" eschatology, has found it necessary to subject this conception to radical qualification. In a little-noticed footnote to his work *The Interpretation of the Fourth Gospel* (Cambridge: Cambridge University Press, 1953), he writes: "The not altogether felicitous term 'realized eschatology' may serve as a label. Emendations of it which have been suggested for the avoidance of misunderstandings are Professor Georges Florovsky's 'inaugurated eschatology' and Professor Joachim Jeremias' '*sich realisierende Eschatologie,*' which I like but cannot translate into English" (p. 447, n. 1). To replace "realized" by "inaugurated," or even "*sich realisierende,*" would seem to be something more than an "emendation."

14. Karl Löwith, *Meaning in History* (The University of Chicago Press, 1949), pp. 195–196.

15. John Baillie, *The Belief in Progress* (Charles Scribner's Sons, 1951), pp. 210–211.

16. Emil Brunner, *Christianity and Civilization* (Charles Scribner's Sons, 1948), First Part, p. 49.

17. Reinhold Niebuhr, *The Nature and Destiny of Man* (Charles Scribner's Sons, 1943), Vol. II, p. 85.

18. See, e.g., Gunnar Myrdal, *Value in Social Theory,* ed. by Paul Streeten (London: Routledge & Kegan Paul, Ltd., 1958); and Howard Becker, *Through Values to Social Interpretation* (Duke University, 1950). See also Will Herberg, "Faith and Secular Learning," in *Christian Faith and Social Action,* ed. by John A. Hutchinson (Charles Scribner's Sons, 1953), pp. 199–216.

Politics has always been one of Will Herberg's consuming interests, for man who exists in history is inescapably a political being. In the following essay he spells out the implications for democracy and the state of a social philosophy based on the Judeo-Christian view of man in history. The biblical faith, he maintains, transfers absolute commitment to what is really absolute, the transcendent God, and brings to political thought a sober view of human nature and a realistic view of history.

The essay that follows was published in *The Drew Gateway*, Vol. XXIX, No. 1 (1959) and is reprinted by permission.

17

SOCIETY, DEMOCRACY, AND THE STATE
A Biblical-Realist View

It is the purpose of this paper to present the outlines of a critical-realistic view of democracy and the state: *critical* in the sense that it attempts to establish its own positions in terms of a radical criticism of the assumptions and conclusions of the received philosophies of politics; *realistic* in the sense that it takes as its fundamental premise and point of departure the depth understanding of human nature and social institutions that characterizes the Jewish-Christian tradition in its authentic—that is, biblical—form. This approach would seem best calculated to bring out and illumine the basic issues of political philosophy, particularly in their relation to the perplexities of our time.

Man, Society, and the State

Classical Philosophy

The *classical* conception of the state, stemming from Plato and Aristotle and deeply influential in the intellectual tradition of the West, is closely linked with certain forms of the philosophy of "natural law." It sees the state as primarily a necessity and expression of human nature, and therefore as natural to man as man;[1] the state is, indeed, regarded as the highest form of human association, with a profoundly humanizing and civil-izing function to perform. Men, it is held, are by nature social;[2] they are by nature unequal—some born to be masters, others born to be slaves;[3] by nature, too, they are diverse and therefore prone to fall into conflicts of purpose and interest. Hence, on the one side there is human association, and on the other its political aspect, the state; the latter serves to sanction and preserve the hierarchical social structure, to control inner con-flict, and, through its laws and institutions, to educate succeed-ing generations for their appropriate place in the life of the community. In the classical view, in other words, the state is simply society itself in its highest aspect, natural and benign, the supreme unifying force in human association.

This conception is certainly an attractive one, but it is open to serious objection. In the first place, it virtually identifies state and society, as may be seen from the easy, matter-of-course way in which the fact of man's sociality is converted into an argu-ment for the "naturalness" of the state. By thus identifying state and society, and always seeing man in his social dimen-sion, classical political philosophy, against its own desire per-haps, reduces the individual person to a mere function of the state. "Greek rationalism," writes Hajo Holborn, "had no or-gan for the free individual. The idea of the right of the individ-ual to possess a sphere of his own was alien to the Greeks. The government was in total control of the community, and what-ever freedom the individual might acquire he could gain only through participation in government. The Greek soul did not demand a field in life all to itself beyond the social order."[4]

Not only does the classical view identify the state with soci-ety, and dissolve the individual totally in the latter; it also takes human inequality as "natural," that is, as original, radical, and ultimate. That is how men are "by nature," and since what is natural is right, that is how men are not merely as a matter of fact, but normatively, as a matter of right. Of course, because of the ignorance of men and the imperfection of human institutions, some happen to be slaves who by nature ought to be masters, and vice versa. These discrepancies should be corrected by the wise legislator, but inequality itself is natural, and therefore normative and right. In classical social philosophy, Platonic, Aristotelian, and Stoic alike, there is simply no vantage point for a political ethic of human equality, and none ever emerges.[5]

Positivism

Side by side with the classical view, and coeval with it, is the *positivist* conception. In Plato's *Republic*, Socrates has his Thrasymachus, who represents an influential strain of thought, both in his own time and in ours. Positivism drops the whole notion of ethical normativity as meaningless. The state is coercive power pure and simple, self-justified by the mere fact of its being and possessing power. Positivism thus eliminates the possibility not only of providing an ethical justification of the state, but even of making any significant moral distinctions among states. Every state, simply by virtue of its possessing dominant coercive power, and insofar as it does possess such power, is "right" and "justified," whatever meaning these terms may have. On such a basis, it obviously becomes impossible to distinguish the state from a super-racket (or in Plato's and Augustine's phrase, a "robber band").

This view is difficult to overthrow by mere logical argument, but it obviously does violence to the basic facts of human experience, since men have always made distinctions among states not merely in terms of the power they wielded, but also and above all in terms of some criterion of the "right" and the "just." The teaching that the state, so long as it has power, can do no wrong because right is the will of the powerful—which is the essence of the positivist view, ancient and modern—is less a philosophy of the state than an *anti-philosophy*, designed to liquidate all efforts to interpret and evaluate the state beyond the mere fact of power.

Biblical-Realist View

As against both the classical and the positivist conceptions of the state, there is the view which is already implicit in the Bible, but which emerges explicitly in the teachings of the church fathers, especially Augustine, and in the earlier Jewish rabbis. It sees the state as the supreme coercive organ of society, or society in its coercive aspect; it understands that the state is made possible by the natural sociality of men, but by no means identifies it with society itself. The individual person transcends both society and state in a dimension of being that relates him directly to God.

In this view, the state is seen as closely bound up with human sinfulness, that is, with man's existential alienation from God in egocentricity and self-will. More specifically, the state is seen first as the *fruit of sin,* emerging out of the pervasive disorder in human affairs which sin brings about; secondly, as a *protection against sin,* that is, a protection against the aggressions, the disorders and conflicts, that sin (egocentricity) introduces into the corporate life of mankind; and finally, as an *occasion to sin,* placing, as it does, power and privilege in the hands of some men, and thus providing them with both the temptation and the opportunity of aggrandizing themselves at the expense of their fellows. It may be worthwhile to examine each of these aspects a little more closely.

The state as the fruit of sin. "Pray for the peace of the government," a first-century rabbi is reported as saying, "for were it not for the fear of that, we should have swallowed each other alive."[6] The state is engendered not out of simple human sociality, which, of course, makes it possible, but out of human *sociality disordered* by the conflict of individual and group self-interest; it is the fruit not simply of human nature, but of human nature twisted and perverted by man's inveterate self-centeredness, which brings him into conflict not only with himself but with his fellow men. This emphasis is of crucial importance, for by denying that the state is in the "order of creation"—that it is an institution intended by God in his plan for mankind—it cuts the ground from under all forms of state worship.[7] The state, however useful, however necessary, however indispensable, is not part of the "original rightness" of things, but rather a consequence of the disruption of that "original rightness." It is an institution of the historical order, with all the ambiguities that this implies.

The state as a protection against sin. ". . . Were it not for the fear of [government], we should have swallowed each other alive." The state is an "order of preservation," an institution that derives its sanction and justification not from its accordance with normative human nature, but from its utility in protecting men against the disruptive consequences of sinful egocentricity, from the service it renders in preserving the social order and assuring some degree of freedom, justice, and security amidst the coercions and intractabilities of life.

The state as an occasion to sin. Philosophers and theologians have long noted the moral peril to which the possession of power and privilege exposes those whom the hierarchical structure places in superior positions. Exercising the supreme coercive power of society embodied in the state easily tempts one to delusions of grandeur, to pride and arrogance, to the tendency to regard one's own interests as the interests of society as a whole. In those upon whom power is exercised, it tends to engender a mean spirit of subserviency, punctuated by outbursts of resentment. It is an aspect of what Buber calls the "cruel antitheticalness" of things that the very same institution that receives its sanction from its being a protection against the disruptive consequences of sin should itself so easily come to serve as a vehicle of sinful self-aggrandizement and irresponsibility.

Because it is so closely linked with the historical order of "fallen" humanity, the state is not, in the tradition of biblical faith, felt to be something inherent in, or coterminous with, the human community. Looking back, the tradition of biblical faith sees an "original rightness" without state or coercion; looking forward, it sees the vision of a "restored rightness" in the eschatological future, in which a transfigured human community will live in freedom and harmony, again without state or coercive institutions. The state, therefore, merely falls into the middle period of biblical *Heilsgeschichte;* it is neither protological nor eschatological, neither in the order of creation nor in the order of redemption, but clearly and properly a provisional historical institution in the order of preservation.[8]

This complex but realistic conception—the Augustinian view, it might be called, recognizing the function and necessity of the state, but refusing to idealize it—is, as I have pointed out, already implicit in the Bible. It emerges in explicit form in the teachings of the fathers of the Church and Synagogue, and dominates the political thinking of the Middle Ages,[9] though in the thirteenth century the classical-Aristotelian view reappears (with modifications) in the philosophy of Thomas Aquinas. Both liberalism and Marxism show their kinship with the Augustinian view in different and characteristically secularized ways.

On the very first page of *Common Sense,* Thomas Paine, articulating the philosophy of eighteenth-century liberalism, declares: "Society in every state is a blessing, but government, even in its best state, is but a necessary evil; in its worst state, an intolerable evil. . . . Society is produced by our wants, and government by our wickedness."[10] Society, in other words, is regarded by Tom Paine as in the order of creation, while the state ("government") he sees as an order of preservation, necessary indeed (in view of our "wickedness"), but at best a deplorable necessity, since it is the fruit of the disorder of society and may well become an instrument of privilege and oppression. This view obviously derives from the biblical-realist tradition, yet it quite as obviously represents a misleading oversimplification of it. For what it does is to idealize society so as to provide a better contrast for the moral dubiousness of the state. A consistent realism will not fail to see that while the state is morally dubious and involved in ambiguity, so is society, so are *all* social institutions: both state and society are aspects of the historical order, of the disordered existence of sinful man. What is given in the order of creation is not the state, not even society in its empirical forms, but man's need for community in order to be himself ("It is not good that the man should be alone" [Gen. 2:18]). A consistent realism will have to insist that even social institutions and practices which are not political— the institutions and practices of economic control in our society, for example—may often prove dangerously oppressive and require political intervention on the part of the state to mitigate the injustice and protect the victims of the oppressive practices. The contrast of the "social" and the "political" principles has its point, but it is a limited and provisional one; if it is pushed too far and made absolute, as so much of old-line liberalism tends to do, it very easily becomes a source of serious confusion in social and political life.

It is easy to detect the lineaments of the biblical understanding of the nature and destiny of man in the historical philosophy of classical Marxism. Marxism, too, sees the state and political institutions as the consequence of mankind's lapse from its "original rightness"—specifically the lapse from the original harmony of primitive community to the disordered class society engendered by private property. It, too, looks forward to the overcoming of the disorder and the restoration of the original harmony in a society in which neither state nor political institutions of coercion will have a place. But because Marxism refuses to know anything of transcendence, and therefore subjects the integral vision of biblical realism to drastic secularization, it falls into a dangerously oversimplified conception of the human predicament and is driven to convert the multidimensional eschatology of biblical tradition into a crude and violent historical utopianism. The demonic consequences of this utopianism need no documentation in this day and age.

The reappearance, though in perverted form, of the biblical-realist philosophy of the state in liberalism and in Marxism bears testimony at once to the perennial relevance of its insights and to the terrible dangers involved in any attempt to secularize it. In its authentic and integral form, however, the biblical-realist philosophy of the state would seem to be the one best fitted to do justice to both the normativity and the actuality, the dignity and the nevertheless conditioned character, of the state and political institutions. It is therefore the philosophy that would seem to promise most for a realistic understanding of democracy.

DEMOCRACY: TWO KINDS AND TWO PHILOSOPHIES

Both as a concept and as a historical order, democracy is infected with a deep-going and pervasive ambiguity. Out of the original democratic "idea" and movement two tendencies have emerged, in which democracy is understood in radically different ways and justified in terms not merely different but incompatible. Much of the confusion in present-day thinking about democracy may be traced to this underlying ambiguity.

Totalistic Democracy

Stemming from Rousseau, and incorporated into certain Continental philosophies of democracy, is the conception of democracy as the "true," the direct and undivided, sovereignty of the people. The fundamental conviction of this school of thought is that the people are "really" rational and good, but are corrupted by evil and oppressive institutions, so that everything would be restored to virtue and happiness could the people but come to rule themselves. Since an enlightened and uncorrupted people can neither be nor do wrong, the true will of the people may be taken as constitutive of the right. Democracy, in this conception, is the unhindered expression of that will (Rousseau's "general will").

In this philosophy, the prime democratic virtues are equality and sociability ("fraternity"). Freedom is conceived as one's integration into the total community. Since, in the democratic order, the state is identical with the people as the expression of their true will, the democratic state (Rousseau insists) "neither has nor can have any interest contrary to theirs; consequently, the sovereign power need give no guarantees to its subjects."[11] Here we see the germ of "totalitarian democracy," the kind of democracy in which the total people incarnated in the state claims absolute jurisdiction over all of life, without limitation, let, or hindrance.[12] In this kind of democracy, "everyone belongs to all and all to everyone. All are slaves and equal in their slavery . . . [since] the chief thing is equality." These words are from *The Possessed* by Dostoevsky, one of the few in the nineteenth century—along with Tocqueville, Burckhardt, Lord Acton, and perhaps one or two others—who saw the inner logic of mass democracy of the Rousseauean kind.

This type of political philosophy, strangely enough, has its contacts with classical tradition, even with Aristotle. Was it not Aristotle who recommended the rule of the many on the ground that "the many, of whom each individual is but an ordinary person, when they meet together, may very likely be better than the few good, if regarded not individually but collectively?"[13] Apparently he never considered that aggregation into groups might have the effect not so much of overcoming the one-sidedness of the individuals who compose them, as of compounding the intractabilities and irrationalities of those individuals in the relative irresponsibility of the mass. Further, there was always the disposition in Greek thought to regard the rightly constituted state as incapable of doing wrong and as naturally designed to absorb and integrate the lives of its citizens.

The Rousseauean tradition has strongly influenced the direction of modern liberalism. Insofar as modern liberalism grounds its defence of democracy upon "trust in the people," upon reliance on literacy and education to produce an enlightened citizenry, and upon confidence in the power of reason and communication to eliminate the disruptive conflicts of social life and achieve social harmony, it reveals its kinship with the Rousseauean ideology, from which indeed it derives its basic outlook. It need hardly be said that there is some truth in each of these dogmas of political idealism; when, however, they are carried beyond the modicum of truth they contain, they become dangerously delusive. The people, in their corporate capacity, are obviously to be trusted, but only up to a certain point; nothing is more hazardous to an ordered society than the unrestrained turbulence of a people turned into a political mob. Literacy and education are surely good things, but we should not forget that the most literate and best educated populace in Europe was most easily seduced by the infamous appeal of Nazism. Reason and communication may well tend to dissolve misunderstandings exasperated into dissension; but what can they do in the face of antagonisms engendered out of real conflicts of interest, where a better understanding of the issues and circumstances might often lead to an exacerbation of the discord, rather than to its mitigation? The inadequacy of the liberal understanding of democracy is too obvious to need reiteration.

Actually, the liberal doctrine in this respect is not so much a philosophy of democracy as a philosophy of anarchy. Insofar as its arguments have any cogency, they would seem calculated to show how unnecessary government, as an agency of coercion, is in a society that has emancipated itself from evil and obsolete institutions, with an enlightened citizenry at last in control of its own destiny. Liberalism, to the degree that it is consistent, should look to the "withering away" of the state with the spread of peace and enlightenment. This is the social gospel of Herbert Spencer, and it is certainly implicit in the liberal presuppositions. Marx, who may best be understood as a Machiavellian power politician before—and a liberal utopian after—the revolution, shared the same conviction about the essential governmentlessness of the right kind of society in which the people have truly come into their own. Neither Herbert Spencer nor Karl Marx had any sense of the deep irrationalities, intractabilities, and conflicts perennial in human affairs, expressed through but not dependent upon the particularities of economics and politics, and therefore not to be eliminated by any political or economic reform, no matter how radical. It is this sense of the perennial predicament of human life in its corporate as well as its personal dimension that the tradition of biblical faith inculcates, thereby helping to open the way for a truly realistic understanding of democracy and the state.

Constitutional Democracy

The conception of democracy that underlies the American democratic system is closely related to the critical-realistic philosophy of the state. It grounds its affirmation of democracy not in a trust in the goodness and rationality of men, but in the very different conviction that no man is good enough or wise enough, no matter how good and wise he may be, to be entrusted with irresponsible power over others. This is a truth mercilessly inculcated by all experience and history; it is also a direct corollary of the biblical-realist teaching about the universal sinfulness of men, for what does human sinfulness mean in this context but that even our best wisdom and virtue are inescapably limited by our creatureliness and corrupted by our self-interest? Both sides of man's nature are thus taken into account: for if it is man's capacity for justice and cooperation that makes society and the state possible, it is man's proneness to conflict and injustice that makes democracy necessary.[14]

This conception of democracy, so utterly different from the Rousseauean, pervades the Federalist papers, particularly those from the pens of James Madison and Alexander Hamilton; it influenced the thinking of Thomas Jefferson;[15] and it has received definitive formulation in the hands of Abraham Lincoln, who pronounced it to be the cardinal principle of the American political system. Answering Stephen A. Douglas in an address delivered at Peoria, Illinois, on October 16, 1854, Lincoln declared:

> Judge Douglas frequently, with bitter irony, paraphrases our argument by saying: "The white people of Nebraska are good enough to govern themselves, but they are not good enough to govern a few miserable Negroes!" Well, I doubt not that the people of Nebraska are and will continue to be as good as the average people elsewhere. I do not say to the contrary. What I do say is that no man is good enough to govern another without that other's consent. I say this is the leading principle, the sheet anchor, of American republicanism.[16]

What Lincoln here calls "American republicanism" we today call American democracy. The "leading principle," the "sheet anchor," remains the same: a contrite and realistic understanding of the possibilities and limitations of human nature in politics.

The ultimate source of this understanding, which underlies our Constitution and constitutional system, was indicated by Lord Bryce in his well-known work on the American Commonwealth. The American Constitution, Lord Bryce pointed out, "is the work of men who believed in original sin, and were resolved to leave open for transgressors no door they could possibly shut."[17] The biblical grounding of the democratic conception, as that is understood in our constitutional tradition, is thus evident. The Founding Fathers, however far from Christian faith some of them may have wandered, were sufficiently close to the Christian tradition to be permeated with a strong sense of biblical realism in dealing with human behavior in politics. Because they were possessed of this realistic sense, they were enabled to avoid anarchy on the one side and despotism on the other, and to erect the constitutional structure that has served us so well these many years.

The Anglo-American realistic understanding of democracy, in contrast to the Rousseauean conception, finds its point of departure in the view of the state as an order of preservation designed primarily to safeguard society from the disruptive forces of individual and corporate self-interest. Some organization of power there must be if the social order is to maintain itself and continue functioning. But power is a dangerous instrumentality: it tends to expand, aggrandize, and absolutize itself. Too drastically restrained, it cannot serve its purpose, and society falls into the peril of anarchy and chaos; sufficiently developed to fulfill its restraining and integrating functions, it tends to overpass its bounds and to culminate in tyranny and oppression. It must be used, and yet curbed. Constitutional democracy is the institutionalization of these insights; it is essentially a political system which strives to combine the necessary use of power for social purposes with institutional safeguards against its abuse by tyrannical rulers, oligarchical minorities, and despotic majorities alike. It stresses not the direct and uncontrolled power of the people, but rather the constitutional forms and limitations of popular rule. It favors the wide distribution of power in society not on the liberal ground that the many are wiser than the few, but in the conviction that the only effective check on inordinate and oppressive power is counter-power, that the only safe way of utilizing power in society is by dispersing it among many diverse social interests in a complex system of checks and balances. Its watchword is the necessary utilization, yet suspicion, of power. "In the question of [governmental] power," Thomas Jefferson, the most "optimistic" of the Founding Fathers, once declared, "let no more be heard of confidence in man. . . . Free government is founded in jealousy [that is, suspicion], not in confidence."[18] This is the authentic spirit of Anglo-American democracy.

Democracy in the Anglo-American sense means not only the institutional and traditional restriction of inordinate power: it involves also the limitation of the jurisdiction and scope of the state to certain areas of social life, and the protection of the citizens against the operations of government even within these areas. In this difficult matter, constitutional democracy operates by what has been called the principle of *subsidiarity*. Primacy emphatically rests with the individual person, and the fullest freedom consistent with justice and order is to be guaranteed to the individual in the pursuit of his purposes and the realization of free community. What the individual can properly do for himself, it is no one's right or business to do for him; what individuals in nongovernmental association can do to achieve their legitimate ends, it is theirs to do. Only when the efforts of individuals and non-state groups are obviously insufficient to meet needs of acknowledged public concern, or when intervention becomes necessary to mitigate gross injustice, is the state called upon to intervene or take over. The bounds of governmental power and jurisdiction cannot be set in advance, for they obviously depend on the shifting structure of social life, but some bounds there must be; otherwise democracy in any intelligible sense is lost in the all-devouring, omnicompetent total state.

This unity amidst diversity, where unity is achieved through the promotion, not the suppression, of autonomous social interests, is the hallmark of democracy in the Anglo-American sense. Rousseauean totalistic democracy requires a uniformity and homogeneity throughout the entire social body: nobody and nothing must be permitted to stand between the individual citizen and the state, nobody and nothing must be permitted to enjoy any degree of autonomy over against the state, which claims to be all-powerful and irresponsible because it is the unequivocal incarnation of the "general will." Our kind of democracy, on the other hand, is predicated on the recognition of the independent legitimacy of social interests and free associations, and on the protection of the inherent rights of individuals and minorities against the pretensions of the state. "In a democracy," the anthropologist Bronislaw Malinowski concludes after a searching inquiry, "no central power exists which controls all aspects of the culture. . . . This autonomy of institutions really contains and embodies all the other principles of democracy. . . . This functional autonomy is realized in the independence of institutions, and makes possible the organization and combination of groups where cooperation is necessary and interests divergent."[19]

In the last analysis, the contrast between the two types of democracy is a contrast between a democracy that limits its pretensions to the political order and therefore recognizes a majesty beyond itself, and a democracy that knows no such limitations but claims an all-encompassing ultimacy that only God can possess. In the Rousseauean conception, as is obvious from Rousseau's own writings and from all of modern history in which Rousseauean ideas are embodied, democracy is understood as both a religion and a church; it is the locus of all ultimate values, the object of all ultimate allegiances, the center of all ultimate meaning. This kind of apotheosis of the political order is familiar to us as it is exhibited in the Nazi or Communist totalitarian mass-state. We ought, however, to recognize that the same tendency to divinize the political manifests itself—in much mitigated form, of course—in our own democracy whenever democracy itself is exalted as the supreme value and object of total allegiance. Democracy cannot, without self-destruction, be made the object of a religious cult, as so many Americans are trying to make it in the hope of developing a spiritual dynamic with which to meet Communism on the ultimate level. Like every other social order or political system, democracy is essentially instrumental and related to a proximate end. Democracy, to preserve itself, must acknowledge a "higher law" and a higher sovereignty; were it to make ultimate pretensions as the highest principle of life, it would turn itself into a demonic self-idolatrizing ideology, repugnant alike to the true democrat and to the man of biblical faith, for it is the essence both of true democracy and of biblical faith that there is no god but God. The strength of American democracy lies in the fact that, as was recently pointed out in a very striking manner, "both the religious believer and the man of secular faith in the United States come close to holding in their hearts the Hebraic commandment: 'Thou shalt have no other gods before me.' [In other words, whatever else one may or may not believe,] one does *not* believe that there is any idea, institution, or individual—a man, a nation, an 'ism' [not even democracy itself]—that one can accept as God. [The essence is that the individual] keep this obdurate recalcitrance in the face of all proposed faiths and ideologies that would give any political thing [even democracy] suprahuman and transcendental value."[20] Genuine democracy must, at least implicitly, acknowledge a majesty beyond itself, or else it will inevitably exalt itself to supreme majesty. Lincoln's phrase, "this nation under God," does not merely reflect the shared conviction of the American people; it expresses the law of life of every authentically democratic social and political order.

CONCLUSION: DEMOCRACY AND BIBLICAL FAITH

Democracy, to be democratic, must find its grounding in something beyond itself. This grounding may most appropriately be found in the convictions and commitments central to the enduring tradition of biblical faith.

1. The democratic emphasis on the individual human being and his rights, as well as on his duties and responsibilities, is grounded in the biblical conviction that man is created "in the image of God" (Gen. 1:26) and possesses a high dignity by virtue of God's "mindfulness" of him (Ps. 8:4–5).

2. The democratic emphasis that power must be limited and made responsible is grounded in the biblical conviction of human sinfulness (that is, egocentricity), which makes no man,

even the wisest and the best, good enough or wise enough to be entrusted with unlimited, irresponsible power over others. This is the final argument against all forms of benevolent despotism, even of the so-called democratic variety.

3. The democratic emphasis that no social order or institution can claim final and absolute significance, and therefore exemption from criticism, change, or reform, is grounded in the biblical conviction that God alone is absolute, and that every human idea, institution, or order stands under his continuing judgment (Isa. 2:12–29; 40:21–24).

Democracy's immense superiority over totalitarianism is not the superiority of a perfect society. Democracy makes no claim to perfection. But it does claim two things for itself: (1) an underlying allegiance to genuinely human values, which totalitarianism either explicitly repudiates or cynically perverts; and (2) a built-in principle of self-limitation, self-criticism, and self-reform, the like of which no totalitarian regime can possess or tolerate. The values of democracy are essentially the values that emerge from our religious tradition; the built-in principle of self-limitation, self-criticism, and self-reform is, in the final analysis, the institutionalization of the prophetic conviction of the sovereignty of God and his continuing judgment upon man and his works. Both are rooted in biblical faith and can find no secure grounding apart from that faith.

NOTES

1. "Hence it is evident that the state is a creation of nature." Aristotle, *Politics*, Bk. I, ch. I, 1253a (Loeb edition).

2. "Man is by nature a political animal" *(ibid.)*. From the argument it is evident that "political" in this context is to be understood as "social."

3. "But is there anyone thus intended by nature to be a slave, and for whom such a condition is expedient and right; or rather, is not all slavery a violation of nature? There is no difficulty in answering this question on

grounds both of reason and of fact. For that some should rule and others be ruled is a thing not only necessary but expedient; from the hour of their birth, some are marked out for subjection, others to rule" (*ibid.*, ch. II, 1254a).

4. Hajo Holborn, "Greek and Modern Concepts of History," *Journal of the History of Ideas*, Vol. X, No. 1 (Jan., 1949).

5. This is true even of Stoicism, which is frequently mentioned as having championed a doctrine of human equality on a pantheist, rationalistic basis. But this is to misunderstand the actual teaching of Stoicism. "Zeno," Margaret E. Reesor points out, "divided men into two classes, those who live according to divine reason and those who do not. . . . The Republic [of Zeno] had as its citizens only good [that is, wise] men. Zeno argued that only the good were capable of being citizens, friends, kindred, and free. . . . There cannot be equality, he maintained, between the men of virtuous and the men of non-virtuous character." *The Political Theory of the Old and Middle Stoa* (J. J. Augustin, 1951), p. 10.

6. M. Abot 3.2. The saying is attributed to Rabbi Hanina, the deputy of the priests who flourished toward the middle of the first century. New Testament parallels will easily come to mind, especially the celebrated statement in Rom., ch. 13.

7. "It would be better in the whole to regard it [the state] as a regrettable necessity, like the soldier, the policeman, or the public executioner. Statism is the worst of all superstitions because it singles out for worship that agency which is compelled, owing to practical exigencies, to practice what the perfecting of life would eliminate." Ralph Barton Perry, *Puritanism and Democracy* (The Vanguard Press, Inc., 1944), p. 601.

8. This entire conception is clearly formulated by Augustine: "It is thus that God created men. . . . 'Let them rule,' he said, 'over the fishes of the sea, and the fowls of the air, and over everything that creeps upon the earth' (Gen. 1:26). He made a man rational, and lord over only the irrational creation, not man over man, but man over the beasts. Therefore, the righteous men in primitive times were shepherds rather than kings; in this God showed what the order of creation desired, and what sin exacted. Sin is the maker of servitude, the first cause of man's subjection to man. . . . Take man as God created him at first, and he is slave to neither sin nor man. Servitude has its institution from that law which commands the conservation and forbids the disturbance of nature's order." *The City of God*, Bk. XIX, ch. xv. See also Oscar Cullmann, *The State in the New Testament* (Charles Scribner's Sons, 1956).

9. "Most medieval scholastics objected to any mastery of man over man, and declared the state to be but the fruit of sin. They only admitted that it was at the same time the divinely instituted remedy for sin." Salo W. Baron, *Modern Nationalism and Religion* (Harper & Brothers, 1947), p. 92.

"The origin of profane history is sought [by medieval German Hasidism] in the fall, which is also defined as the cause of force and social inequality in relation to men." Gershom G. Scholem, *Major Trends in Jewish Mysticism* (Schocken Books, 1941), p. 90.

10. Moncure Daniel Conway, ed., *The Writings of Thomas Paine* (G. P. Putnam's Sons, 1894–1896), Vol. I, p. 69. This is a classical eighteenth-century formulation. In nineteenth-century liberalism, "society" begins to be interpreted primarily as the economic order, while "government" ("politics") remains the *bête noire.*

11. Jean-Jacques Rousseau, *The Social Contract,* Bk. I, ch. vii; see *Social Contract· Essays by Hume, Locke, and Rousseau,* intro. by Ernest Barker (Oxford University Press, 1947), p. 260.

12. See J. L. Talmon, *The Origins of Totalitarian Democracy* (London: Seeker & Warburg, 1952).

13. Aristotle, *op. cit.* Bk. III, ch. VI, 1281b. As against this notion, note the thesis of Reinhold Niebuhr's work given in the title *Moral Man and Immoral Society* (Charles Scribner's Sons, 1932).

14. See Reinhold Niebuhr, *The Children of Light and the Children of Darkness: A Vindication of Democracy and a Critique of Its Traditional Defense* (Charles Scribner's, Sons, 1944), esp. Ch. 2.

15. "Sometimes it is said that man cannot be trusted with the government of himself. Can he, then, be trusted with the government of others? Or have we found angels in the form of kings to govern him?" Thomas Jefferson, *Messages and Papers,* ed. by James D. Richardson (Washington, 1910), Vol. I, p. 332.

16. T. Harry Williams, ed., *Abraham Lincoln: Selected Writings and Speeches* (Chicago: Packard & Co., 1943), pp. 36–37. This may be compared with a recent statement by Reinhold Niebuhr: "No one is good enough or wise enough to be completely entrusted with the destiny of his fellow men." *Christian Realism and Political Problems* (Charles Scribner's, Sons, 1953), p. 11.

17. James Bryce, *The American Commonwealth,* 2d ed., rev. (London: The Macmillan Company, 1889), Pt. I, ch. xxvi, sec. viii.

18. Kentucky Resolutions, 1798.

19. Bronislaw Malinowski, *Freedom and Civilization* (Roy Publishers, 1944), p. 229.

20. Elliot E. Cohen, "The Free American Citizen—1952," *Commentary,* Vol. 14 (July–Dec., 1952).

The absolutizing of the state, which has come to be known as totalitarianism, is a recurrent threat to any nation, including the United States, but in the twentieth century this form of government has become a reality in Europe and elsewhere. It is significant, then, that the following essay was originally given as an address at an international conference held in Wiesbaden, Germany, September 6–9, 1966. The address shows that Herberg's understanding of biblical and historical Christian theology makes him a relentless critic of totalitarianism in any form. The essay is a companion to the preceding one, which was addressed primarily to constitutional democracy as it has developed in the United States.

The following essay was published in *Modern Age,* Vol. XI (1966–67), and is reprinted by permission.

18

CHRISTIAN FAITH
AND TOTALITARIAN RULE

The twentieth century is the age of totalitarianism. Not only does a great portion of the human race live under pervasive totalitarian rule, but totalitarianism emerges as a crucial problem at every level of twentieth-century life, and is largely at the source of the great conflicts—economic, political, and spiritual—that are tearing apart the contemporary world.

What has Christianity to say about this massive historical reality that gives our century its characteristic aspect? The utterances and interventions of influential Christian spokesmen in recent decades, for the most part, can hardly be regarded as contributing to the clarity and responsibility so desperately needed in this time of crisis. The confusion in the churches is itself a major factor exacerbating the crisis and facilitating the advance of totalitarianism on many fronts. The effort to achieve a Christian understanding of totalitarianism, therefore, involves a drastic criticism of many things that have been said and done by the churches, and in the name of the churches, in their fateful confrontation with totalitarianism.

I

Our Western political institutions, especially our Western political conceptions, derive, in large part, from the experience of the ancient Greek city-state, and from the political philosophy developed around it. For Aristotle, it will be remembered, the *polis*, the State, was "by nature." Man, according to Aristotle, was "by nature a political animal," that is, a being with a nature that demanded organized community for its proper life, and was always straining to establish it. Indeed, for Aristotle, as for Plato before him, and for the intelligent, educated Athenian of their time, the *polis* was, in fact, the *human-making* institution, in which man's human potentialities could be actualized and perfected. The full perfection of humanness could be achieved only within and through the *polis*. When the Greek city-states began to lose their autonomy and vitality, political philosophers began to talk of a "universal *polis*," a *polis* of the cosmos, a cosmo*polis*—sometimes identified with the Roman Empire, sometimes conceived as a "heavenly city" of the wise and the virtuous. But Greek political philosophy still remained essentially *polis*-thinking.

Greek experience, and Greek philosophy founded on this experience, did not, and apparently could not, distinguish between society and State. Man's sociality, which makes society "natural" to him, was made to cover the coercive organization of society as well. In Greek political thought, therefore, there was a strong totalistic element: the pervasiveness of society in bringing forth, educating, and molding the individual into a civilized human being was easily understood as the total jurisdiction of the State as a mind- and character-forming power. Even Aristotle, a careful, moderate, and realistic thinker, complained that

> in most states, these matters [education, occupations, domestic affairs, etc.] have been neglected [by the authorities]; each man lives as he likes, ruling over wife and children in the fashion of the Cyclops. The conclusion to which we come is that the best course is to have a system of public and proper provision for these matters.[1]

In any well-conceived community, in other words, such matters as marriage, vocation, and domestic life would properly fall under the jurisdiction and control of the State. The fact is that,

in principle—though fortunately not always in practice—
Greek political rationalism, as Hajo Holborn points out,

> had no organ for the free individual. The idea of the right of
> the individual to possess a sphere of his own was alien to the
> Greeks. The government was in total control of the community,
> and whatever freedom the individual might acquire, he could
> gain only through participation in government. The Greek soul
> [apparently] did not demand a field all to itself beyond the social
> order.[2]

The distinction between society and the State was well understood by the Jews of the time as a result of their own
experience and the traditions about the kingship coming from
the Old Testament; the early church fully shared their way of
thinking. Community, conceived in terms of ever-widening
circles of covenant, was part of God's creation, and therefore
(using the Greek vocabulary) "natural" to man. But the State,
as the *coercive* organization of society, most emphatically was
not. The State, with its vast, complex machinery, was the
outcome not of human nature but of human *sin*. And yet it
was ordained of God, indirectly but no less truly. Here is how
Paul, in that celebrated thirteenth chapter of Romans, con-
ceives it:

> Let everyone be subject to the governing authorities, for there
> is no authority but from God, and the powers that be are
> ordained of God. Therefore he who resists the authorities resists
> what God had ordained, and those who resist will incur judg-
> ment. For rulers are not a terror to good-doing, but to evil-
> doing. Would you have no fear of the magistrate who is in
> authority? Then do what is good, and you will have his approval,
> for he is God's minister for your good. But if you do evil, be
> afraid, for he does not bear the sword in vain; he is the minister
> of God to execute his wrath on the evil-doer. Therefore, one
> must be subject [to the authorities] not only to avoid God's
> wrath, but also for the sake of conscience. For the same reason
> you also pay taxes, for the authorities are the ministers of God.
> . . . (Rom. 13:1–6.)

What one may call the theopolitical logic here is clear enough. Were it not for man's sinfulness, were it not for man's propensity to do evil, there would be no necessity for the coercive State, for the magistrate with his sword. But since man is sinful and prone to evildoing, God, in his infinite mercy, has instituted the political order as an *order of preservation*, to save mankind from itself, to save it from destroying itself through its sinful self-aggrandizement. Hence, the State authority, from the Emperor down to the local magistrate, is carrying out a divine vocation: the ruler is, in Paul's forceful language, a "minister of God," though he may not himself know or acknowledge it—remember that the "public authorities" Paul is talking about are the pagan Emperor Nero and his pagan officials throughout the Empire! The magistrate with the sword is necessary and must be obeyed by the Christian out of his Christian conscience; but he is made necessary by the dreadful consequences of human sinfulness, and he is to be obeyed not on his own claim but out of obedience to God.

Paul's sweeping injunction, "Obey the governing authorities!" finds its own limitations elsewhere in the New Testament. There is, first, Peter's declaration, "We must obey God rather than men" (Acts 5:29); this, however, was strictly limited in scope, meaning that a Christian could not obey the magistrate when the magistrate called to idolatry, or forbade the proclamation of the gospel. Much more fundamental was the teaching that emerges out of Rev., ch. 13. In contrast to Rom., ch. 13, which defines the *legitimate* government, ordained by God, as a divine order of preservation, Rev., ch. 13, defines the *illegitimate* government, which is an agency not of God, but of the Devil. Here is the operative section:

> Then, out of the sea, I saw a Beast rising. . . . The Dragon conferred upon it its power and rule. . . . The whole world went after the Beast in wondering admiration. Men worshiped the Dragon who had conferred his authority upon the Beast; they

worshiped the Beast also, and chanted: "Who is like unto the Beast? Who can stand against him?" (Rev. 13:1–5.)

This powerful passage has a reference that is directly political. The Dragon, of course, is Satan. The Beast is the Roman Empire, or the Emperor. Here, the "public authority," which Paul had seen as the minister of God, is denounced as a servant of the Devil. And how is its diabolical character discerned? By its self-exaltation against God! Instead of confining itself to its God-ordained function of preserving society against sinful evildoing, it now claims to be worshiped and exalted. (The chant, "Who is like unto the Beast? Who can stand against him?" is, of course, a devilish parody of the Song of Moses, Ex. 15:1–18: "Who is like unto Thee, O Lord . . . ?") Because it claims for itself what is owing only to God, the State is no longer to be obeyed as an order of preservation, but is to be opposed as an agency of Satan, in rebellion against God. This is the *illegitimate* State—in fact, the anti-State.

The Pauline conception of the State as an institution not of the created or "natural" order but of the sinful world, ordained to protect mankind against itself, came to govern the thinking of the Western Fathers, most thoroughly the thinking of the great Augustine. For Augustine the political order, embodied in the coercive State, is emphatically not "by nature," as an order of creation. On the contrary, it is *propter peccatum*, "because of sin." In the order of creation, there is no rule of man over man; that emerges, as Paul had shown, out of the necessity for curbing man's evildoing, his sinful self-aggrandizement which, uncurbed, would destroy the entire human race. The State is, therefore, not only *propter peccatum;* it is also *remedia peccati*, a remedy for, a protection against, sin. One must, therefore, obey the public authorities, except when they order something *contra legem Dei*—which to Augustine and the other Fathers meant, as in the New Testament, a call to idolatry, a prohibition to preach the gospel, or both. Under such circumstances, the Christian would have to obey God rather than man; but his disobedience to earthly authorities would always remain passive, leading to martyrdom. Of the distinction between the legitimate and the illegitimate State, there is only the most shadowy suggestion; to Augustine it seemed so little relevant to the new age of the Christian emperors.

We cannot sufficiently admire the profundity and realism of this biblical-patristic view of the State. To the Christian, it should be self-evident that political power, to be in any sense legitimate, must ultimately come from God, the true Sovereign Lord. Where else is the legitimacy of an arrangement that gives some men power over others to come from? From the mere will and power of the ruler—whether monarch or people? That would be the sheerest idolatry. If I am to recognize the legitimate authority of the rulers, be they kings or parliaments, I must see these rulers, whether they themselves acknowledge it or not, as ministers of God, and their authority as authority coming from God, conferred upon them for preservative purposes. This view carries with it, let us never forget, implicit limitations on the scope of this authority of the State: if those limits are passed or violated, the State loses its legitimacy and becomes a diabolical agency for the oppression and subversion of mankind.

But our admiration of the profundity and truth embodied in the Pauline-Augustinian doctrine cannot blind us to one glaring defect. For, if the State is justified by the necessity of curbing the evildoing that comes out of the sinful self-aggrandizement of men, how is it that the ruler—whether prince or parliament—is overlooked? Is not the ruler a man, a sinful man, driven on, as are other men, by sinful self-aggrandizement, by the *libido dominandi,* the "lust for dominating," which Augustine sees as the paramount "law" of the Earthly City? Does not the ruler, therefore, need curbing on his part as well? This germinal idea of a constitutional order setting restraints on the power of rulers, however legitimate, seems to have been completely overlooked until the Middle Ages—or, perhaps, not entirely overlooked since there was some notion of the Church acting as a check on the inordinacies of the State. In any case, the groundwork of the Christian understanding of the State, its nature and its limits, was firmly laid.

II

This conception, however, did not fully satisfy Thomas Aquinas in the thirteenth century. He was engaged in a massive enterprise of reconciling, by proper distinction and redefinition, the philosophical and the Christian traditions—Aristotle with Augustine, Augustine with Aristotle. And so he revived the Greek doctrine of the State as existing "by nature," while retaining the Pauline-patristic teaching of the State as an order of preservation made necessary by sin. Thomas effected this reconciliation by an acute distinction. There are two kinds of subjection of man to man, he said. The first is *subjectio civilis*, civil subjection—the kind made necessary by the very nature of civil society, in which the various positions and tasks would require some sort of public authority for their allocation, even if every citizen were a saint. This kind of subjection is "by nature," and is presumably the kind Aristotle had in mind in his book on politics. On the other hand, men are obviously and emphatically not all saints: they are sinners, acting out of sinful self-aggrandizement, and they have to be curbed in their evil-doing. Here the subjection is *subjectio servilis*, servile subjection—the kind Augustine had in mind. Hence, therefore, the State exists both by nature and by sin.

The tenability of this appealing synthesis has been much argued. For our purposes, however, no conclusion on this question is necessary. What is most emphatically necessary is to note that, for all his desire for reconciliation, Thomas brought out even more clearly the fundamental points of difference between the Greek and the biblical views. Although Aristotle did not, and could not, distinguish between society and State, Thomas could and did. He translated Aristotle's characterization of man, *"zoon phusei politikon"* ("by nature a political animal"), into Latin as *"animal naturaliter sociale et politicum"* ("by nature a social and political animal"), thus making the vital and far-reaching distinction between society and State. But even more important—of really fundamental importance, as Jacques Maritain has pointed out—is Thomas' emphasis on the transcendence of the human person beyond all social collectivities and institutions, beyond society itself. Consider these two texts from St. Thomas:

> Every individual person is related to the entire community as part to whole.[3]

> Man is not ordained to the body politic according to all that he is and has.[4]

Here we have the first clear and explicit challenge to totalitarianism. Although by nature part of civil society, the individual person is not to be swallowed up whole in society or State. On the contrary, by virtue of certain aspects of his being —what Kierkegaard was later to call his "God-relationship"— man as such is elevated above political society and the social order. It is man's ordination to the divine that thus raises him above everything social and political that would totally engulf him. Who denies this, denies both God and man.

Not only does St. Thomas make explicit the Christian rejection of totalitarianism, which is radical and uncompromising; he also makes quite plain the meaning of legitimate and illegitimate government. Government is instituted by God, but the divine ordination may operate through a variety of ways and institutions, ranging from dynastic succession to popular election. The ruler must remember that he is there to keep order, dispense justice, and maintain the law, which is his to make only to a very limited degree. The ruler must be careful that, on the one side, he does not go *contra legem Dei*, against the law of God; and, on the other, he does not drive *ultra vires*, beyond his proper powers, as these are defined by natural and public law, by custom, tradition, character, coronation oath, and the like. If he avoids violating the divine law, and if he keeps within what may now be properly called the constitutional limits of his power, as publicly defined, he is a legitimate ruler and is entitled to honor and obedience without qualification. But, if he deliberately, systematically, and incorrigibly insists on violating the divine law and on running beyond his constitutional powers, he becomes an illegitimate ruler, a tyrant. And against tyrants, as is well known, St. Thomas allows rebellion (on the part of the magnates of the community) and even tyrannicide as a last resort. With St. Thomas, the Christian doctrine of legitimate government over against tyranny is well established. The Reformers did not go beyond: both Luther and Calvin called for unqualified obedience to constituted authority, so long as it remained legitimate in the biblical-Augustinian sense; both permitted resistance when the ruler went *contra legem Dei;* and both required that this resistance be passive, leading to martyrdom—though both allowed a loophole, subsequently enlarged by the Calvinists, to permit armed rebellion and tyrannicide, along Thomist lines. In addition, however, Calvin's keen sense of the involutions of sin as *libido dominandi* led him to make an explicit argument in favor of republicanism, or government by committee, over against government by the will of a single ruler.

> The vice or imperfection of man [Calvin argued], therefore renders it safer and more tolerable for the government to be in the hands of many, that they may afford each other mutual assistance and admonition, and that, if anyone arrogate to himself more than is right, the others may act as censors and masters to restrain his ambition.[5]

III

Direct and conscious confrontation with totalitarianism did not arise for the mass of Christians in Western Europe and America, and for the Church as such, until the appearance of Nazism as a massive power on the continent of Europe. To be sure, totalitarianism had emerged earlier both in Soviet Russia and in fascist Italy, but it had emerged slowly, and concern over it was pushed to the background by excitement over other aspects of the new regimes (the atheism of Soviet Communism, e.g., or the imperialist adventures in Africa on the part of the Mussolini regime). Indeed, in Germany itself, it was not until 1935 that Karl Barth came to realize that the Nazi State was not an ordinary State in the sense of Rom., ch. 13—legitimate, to be prayed for, though unfortunately harassing the Church and acting with painful injustice in many ways. In fairness, however, it must be noted that it was largely the writings of Karl Barth in the years that followed that revealed the inner nature of totalitarianism and its demonic character from the Christian standpoint—though Barth's strange reversal at the end of the war, when totalitarianism came to be represented by Communism rather than Nazism, has no doubt been a major factor contributing to confusion and demoralization in Christian ranks throughout the world.

What is it that characterizes totalitarianism as a special kind of State, a State radically different from the kind of State designated as legitimate in the tradition of Paul, Augustine, and Thomas?

1. The totalitarian State by its very nature recognizes no majesty beyond itself: it exalts itself as its own highest majesty, its own god, and demands to be "worshiped" as such. In short, it demands for itself what is owing only to God: worship and absolute submission.

2. The totalitarian State, in line with its own self-absolutization, claims jurisdiction over every aspect of life, public and

private: "Everything in the State, and through the State; nothing outside the State." In principle, the State swallows up society; State and society swallow up the individual person; and, in practice, every device of modern mass control is employed to implement the totalitarian claim. Nothing outside the State, nothing truly voluntary or private, can be tolerated.

3. The totalitarian State refuses to recognize in man any dimension of his being or doing that carries him beyond the totalitarianized social order. For man to claim such a dimension of being is regarded—quite logically in its own terms—as the most radical challenge possible, not merely to the regime, but to the totalitarian idea and system as such.

Such is totalitarianism in its essence. It is not merely an oppressive regime—indeed, in principle, it does not have to be particularly oppressive at all, at least not to large sections of the population. What is involved is something much more fundamental. The old-fashioned despot demanded obedience, taxes, and manpower for his armies. The totalitarian regime wants much more: "It's your soul they want," as someone once put it, referring to the Nazis. It is total possession of the whole man they want, and they will brook no rivals in engaging man's loyalties, hopes, and affections. The totalitarian rulers will sometimes tolerate less than they demand in principle; but this "moderation" is only temporary, pending more favorable conditions. A real abatement of their total claims is not to be expected.

No extended argument is needed to show that the totalitarian State, thus described in its essence, is the contemporary embodiment of the *illegitimate* State pictured in Rev., ch. 13 and further defined by Augustine and Thomas. It deifies and exalts itself; it demands a quasi-religious commitment on the part of its subjects; it runs constantly *contra legem Dei;* and it operates systematically *ultra vires,* beyond the inherent constitutional limits of States. Finally, it refuses to recognize, and strives incessantly to destroy, man's personal being and his God-relationship.

But we cannot leave it at that. Every established order, every society, and every political system has its inner totalistic strivings. Søren Kierkegaard, himself a thoroughgoing political conservative, was among the first to see this. Over a century and a quarter ago, he pronounced these impassioned words:

> The deification of the established order is the secularization of everything. . . . In the end, one secularizes also the God-relationship. . . . [This God-relationship] must be, for individual man, the absolute; and it is precisely this God-relationship of the individual that puts every established order into question. The established order refuses to entertain the notion that it might consist of . . . so loose an aggregation of individuals, each of whom severally has his own God-relationship. The established order desires to be totalitarian, recognizing nothing above it, but having every individual under it, and judging every individual who is integrated in it.[6]

"The established order desires to be totalitarian," exalting itself, and demanding everything. But there is a difference: the legitimate state, especially the modern constitutional state, possesses built-in institutions and traditions of resistance to these totalitarian "desires" and strivings, while the totalitarian State is the very political embodiment of these totalistic potentials, and lives only to promote and implement them.

IV

On the basis of this analysis, what is indicated as the Christian attitude toward totalitarianism, the totalitarian State, and the actual totalitarian regimes in operation today? Certain points, I think, deserve emphasis.

1. Since the totalitarian State is so obviously the diabolical State of Rev., ch. 13—the illegitimate State of Christian tradition—the Christian as Christian owes it no allegiance, no support or obedience whatever. On the contrary, the Christian as Christian stands in radical opposition to the totalitarian State

and all its works, for the totalitarian State is, in fact, an instrument of the Devil against mankind. It is war without possibility of compromise.

Many Christians find it hard to understand or go along with this notion. Some Christian leaders have even allowed themselves to become so bemused with the idea of "socialism," as a kind of wave of the future, and with the "liberal" delusion that the "enemy is always at the Right," that they cannot see the flagrantly totalitarian character of the Soviet, East German, Chinese, and other Communist regimes, because these regimes are allegedly to the "Left." These leaders tend to adopt attitudes running from friendly "neutralism" and "critical cooperation" to outright support. I will not elaborate further, but I venture to say that this betrayal of the Church will not, in the end, pass off entirely unrequited.

But for large numbers of Christians, these are not the considerations that make them so embarrassed by the intransigent opposition to totalitarianism that I have suggested as the truly Christian attitude. The fact is that many Christians, especially on the Continent, have been so habituated to the Pauline doctrine of Rom., ch. 13, that opposition to government, let alone such intransigent opposition, is entirely out of their field of vision; they cannot conceive that something like it might become their Christian duty. They cannot see that the totalitarian State is a very different kind of thing, a diabolical thing, a device of the Devil. We are now paying for the superficial, unreal, even plainly misleading political education of the Church in recent decades and centuries.

2. This radical opposition to totalitarianism as the work of the Devil does not itself entail public disobedience or outright rebellion at every point. It does entail a total inner withdrawal of allegiance and obedience. But let us not forget that along with this inner posture of radical opposition there are considerations of prudence and worldly responsibility that cannot be ignored. Revolution against the totalitarian State is, in princi-

ple, always justified in the Christian conscience; but the actual
translation from principle to action must depend on a careful
and realistic assessment of the situation. I do not want to lay
down rules: sometimes a demonstrative action without much
hope of success may be in place; but sometimes, too, prudence
may have to be exercised to a high degree. All this must
necessarily be left to the conscience and good sense of those
who live and suffer under totalitarianism.

3. There is still another consideration of far-ranging importance. The primary function of the State, it will be recalled, is
to curb evildoers, and to assure the community its security and
justice. The totalitarian State is prone to pervert even this
elementary function, politicizing its justice and converting the
security it affords into a weapon of State control. But in totalitarian countries, as in all others, the elementary preservative
services must be carried out or else the society itself would go
under. Fires must be put out, traffic must be regulated, theft,
burglary, and nonpolitical crimes of violence must be suppressed, and so on. Now it seems obvious to me that responsible inhabitants of a totalitarian country, no matter how uncompromising their opposition to the State, would have to give
some support to the activities of the State in these elementary
preservative areas. Augustine somewhere speaks of a man held
captive for ransom by a robber band, and therefore obliged to
live in the robber community for months, perhaps even for
years. Obviously, he will feel it necessary and proper to support
the efforts of the bandit leaders to maintain order in the bandit
community, preventing violence, fighting fires, dispensing its
very limited and partial kind of justice ("Even a robber band
has its justice," as Plato pointed out). The captive will do this
without in the least recognizing the legitimacy of the bandit
government, or abdicating his right to escape if possible, or
helping destroy the entire bandit enterprise, if circumstances
prove favorable. This kind of "cooperation," if "cooperation"
it can be called, is very different from the cooperation offered

by many radical Christians to the totalitarian regime. The cooperation they offer in East Germany, e.g., is to help build "socialism," the name given to the State-controlled economies of such countries. In the one case, the totalitarian program is being supported and promoted; in the other case, it is only those activities of the State without which it would be impossible to live that come into consideration.

These conclusions are not, I admit, particularly sensational; and I do not want them to be. They are simply some of the more obvious conclusions one may draw from the fundamental Christian understanding of the State, the legitimate State of Rom., ch. 13, and the illegitimate, self-deifying State of Rev., ch. 13. We might put it this way:

The Christian acknowledges the legitimate State of Rom., ch. 13—whether democratic or not—as a divine order, and is bound in conscience to obey it, unless it commands what is *contra legem Dei*, against the law of God. On the other hand, the illegitimate State depicted in Rev., ch. 13—in our time, the totalitarian State—must be denied the allegiance and support of the Christian. There is no obligation in conscience to obey it; though, where it serves an elementary preservative function, the Christian can support these activities without commitment. This, I think, is basic.

One final point: we must not fall into the egregious error of identifying the legitimate State with the democratic State. The legitimate State is not identifiable with any particular system, and can find expression in any one of a variety of regimes, provided it meets the requirements I have described. The absolute monarchy of the eighteenth century was certainly not democratic; but it was quite legitimate in the proper sense: (1) it recognized a higher majesty beyond itself; (2) it did not claim total jurisdiction over all of life, many areas being left, in theory and practice, to institutions and agencies outside the State, or to the individual himself; (3) it never questioned the reality of the God-relationship that raised the individual human being at some point beyond every social order, including the absolute monarch's own political order; and (4) it acknowledged the preservative function of the State, and fulfilled it with not inconsiderable success. There are self-styled democracies that have not met, and do not meet, these requirements nearly as well. So let us keep clearly in mind what we really mean when we speak of legitimate and illegitimate States.

In the last analysis, the struggle against totalitarianism and the totalitarian State is, for the Christian, a religious struggle, a struggle for men's souls. For the totalitarian State is not simply a political institution; it is, as Karl Barth saw so clearly when it was a matter of Nazism, an "anti-Christian counter-church," making an "inward claim," and "demanding the adoption of a particular philosophy of life" utterly opposed to Christianity. With this kind of State no Christian who is serious about his Christian faith can make his peace.

NOTES

1. Aristotle, *Nicomachean Ethics* 14:1180a, 14.

2. Hajo Holborn, "Greek and Modern Concepts of History," *Journal of the History of Ideas*, Vol. X, No. 1 (Jan., 1949), pp. 3–13.

3. *Summa Theologica*, II-II, qu. 64, art. 2.

4. *Ibid.*, I-II, qu. 21, art. 4, ad 3.

5. *Institutes*, IV.xx.8.

6. Søren Kierkegaard, *Training in Christianity*, tr. by Walter Lowrie (Princeton University Press, 1951), p. 92.

In the 1950's the United States was swept by a revival of religion which reached the proportions of a "boom." People flocked to churches, and there was even "religion along the Potomac"! In the eyes of sensitive religious leaders, however, there were certain aspects of the religious awakening that were disappointing. In March, 1959, Henry P. Van Dusen, then president of Union Theological Seminary in New York City, published an article in the *Union Seminary Quarterly Review* in which he expressed his misgivings. "The 'revival of religion,'" he said, "has thus far been paralleled by no corresponding resurgence or recovery of morality. . . . [This] is the most disturbing, confounding contradiction of our present moral and spiritual situation." Sympathetic with this observation, the editors of that quarterly invited Will Herberg to write an essay dealing with the problem. Herberg's essay, which criticizes moral relativism and "situational ethics," pleads for a new and deeper understanding of moral law. The essay appeared in the March, 1960, issue of the *Union Seminary Quarterly Review* (Vol. XV, No. 3), and is reprinted by permission.

19

RELIGIOUS REVIVAL
AND MORAL CRISIS

It has become a platitude, yet it remains a paradox, that America is at once the most religious and the most secular of nations. No matter what criterion we may employ to judge religiousness, we will discover that the nation is in the grip of a religious upsurge without parallel in this century. Religious identification is well-nigh universal; church affiliation is at an all-time high and church attendance is keeping pace, though at some distance; Sunday school enrollment is rising rapidly, while religious schools are growing and gaining favor with all groups; clergymen are rated as "doing most good" by a larger proportion of the American people than for all other professional categories put together; serious religious books, courses in religion in colleges and universities, and even classic works in theology are enjoying an intellectual prestige and popularity unknown for many decades. There would seem to be little doubt that, in the course of the past twenty years, the familiar modernist trend away from religion has in important ways been reversed; religion in America is staging a comeback which many, a generation ago, would have regarded as virtually unthinkable.

But if the trend away from religion has, for the time being at least, been reversed, the trend toward secularism has not—and therein lies the paradox. What we have is an upsurge of religiousness amidst an advancing secularism, the simultaneous advance of both secularism and religion in our culture. The evidence for this side of the picture is as impressive, though by no means as easy to display, as the evidence for the other side. Americans are religiously identified and church affiliated, valuing religion very highly and eager to have their children receive what they think of as religious education; yet it is perfectly clear that they know less than ever about the teachings and traditions of the religions they profess, and that the goals they pursue and the values they live by are derived, and often avowedly derived, from other sources. The very same Americans who say they regard the Bible as the "inspired word of God," and who distribute it very assiduously, show an incredible lack of interest in the contents of the Bible, to the point indeed where almost half do not seem to know so much as the title of a single book of the New Testament or, for that matter, of the Bible as a whole. The very same Americans who fervently believe that religion is a "very good thing" also admit that their religious beliefs have little or nothing to do with their views on economics, politics, or other everyday affairs of life. What we are confronted with in contemporary America is the paradox of the religiousness of an essentially secularistic people, or alternatively, the secularism of a people who think very highly of religion and are closely identified with the churches.

Perhaps nowhere is this paradox more striking than in the discrepancy between the religious upsurge we have noted and the deep moral confusion in which our culture is involved, which latter seems to have reached the point of actual crisis. It is not easy to document this aspect of our religious situation. Overt expressions of moral decay are notoriously hard to isolate and even more difficult to interpret. The alarming rise of juvenile delinquency, for example, is of course a moral problem; but it is impossible to tell how much of it is the consequence of a general moral decay in our society, and how much is due to the painful process of immigrant acculturation, so familiar in our history. The frequently recurring scandals in public life are shocking enough,[1] but have we any reliable way of comparing the state of public morality thus disclosed with the comparable condition a century or half a century ago? Yet with all these qualifications, we cannot escape the impression that we are today involved in a serious moral crisis, which is expressed primarily not in the widespread violation of accepted moral standards (when has there been a lack of that?), but in the disintegration of these moral standards themselves. If moral crisis there is, it would seem to be manifested most profoundly in the advanced state of decay of our traditional activist morality of duty, and its rapid supersession by a morality of enjoyment and consumption, by a "fun morality," as one observer not long ago put it. The situation is actually more complicated than that, as we shall see, but here at least we touch upon something that suggests the depth and dimensions of our moral crisis.

How are we to bring these together into some sort of coherence—religious revival, on the one side, and moral decay on the other? I must confess that I am thoroughly at a loss about many aspects of the problem, but I do think that some light might be cast by a careful analysis of the actual nature of the religious revival under way today and its implications for the moral life. In other words, I am of the opinion that there is something about the current religious revival that, so far from challenging the moral decay of our culture, actually in a way tends to contribute to it, even to promote it. And this is happening, though in different ways, both where the religious revival is at its shallowest and where it is at its deepest. In both cases, religion and morality find themselves in a kind of conflict and tension that we, with our naive assumption that all "good" things must be in harmony, cannot really understand. A closer look at the problem might yield some insights of value.

I

Actually, what we have under way today is not one religious revival, but two—closely interrelated, but different in depth, character, and scope. The first is the mass phenomenon to which so much attention has been called. It might be designated as the sociological revival of religion-as-belonging.[2] On this level, religion serves the very important social and psychological function of providing a context of belonging in a fluid and mobile society in which earlier contexts are rapidly becoming irrelevant. There was a time when Americans defined their identity—that is, answered the questions, "What am I? What is he?"—in terms of race, ethnicity, region, and similar categories. Race was and still is the predominant form of identification where nonwhite groups of the population are involved. But for the mass of our people it was ethnicity—what we generally call "nationality"—that served as a context for self-identification and social location through much of American history. Americans identified themselves and their neighbors as "Irish," "Germans," "Poles," "Italians," "Jews" (then understood in an ethnic sense), and "Yankees" (a kind of quasi-ethnic term designating the old inhabitants of earliest migrations).

With the establishment of stable and thoroughly American third generations, however, ethnic identifications began to lose much of their force and relevance. Through the complex dynamics of the American cultural process, they have been replaced by forms of identification that are religious in a very curious sense. Definition of identity within the overall totality of American life is now taking place increasingly in terms of a tripartite religious belonging—Protestant, Catholic, Jew. Although ethnicity and region still play their part—and of course race too, in the case of nonwhites—Americans today tend more and more to identify themselves and their neighbors as "Protestants," "Catholics," and "Jews," understood as the three ways of being an American and being religious in the American way. One of the chief reasons for the near-unanimity of religious identification among Americans, and therefore one of the chief factors in the present upsurge of religion in this

country, is that religious identification has become the culturally appropriate way of defining one's identity as an American
under contemporary American conditions.
All this is of importance to our inquiry for two reasons. In
the first place, it suggests that the current religious revival,
insofar as it is related to this factor of identification, is theologically speaking a mere surface phenomenon, however significant
it may be sociologically. To serve its sociological purpose, the
religion of belonging need have no serious religious content; in
fact, it may actually serve its sociological function better the
more vacuous and contentless it is, since religious content,
especially if taken seriously in the life of faith, may well disturb
the adjustment which it is the purpose of this kind of religion
to achieve. The paradox of religionless religion, which has
baffled so many observers, now begins to assume a more intelligible aspect.

But there is still another, and perhaps even more important,
reason why this analysis is pertinent to our problem. For the
urgency with which Americans are turning to this religion of
belonging points to the anxious search for social identification
and the deep need for "togetherness" that have become so
pervasive in our culture. Americans are indeed undergoing a
profound change in cultural character type. To use David
Riesman's suggestive and imaginative categories,[3] the inner-
directed culture, hitherto so characteristic of American life—
a culture which prized self-reliance, achievement, and the reso-
lute pursuit of personally affirmed goals or ideals, all summed
up in the magic words "character" and "conscience"—is rapidly giving way to a culture in which the highest good is
sociability, adjustment, and "getting along with people." This
is the other-directed culture of which Riesman speaks; it tends
to emerge against the background of an economy of plenty,
with emphasis on leisure and consumption, just as inner-direc-
tion tends to emerge against the background of a dynamic
production-minded society. American life is today involved in

the transition from the one to the other, and all aspects of our culture, including religion and morality, reflect this process.

In a situation defined by the other-directed need for sociability, where isolation from the peer group brings intense anxiety, the kind of religion I have described is bound to thrive, for this kind of religion brings, as nothing else can, that sense of belonging and reassurance amidst the anxiety of isolation (the loneliness of the "lonely crowd") which the other-directed man so urgently needs. At least in part, therefore, the current upsurge of religion in this country comes as a consequence of the other-directed man's craving for "togetherness."

The implications of all this for morality are curiously equivocal. Of course, the other-directed craving for sociability makes for conformity—for a kind of compulsive conformity, in fact —and that means a conformity to established moral standards as well. But what kinds of standards, what kinds of norms and values, are these that emerge in an other-directed culture? Not the norms and values of duty, character, and achievement, which marked the older, inner-directed type of society, but the norms and values of tolerance, sociability, and good judgment. Not the "good man," but the "good fellow," becomes the ideal. The whole passage from Professor Leo Strauss, in which this point is made, is worth quoting:

> There exists a very dangerous tendency to identify the good man with the good sport, the cooperative fellow, the "regular guy," i.e., an overemphasis on a certain part of social virtue and a corresponding neglect of those virtues which mature, if they do not flourish, in privacy, not to say solitude. . . . By educating people to cooperate with each other in a friendly spirit, one does not educate non-conformists, people who are prepared to stand alone, to fight alone.[4]

This ethic of the "good fellow" is indeed a broad and tolerant ethic: it implies a tolerance of everything and anything, provided only it does not upset sociability or imperil good adjustment. For that very reason it cannot understand, or even tolerate, the old-fashioned ethic of honor, duty, and virtue, which it finds intolerably narrow, moralistic, and even (this is its favorite term of opprobrium) "neurotic." On the other hand, the earnestly and ingratiatingly "friendly" man is forgiven everything, and so is the "victim of circumstances," who needs only to be "understood" to be exonerated of all responsibility. The Charles Van Doren affair might serve as a most instructive case study of our emerging ethic of sociability.[5] Professor Hans Morgenthau has called attention to the alarming decay of professional conscience among academicians which Mr. Van Doren's deceptions and the tolerant reactions of so many intellectuals reveal.[6] I have myself heard more than one person plead on behalf of Mr. Van Doren that, after all, he did not "hurt anybody," and besides he was always so "sincere"!

The new ethic of the "good fellow" is opposed, at every point, both to the ethic of virtue derived from classic Greek philosophy and to the prophetic ethic of responsibility in biblical revelation. Yet it is often vindicated in religious terms and held as part of their religion by millions of people who are sincerely religious. It is so easy to confuse the spurious sociability of "togetherness" with the authentic community of love, the contentless tolerance of "getting along with people" with the searing consciousness of the divine forgiveness, the anxious need to be liked with the abiding concern for one's neighbor.[7] But this confusion ought not to mislead us. High religion may reach beyond the moral, but it never sinks below it. It sees all of man's righteousness as "filthy rags" over against the divine holiness, and all of men's best efforts as standing under the judgment and needing the mercy of God. But it never devaluates righteousness or blurs the distinction between right and wrong. It sees morality transcended and duty overcome in love, but transcended and overcome only by being taken up and elevated to a higher plane. It knows nothing of the evacuation of duty and morality that is the substance of the new ethic of sociability and good fellowship. In this new ethic it sees quite literally the demoralization of life.

Contemporary religion is very far indeed from being high religion in this sense. Contemporary religion is incapable of creating the man of virtue or the man of responsibility. Despite all the petty moralisms with which it is entangled, it possesses no moral rigor and makes no moral demand. It too shares the ethic of "togetherness" which makes the sociable, cooperative fellow identical with the good man. It is therefore incapable of stemming the moral decay that afflicts us; it is indeed often itself a factor in promoting this moral decay. No wonder, then, that religious revival and the demoralization of life can go hand in hand, each reinforcing the other.

II

But contemporary religion is not all of one piece. Running across and even counter to the mass upsurge of religiousness I have described, there is another kind of religious revival that is often overlooked. It is a religious movement that goes deeper, and gains its strength from the primordial quest for self-understanding and meaning in life. This kind of religious stirring I have found largely among the younger people on the campuses or in the suburban communities that have become virtually extensions of the campus. H. Richard Niebuhr has well described the kind of religious mood and religious concern I have in mind:

> Present-day youth has to rest its large-scale securities on deeper foundations [than earlier generations found satisfactory], and this is probably the source of much of its religious interest. . . . Some of it is finding no greater security than an Epicurean philosophy of chance offers; but much of it is getting down to bedrock and finding a foundation on which life can rest unmoved, if not unshaken, in these stormy times. There is a

venturesomeness in this quest, but it is a hidden thing, and not apparent to those who think of risk only in terms of risked capital or risked lives. In this respect, once more, youth today, so far as it represents this movement of the human spirit toward a less vulnerable faith in life than that which has been tested and found wanting, is more representative of a period of history than merely of itself.[8]

Obviously, this existential kind of religious concern does not share the moral superficiality of the religion of sociability and belonging, but it brings its own problems, and almost for the opposite reasons. Whereas what I have called the sociological surface of revival of religion promotes a religiousness without religion and an ethic without morality, this depth movement in religion aspires to authenticity of being and regards conformity and adjustment as the deepest perils to the self. Where one adjusts, the other strives to upset every adjustment that does not come from within. And for that reason, it cannot avoid putting morality itself into question.

Morality in the first place means custom. A child brought up in what we like to think of as a normal family quite unconsciously adopts the customs and standards of the family and the surrounding society as its own moral system, and at a certain age can be quite rigid and moralistic about it. Religion, where it is present, goes along with the customary moral system, and usually becomes an important part of it. At any rate, on this level, there is no conflict between religion and morality; one tends to sustain the other because they are both parts of a conventional pattern, absorbed as the child absorbs its entire social heritage.

It is with this social heritage in the form of the "customs of the family" that the child grows up. We will not follow the story in any detail because we are interested in only one aspect of it. Suppose the young man or woman—I am thinking of young men and women of college age—comes to develop a deep and personal religious concern. This may happen in many ways, not only as the outcome of an inner religious "experience," but also as the outcome of an intellectual encounter with the newer religious thinking that can prove so exciting to a fresh and inquiring mind. We need not call what happens "conversion," but it is often a profound and liberating experience, transforming one's entire outlook and way of thinking. The conventional religion of the family, precisely because in most cases it is little more than conventional, now tends to appear insipid, flat, and superficial, devoid of existential passion or intellectual challenge—in a word, it appears merely external and inauthentic. The two kinds of religion—conventional religion and existential religion—are not as a rule in a continuum; one emerges over against the other, often in conscious opposition to it. Clearly, insofar as this happens, the newer religious concern of the young person may prove a deeply disturbing factor in the established religious life of the family and community, for this newer religious concern contains a good deal of the kind of skepticism about faith which calls everything habitual or conventional into question, and will not permit anything established to remain unquestioned.

Even more is this true of established morality. Existential religion is not, at least not in its immediate aspect, a settling or stabilizing force. On the contrary, it is something that tends to engender a deep spiritual disquiet, a profound restlessness and dissatisfaction, a distaste for conventional forms and standards that, from a certain point of view, looks more like moral chaos than the kind of settled morality religion is supposed to bring. The whole conventional system of values, with its familiar injunctions and prohibitions, is suddenly called into question, and in the resultant confusion, it sometimes appears as though everything has collapsed. I remember one young man who was a good, well-behaved boy in the usual sense until, sometime in his junior year at college, he came up against the newer religious thinking, particularly the writings of Paul Tillich. *The Shaking of the Foundations* indeed shook him to his foundations, and his confrontation with the unyielding ulti-

macy of the "ultimate concern" came to him as a blinding
revelation of the relativity of all moral standards and of the
danger of losing oneself in the routine conventionalities of life.
As a consequence, he became what we would now call a "beat-
nik," and said and did things that would have been inconceiva-
ble to him the year before. His parents were naturally much
distressed at this turn of events, and simply could not understand how religion could lead their boy into ways so utterly
"irresponsible." What they did not realize was that his kind of
religion was not their kind of religion, and that amidst all his
irresponsibility there was a curious kind of responsibility, for he
could not help responding to his newly awakened concern for
the truth and going in search of authenticity, even if that
meant impatiently brushing aside the conventional values and
conformities of behavior by which he had hitherto lived.

Existential religion is a spiritual radicalism, and therefore
often upsets the conventional patterns of conformity, even the
conventional patterns of religion and morality. Fortunately,
this is not the last word. Beyond the unstabilizing tendency of
radical religion, and all religion is radical insofar as it is existential, there is at least the possibility of a higher stability of life
lived from out of one's inwardness, gaining clarity and power
from that inwardness. The young man I was speaking about
finally achieved this kind of stability. That was fortunate—or
rather it was a divine grace. Not all such experiments in self-
searching are so dramatic, or turn out so well; some, indeed,
prove abortive or disastrous. But there is no escaping this kind
of self-searching once the question of the authenticity of life
has been raised by a deep religious stirring. And with existential
self-searching comes something very close to moral chaos.

III

The purpose of these remarks has been to cast some light on
the strange and contradictory relationship between religion
and morality in present-day America. Religion is generally ex-

pected to sustain and bolster morality, but today it seems to be doing the very opposite. And, curiously enough, it is both the best and the worst of religions that operate in this way. The mass religion of belonging makes for an ethic that dissolves all sense of right and duty into an indiscriminate and undiscriminating sociability. At the other extreme, the existential religion of personal authenticity makes for a radical individualism that spurns all norms and standards as deadening objectifications of the spirit. Between them, the moral confusion of the time is doubly confounded.

This strange conclusion—that both the best and the worst in contemporary religion contribute to our moral confusion— has its lesson for the theologian. This lesson is that some stable structure of moral values, undergirding conscience and character, would seem to be necessary if the sense of right and wrong in any form is to be preserved. The goodness of "the good sport, the cooperative fellow, the regular guy" is not the goodness of the good man; nor is the responsibility of the self in its inwardness identical with the responsibility of social man in his community. An ethic of sociability, which makes adjustment and "togetherness" into a condition of blessedness, will not serve; but neither will a purely "situational ethic" in which there are no normative structures and the only criterion of responsibility is the authenticity of decision. One leads to moral vacuity, the other to moral chaos. It is the attrition of the normative structures of the moral law, whether understood as natural law or divine law, that is at the root of the present moral crisis, and this process our religion promotes rather than hinders. Of course, much of our religion is "moralistic," but moralism is not the same as morality; it is often an aspect of morality in disintegration. What our religion, in its best as in its worst aspects, does not possess is the capacity to affirm and sustain the moral law and yet bring it under the judgment of a holy God. Until it somehow acquires this capacity, it will have no resources with which to cope with the moral crisis of our time.

NOTES

1. Here I have in mind not only grossly improper practices of government officials but also the unsavory mess uncovered by the recent television quiz program inquiry. [In this "pre-Watergate" statement, Herberg refers to corruptions evident in 1960 and particularly the Charles Van Doren television scandal, alluded to later in this essay.—Editor]

2. [In the following paragraphs, Herberg summarizes the thesis developed in his book *Protestant—Catholic—Jew* (Doubleday, & Co., Inc., 1955; 2d ed., 1960).—Editor]

3. See David Riesman, *The Lonely Crowd* (Yale University Press, 1950).

4. Leo Strauss, *What Is Political Philosophy? and Other Essays* (Free Press, 1959), p. 38.

5. Charles Van Doren was a college professor who, in the late 1950's, appeared on the television quiz program "The 64,000 Dollar Question." Because of his popularity, the producers of the program ensured his continued appearance on the program by secretly supplying him in advance with answers to questions that he was asked. The subsequent discovery of this deception evoked a great public outcry.

6. Hans Morgenthau, "Reaction to the Van Doren Reaction," *The New York Times Magazine*, Nov. 22, 1959.

7. An instructive example of this confusion may be found in the campus reaction to the recent scandal at a great university, in which a number of students were accused of having sexually abused a fourteen-year-old girl. By and large, the reactions, as reported in the press, fell into two categories: (1) "It'll give the institution a bad name," "What will they think of it at home," etc.; and (2) "Let's not act holier-than-thou. . . ." Nowhere in the published comments was there any suggestion that something *wrong, wicked, sinful* had been done, that there had been a violation of the moral law. Many no doubt felt that way, but they did not have the appropriate vocabulary; the words "wrong," "wicked," "sinful" would have seemed intolerably narrow, self-righteous, and moralistic to them. They could think only in institutional or "permissive" terms.

8. H. Richard Niebuhr, "On Our Conservative Youth," *Seventy-Five* (Yale Daily News, 1953), p. 90.

In the following essay, based on a paper presented on March 31, 1967, at a meeting of the Philadelphia Society in Chicago and published in *Modern Age,* Will Herberg gives a "conservative" defense of the American constitutional tradition. His conservative political philosophy may be understood in the light of an earlier essay in which he spoke of his conversion from political radicalism (Marxism) and of the influence of Reinhold Niebuhr on his thinking (*Union Seminary Quarterly Review,* Vol. XI, May, 1956). In that essay he observed that Niebuhr's earlier "prophetic" radicalism culminated in a "new conservatism." Herberg insisted that there is an inner theological connection between the two phases of Niebuhr's thought, not a real reversal. "For the 'prophetic radicalism,' " Herberg said at that time, "implied a radical relativization of all political programs, institutions, and movements, and therefore a thoroughgoing rejection of every form of political rationalism." In the same manner, perhaps, one may perceive an "inner connection" between Herberg's prophetic understanding of democracy and his sharp critique of the Great Society.

This essay was published in *Modern Age,* Vol. XI (1966–67), and is reprinted by permission.

20

THE GREAT SOCIETY
AND THE AMERICAN
CONSTITUTIONAL TRADITION

My objection to the Great Society is not primarily an objection to its economic and social aspects, though these alone are, by and large, sufficiently objectionable. My objection to the Great Society runs deeper. It goes to the very idea itself, and it holds not only against President Johnson's Great Society, but also Governor Rockefeller's Just Society, and Governor Reagan's Creative Society, if indeed this last means anything more than letting people alone to take care of their own affairs. My objection is to the very idea that it is within the scope and competence of the federal government, under our system, to devise and impose upon the country a special kind of society, however pleasing that might be to the President, to the Congress, or even to the people themselves. It is not, I believe, within the proper powers of the federal government for it to undertake any such project. The very idea, it seems to me, flies in the face of the American constitutional tradition, which alone gives legitimacy to our entire political system.

There are limits to the federal government's competence under the Constitution; indeed, there are limits to the competence of any government that claims to be legitimate; and trying to create new societies, with new men in them, is far beyond such limits. The Great Society, as concept and project, is fundamentally *ultra vires* ("beyond its proper powers") for a constitutional government such as ours.

What is the essential difference between the constitutional state, as we know it, and the totalitarian state? Well, there are a number of differences of quite fundamental importance. The totalitarian state—the very word "totalitarian" testifies to this —makes the claim, in principle, to total jurisdiction and control over all the individual's activities, public and private; the constitutional state, on the other hand, is by its very nature limited, *self*-limited. Again, the totalitarian state recognizes no higher majesty beyond itself—it is, in fact, its own highest majesty—while the limited-power constitutional state recognizes, even if sometimes only implicitly and negatively, a majesty beyond itself, some intrinsic limit to its own pretensions, whether it be the natural law, the divine law, or whatever. These, and other differences like them, can all, I think, be summed up in this fundamental confrontation: The totalitarian state normally espouses its own public conception of the "good life" for man and society, and proceeds to enforce this conception by every means in its power; the constitutional state, on the other hand, does not pretend to any such total conception of the "good life" of its own—it strives merely to provide men, and groups of men, with sufficient freedom to follow their own, often diverse, conceptions of the "good life" within the limits of public order. Here is the area of irreconcilable opposition.

Now, I ask you to consider for a moment in which direction it is that Great Society ideas and programs, in their very nature, are straining. Is it not moving in the direction of totalistic new-modeling of society? I am not suggesting in the least that the United States is going totalitarian in chasing the *ignis fatuus* of the Great Society; our country, thank God, is still thoroughly sound at heart, and Great Society programs have a way of discrediting themselves through their own vices. So far, Great Society projects have been little more than a continuation of the political "spending" programs that came in with the New Deal—that, and a lot of talk. But the talk is altogether of the wrong kind; it is talk calculated to produce a superheated vision of a state-conceived, state-operated welfare society, where everyone will somehow be taken care of by Washington from the cradle to the grave. The very conception of government is being systematically, and almost openly, subverted in a direction radically hostile to our constitutional tradition.

This is not merely a question of politics, though that would be grave enough. It is, at bottom, a philosophical, even a theological, question. "What is it to have a god, what is God?" Martin Luther once asked. And he answered: "God and faith go together. That which you depend on most absolutely, that which you turn to most entirely, when in distress and bitter need, that is your god!" What is it that we are becoming more and more accustomed to look to when in need and distress? From whom, indeed, is it that we are becoming more and more inclined to see "all blessings flow"? From Washington, of course, which is striving so hard to envelop us in the warm security of an expanding welfare state. The present-day Great Society envisions itself as a kind of divinized Welfare-Bringer; like the Hellenistic monarchies of another age, it proclaims itself as *Euergetes*, or Benefactor, mediating the gifts of the gods to a grateful people. The analogy is too striking not to be more than a mere polemical device.

Two years ago, you may remember, storms and floods devastated parts of the Midwest, and destroyed, with much else, a number of Amish settlements. Almost immediately, Amishmen from nearby states responded, and came to the assistance of their stricken brethren, rebuilding homes and community edifices through their own efforts. A television documentary reported this event. Here is part of what the commentator said: "These days, when people are in trouble, there is one direction in which they look—the federal government. But the Amish people don't look to the federal government for help; they look to each other in their church and community." This commen-

tator spoke perhaps more wisely than he knew, for in the story
he was telling and the scene he was presenting, there was a
direct confrontation of two irreconcilable ways: individual and
community self-help, in line with our best traditions; and
forever looking to the federal government for comfort and
assistance, like helpless dependents upon a powerful and benevolent patron.

Once basic constitutional restrictions are ignored, no limits
can be set upon the all-embracing solicitude of the federal
government. Food, clothing, shelter: all these, of course. But
man does not live by bread alone. So education, too, is to be
dispensed from the Great Cornucopia. And, beyond education,
spiritual blessings as well. . . . It is not for nothing that President Johnson so often refers to the Great Society he is so intent
upon building as the City of Hope, in which the forlorn deni-
zens of the urban wasteland are to receive new life. And, as if
that were not enough, not too long ago a conference of educators and clergymen appealed to the President to do something
to "restore some meaning and purpose to millions of lives."
Words like these tell their own story—educators and clergymen (clergymen, mind you!) pleading with the President to
make the Great Society serve as an order of redemption, con-
ferring meaning and hope—in short, a church. Surely, further
than this no welfare state, no Great Society, can go in its
inordinate pretensions!

These philosophical considerations are not so remote as may
appear at first sight. For it is an inseparable and inviolable part
of our constitutional tradition that the government, while
friendly and encouraging to the religion, or religions, of its
citizens, may not itself become the object of religious devotion;
it must on no account allow itself to be divinized and to engage
the citizen's highest hopes and expectations. The government,
to be constitutionally legitimate, must be content with being
a power of the middle range, restricted to the rather prosaic
functions proper to it, without pretending to be the seat of the

citizen's highest values, as it is in so many Continental political philosophies and systems, and as it would be in a fully developed Great Society set up and operated by the state.

Fifteen years ago, in 1952, Elliot Cohen, the original editor of the magazine *Commentary,* published his now classic essay "The Free American Citizen." Mr. Cohen wrote:

> It seems to me that the free citizen, religious or nonreligious, does have at least one shared conviction. Whether he professes to believe in God, or professes not to believe in God, he has a conviction that there is no god but God. To put it another way: I believe that both the religious believer and the man of secular faith in the United States come very close to holding in their heart the Hebraic commandment: "Thou shalt not have other gods before me." I take this to mean that, whether one believes in some transcendent power or not, one does *not* believe that there is any idea, institution, or program that we can regard as God. . . . [The essence is that the individual] keep this obdurate recalcitrance in the face of all proposed faiths and ideologies that would give any political thing supreme value.[1]

Yes, this is the creed of the "free American citizen." Can it also ever be the creed of the grateful beneficiaries of a state-operated Great Society?

The vision of a Great Society engineered by the federal government is usually found closely associated with the demand for a "sense of purpose" to be developed and projected by the same authority. But this is likewise a radical departure from our basic constitutional system. The federal government is not, and was never meant to be, a moral agency to give the people an inspirational lead.[2] "If people want a sense of purpose," an eminent British statesman recently said, "they should get it from their archbishops and their Church. They should certainly not try to get it from their politicians and their government." How right he was! Life without purpose is a mean and paltry thing. We all want to inform life with a sense of purpose that will give it significance and value. But the sense of purpose, if it is to come at all, must come to each of us from the deepest sources—from our faith, from our "philosophy of life," from our religious and moral convictions. To look to the state to supply it to us is once more to "religionize" the state, which is against both sound religion and responsible politics. It is something the Founding Fathers and the makers of our constitutional republic never contemplated as a function of the state.

We may see the whole in the part. The continuing controversy over public education in this country is not without its relevance to the larger issue of the Great Society. In sharp opposition to what might be called the French, or Continental, philosophy of education, which sees the rising generation as wards belonging to the state, and the state itself as possessing a "natural" and proper educative function *(l'état enseignant)* with a prior right to form the minds of the children, the American philosophy sees the children as belonging to the parents and family, and asserts the right of the parents, or whomever the parents may designate (tutors, independent schools, church schools), to bring up and educate their children. The government may step in only as a last resort to supply facilities and teachers not otherwise available. Over a hundred years ago, John Stuart Mill, the great liberal of the nineteenth century, eloquently presented this view in his essay *On Liberty:*

> That the whole, or any large part of the education of the [children] should be in State hands, I go as far as any one in deprecating. All that has been said of the importance of individuality and diversity in opinions and modes of conduct, involves, as of the same unspeakable importance, diversity in education.[3]

Mill felt that the state might well require universal education, but should not itself conduct schools. Rather, the state should subsidize the education of children in independent schools chosen by the parents where parents could not afford to educate their children from their own resources. Whatever might be the need for state aid, one thing could *not* be permitted in a free state, and that was the state taking over for itself the function of educating the rising generation and forming its minds in line with state doctrine. The state has no business having an official doctrine about the good life, and even less business trying to indoctrinate the people with it.

So strongly did Mill feel about freedom and parental rights in education that he, an unwavering agnostic, even favored religious education, where desired by the parents. "There would be nothing," he declared, "to hinder them [the children] being taught religion, if their parents chose, at the same schools where they were taught other things."

For historical reasons with which we are familiar, it proved impossible to avoid a large-scale establishment of state schools in this country. But the original commitment that the children *by right* belong to the parents and family, not to the state, for indoctrination, has never been quite abandoned, despite the totalistic dreams of large numbers of professional educationists. In 1925, the United States Supreme Court—in happier days —struck down an Oregon statute which in effect required parents to have their children educated in public schools, and in public schools only. Here is the operative paragraph in the Oregon decision:

> The fundamental theory of liberty, upon which all governments in this Union repose, excludes any general power of the state to standardize its children by forcing them to accept instruction from public teachers. The child is not the mere creature of the state; those who nurture and direct his destiny have the right, coupled with the high duty, to recognize and prepare him for additional obligations.[4]

Another Supreme Court decision, nearly twenty years later (the Massachusetts Jehovah's Witnesses case of 1944) went even further:

It is cardinal with us [the Supreme Court] that the custody, care, and nurture of the child reside first in the parents, whose primary function and freedom include preparation for obligations the state can neither supply nor hinder.[5]

A state system of education, with state control of the rising generation, is an essential element of any fully developed Great Society, and the Oregon and Massachusetts decisions were certainly a blow to such totalistic pretensions. In the matter of education, these historic decisions went far to vindicate the right of individuals, or groups of individuals, to devise and pursue their own ways of life, free from any pressure by the state to comprehend them in an official scheme of purposes, values, and ideals.

Let me now try to bring to some sort of conclusion these somewhat sketchy remarks of mine. Actually, I have had only one point to make, and that is the point that the function of government in our constitutional system is not to provide its citizens with an official program for the good life, an official vision of the Good Society, an official answer to the human yearning for a sense of meaning in life, or an official guarantee of security and hope. The urge to come to the people with such promises and programs is, today, largely one emanating from the federal government; with some exceptions, the several states do not seem to have either the inclination or the resources to launch out into this kind of salvationary politics— though we should never forget Upton Sinclair's EPIC ("End Poverty in California") campaign a generation ago.[6] It is these pretensions of the federal government to come to the people with an official program of well-being, meaning, and hope that I find so disturbing. I am not, at this point, criticizing the particular projects advanced under the Great Society—some are new, some are old; some may make sense, others obviously don't; all seem to involve free and easy spending. What bothers me, and I have been trying to say this throughout this essay, is the banner under which they are brought forward—the banner of a state-conceived, state-promoted Great Society. Such a pretension I find to be fundamentally at odds with the underlying conceptions of our American constitutional tradition.

NOTES

1. Elliot E. Cohen, "The Free American Citizen," *Commentary*, Vol. XIV (July–Dec., 1952), pp. 219–230.

2. George F. Kennan, however unsatisfactory his views on foreign policy may be, is very clear about the nature of government in the American constitutional tradition. "The process of government," he writes, "is a practical exercise, not a moral one. Primarily, it is a sorry chore, consisting of the application of restraint by man over man, a chore made necessary because of man's irrational nature, his selfishness, his obstinacy, his tendency to violence. . . . A government is an agent, and no more than any agent may it attempt to be the conscience of its principals " *Realities of American Foreign Policy* (Princeton University Press, 1954), p. 48.

3. John Stuart Mill, *On Liberty and Considerations on Representative Government*, ed. by R. B. McCallum (Oxford: Basil Blackwell, 1946), p. 95.

4. *Pierce v. Society of Sisters*, 268 U.S. 510 (1925).

5. *Prince v. Massachusetts*, 321 U.S. 158 (1944).

6. [Upton Sinclair was a "muckraking" author and political activist whose long career in the Socialist Party culminated in his organizing the EPIC ("End Poverty in California") movement in 1933. In 1934 he was defeated in his campaign on this platform to become governor of California.—EDITOR]

DATE DUE